Classic MOTORSPORT *Routes*

RICHARD MEADEN

MOTORBOOKS

Classic
MOTORSPORT
Routes

This spread: One of the superb images by Louis Klemantaski of Peter Collins at the wheel of his Ferrari during the 1956 Mille Miglia.
Previous page: Bob Finney driving his Frenzel Special to victory at Pikes Peak in 1955.

Foreword

by VIC ELFORD

From a varied career in motorsport covering everything from rallies to endurance racing; hillclimbs to Formula 1, I was lucky enough to be able to enjoy many of the actual roads described in Richard Meaden's new book, *Classic Motorsport Routes*.

Perhaps the most classic is the Targa Florio in Sicily. First organized by Count Vincenzo Florio in 1906 over a route covering 277 miles (446km), this was filtered down over the years till it found its permanent home on the 44.6-mile (71.4-km) Little Madonie circuit. Little has changed since the last time it was run in 1973 and it still makes for a wonderful afternoon drive. What took us about half an hour under racing conditions will probably take two to three hours at a comfortable touring pace and the mountain scenery makes it well worthwhile. Take time out in the village of Collesano to visit the Targa Florio museum and then enjoy a refreshing drink in the corner café where you will find racing pictures on the walls, some of them signed by Nino Vaccarella and me.

But Richard's book isn't just about the Targa Florio. I have driven in earnest over many of the roads he describes and can promise that they are all well worth the effort and even merit a little side-track from your original destination.

Closer to home, Spa-Francorchamps in the Ardennes is still a classic high-speed example of what racetracks were just a few years ago. Follow the route of the original circuit and you will find 8 miles (13km) of blindingly fast stretches with long climbs and frightening descents. From the very bottom of the circuit at Stavelot, Formula 1 and monster sports cars like the Ferrari 512 and Porsche 917 would be flat out at about 200mph (322kph) all the way back to Blanchimont. Then imagine doing that in pouring rain; although you probably won't even need to use your imagination, since with the track deep in the Ardennes it is usually raining more often than not anyway! Have a look at Eau Rouge, perhaps the most daunting corner in all of motor racing. It is the only part of the original circuit that is not part of the public road so you cannot drive through it; but then once you have seen it you probably would not want to drive through it at 180mph (290kph) anyway.

Mont Ventoux in the beautiful Luberon region of France is a spectacular 6,000ft (1,800m) cone rising out of the vines and lavender fields. The original hillclimb starts in the tiny town of Bedouin and races through the trees for 8.7 miles (14km) to the Chalet Reynard. From there you can take the road that descends to the town of Sault. In winter this is the only option due to snow, but in summer you can take the more courageous alternative and continue to the observatory at the very top. Emerging from the tree line, these last few miles are spectacular as the road winds around the moonscape-like edge of the mountain. You will soon understand that only the very brave who *really* knew the road could beat the clock on this part of the climb. Now there are guardrails at strategic places, but years ago there was nothing between a mistake…and a long, bumpy, painful crash to the valley below.

For the many other classic routes that Richard describes…I'll leave you to explore them yourself.

Right: Vic at the wheel of his Cooper T86B-BRM in the 1968 British Grand Prix at Brands Hatch

Contents

Introduction

by RICHARD MEADEN

It was a holiday as a car-obsessed teenager that sparked my fascination with great old racing circuits. Memory fails me when I try to name the exact year of the vacation, but it must have been around 1986. That was two tantalizing years before I passed my driving test, and consequently meant the road trip involved no driving on my part, yet that fortnight-long tour remains one of my fondest and most vivid car-related memories.

It all began with a detour through Reims to explore the flaking but fabulously evocative remains of the old GP circuit. I'd never seen anything like it and spent hours clambering (somewhat perilously) up the derelict control tower and grandstands, hoping with breathtaking naivety to stumble upon some priceless relic. Needless to say I didn't find anything, but I wasn't disappointed, for by the time we left I'd realized Reims – every last fading, crumbling inch of it – was that priceless relic.

In the days that followed we also visited Spa-Francorchamps, driving as much of the old and current GP circuit as we could find (and rather more than we were strictly allowed to explore!), before continuing into Germany to the Nürburgring for a few tourist laps of the Nordschleife. For me it was the highlight of the trip.

It's more than two decades since that formative fortnight, yet it's grip on me remains as strong as ever. Not only do I hold it solely responsible for my studying *Autosport* and *Motor Sport* magazines when I should have been reading Tudor and Stuart history, but I also blame it for me subsequently finding the idea of a 'proper job' completely abhorrent, leaving me with little option but to become a motoring journalist.

Since then I've been fortunate enough to enjoy 15 years of travelling the world driving fabulous cars on magnificent roads for countless magazine assignments. Of those by far the most memorable have been the times when I've been able to experience roads that have played starring roles in the history of motorsport, and it's these unique roads to which *Classic Motorsport Routes* is dedicated.

While many are from a bygone era, some live their double lives to this day. Either way, the feeling you get as the realization dawns that you're actually driving on a road that was once part of the Targa Florio course, or find yourself following in the wheeltracks of all-time Grand Prix greats like Tazio Nuvolari or Jackie Stewart, or scrabbling up a mountain once stormed by Ari Vatanen or Walter Röhrl, is indescribably exciting.

I've been back to Reims and Spa many times since that fantastic holiday, and I've even raced on the Nürburgring Nordschleife, yet the thrill of returning to these legendary venues remains as strong as ever, as does the desire to experience those routes I've not yet had the chance to visit.

I hope I've managed to capture at least some of that feeling in *Classic Motorsport Routes*, and that you are sufficiently inspired to make some pilgrimages of your own. Many of the circuits have long been consigned to history, but as you'll soon discover the memories you take from them last a lifetime.

ACKNOWLEDGEMENTS

It would have been impossible to complete a project like *Classic Motorsport Routes* without the help and support of countless others. Fortunately, while the routes featured are often literally a world apart, motorsport enthusiasts are a tight-knit bunch, and it's thanks to this shared passion that I've been able to call on the help and support of many knowledgeable people.

First and foremost my thanks go to Vic Elford, both for his enthusiasm for *Classic Motorsport Routes* and for doing me the honour of writing its foreword. As one of the greatest all-round drivers in the history of the sport and a fierce competitor on many of the featured routes there's surely no more appropriate contributor than he.

I thank leading rally photographer Colin McMaster for an endless supply of anecdotes and an encyclopaedic knowledge of classic and modern WRC routes, and Steve Webb at SWRT for finding some truly awe-inspiring in-car footage of Rally Finland's Ouninpohja stage. I thank another great photographer – Jakob Ebrey – and Colin Pagan for their pinpoint descriptions of the Jim Clark Rally stages, and Gethin 'It's all flat-out through here' Jones for his colourful description of the Manx Rally's most memorable stages.

Thanks also to Lydia Richards and Octagon for providing every possible scrap of information regarding the Targa Tasmania and to Sylvianne Peter for unearthing invaluable route information for the Tour de France Auto.

Thanks must go to my friends and colleagues Chris Harris, for confirming details of the old Spa-Francorchamps circuit, and Jethro Bovingdon for relaying his first-hand experience of Bathurst's Mount Panorama circuit.

I'm also much obliged to Andrew Frankel and Gordon Cruikshank for their help with some of the more obscure hillclimb routes, and to Martin Holmes for sparing the time to share his unrivalled experience of rallying past and present.

Special thanks go to Paul Mitchell and Nick Otway at AA Publishing, both for the book commission and for their sustained efforts throughout the long and arduous production process, and to my long-suffering wife, Emma, for her patience and understanding during the many months she lost me to *CMR*.

However, the biggest debt of gratitude is owed to those successive generations of heroic drivers who pitted their considerable skills against the 30 spectacular routes featured in this book. Without their towering success and sometimes tragic sacrifice we would have no legendary routes to explore. The compelling significance of these roads is their enduring legacy.

World Map

THE GREAT ROAD RACES

1 La Carrera Panamericana – Mexico
2 Mille Miglia – Italy
3 Targa Florio – Sicily
4 Targa Tasmania – Tasmania, Australia
5 Tour de France Automobile – France

ROAD CIRCUITS

6 Isle of Man TT Course – Isle of Man
7 Le Mans – France
8 Mount Panorama, Bathurst – Australia
9 Pau – France
10 Ulster TT – Northern Ireland

RALLIES

11 Circuit of Ireland – Ireland
12 Jim Clark Rally – Scotland
13 Manx Rally – Isle of Man
14 Monte Carlo Rally – Monaco/France
15 Rally Finland – Finland
16 Tour de Corse – Corsica, France

GRAND PRIX CIRCUITS

17 Spa-Francorchamps – Belgium
18 Reims – France
19 Nürburgring Nordschleife – Germany
20 Pescara – Italy
21 Monaco

HILLCLIMBS

22 Grossglockner – Austria
23 Klausen Pass – Switzerland
24 Mont Ventoux – France
25 Pikes Peak – Colorado, USA
26 Rest and Be Thankful – Scotland

RECORD BREAKING

27 Bonneville Salt Flats – Utah, USA
28 Frankfurt-Darmstadt Autobahn – Germany
29 El Mirage, Mojave Desert – California, USA
30 Silver State Classic – Nevada, USA

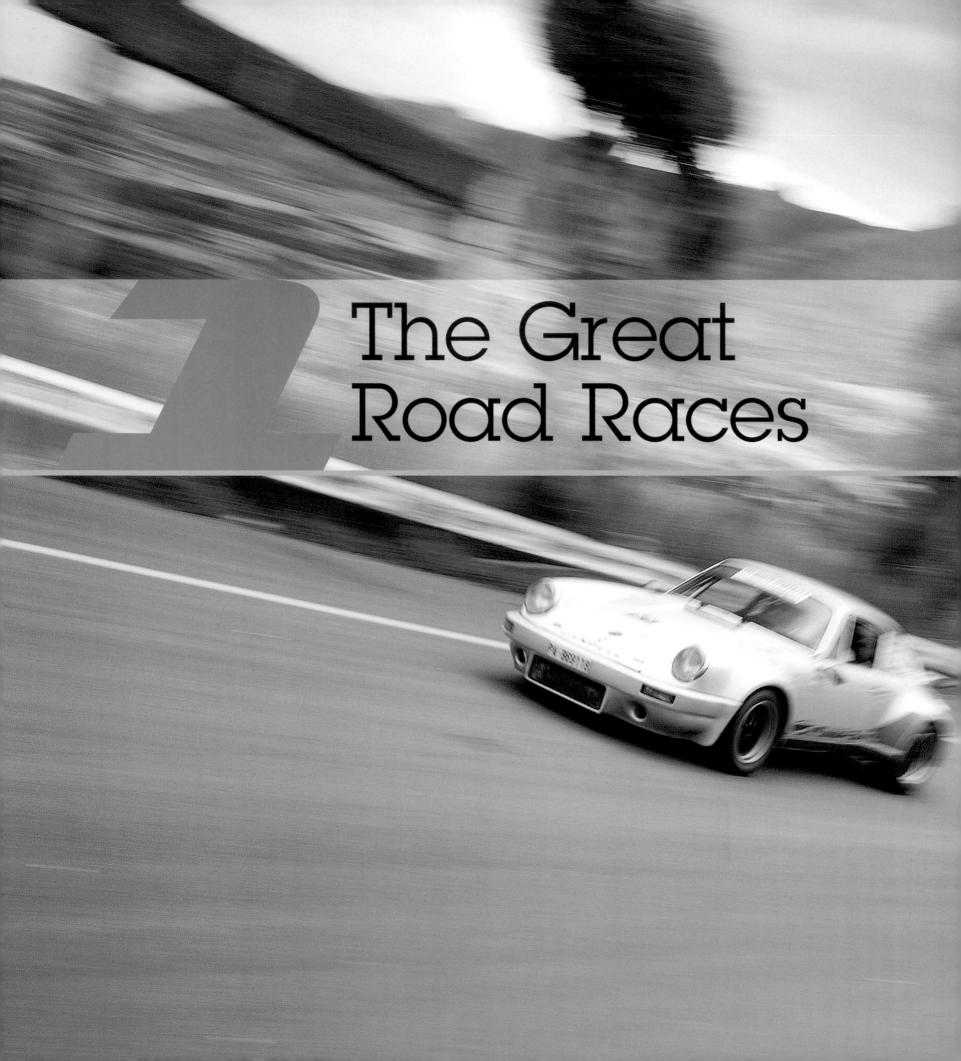

1. The Great Road Races

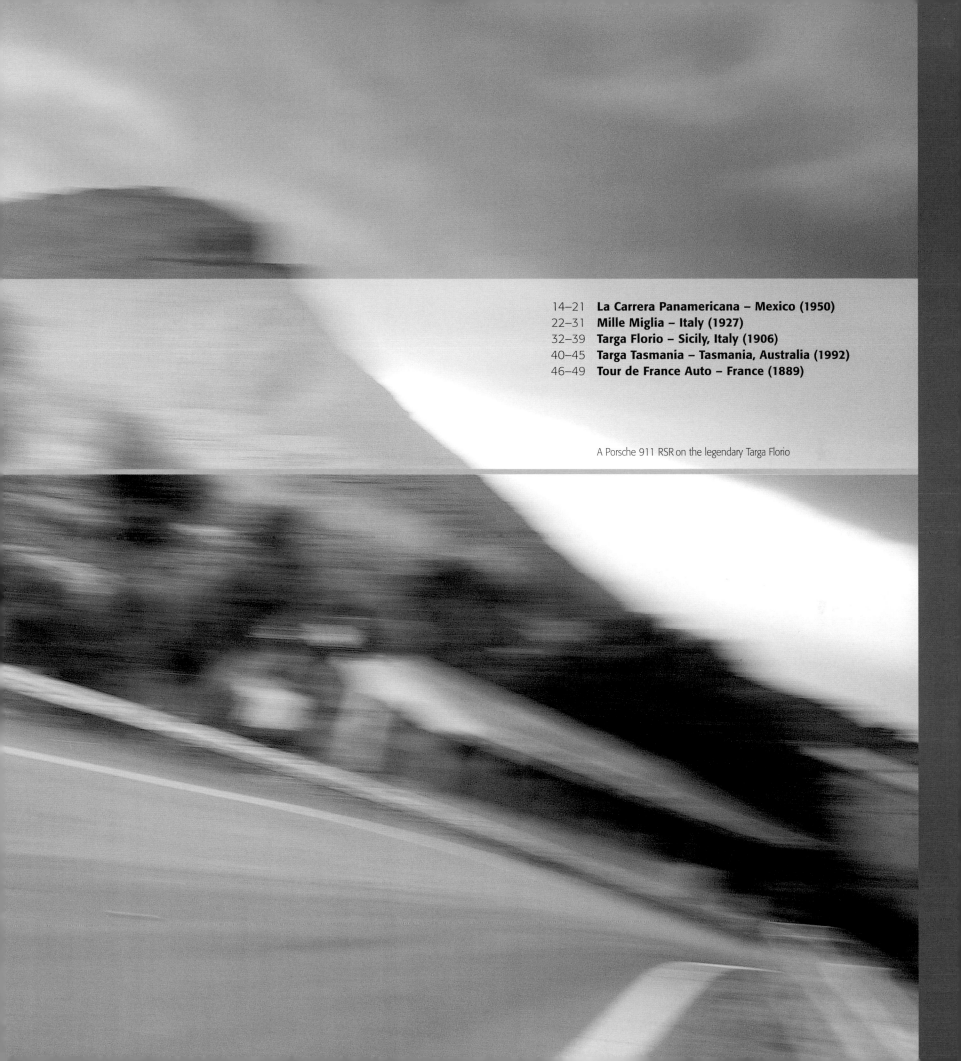

A Porsche 911 RSR on the legendary Targa Florio

LA CARRERA PANAMERICANA

DISTANCE: 2,000 MILES (3,200KM) **FIRST RACE:** 1950 **LOCATION:** MEXICO

More than half a century has passed since the final running of the Carrera Panamericana, yet its epic scale and brutal nature have ensured this short-lived Mexican road race is still regarded as one of the fiercest challenges in motorsport history.

The Carrera was conceived by the Mexican Ministry of Transport as a spectacular way to celebrate completion of Mexico's portion of the Pan-American Highway. Although the Highway is now commonly acknowledged to be more of a concept than a single, defined route, Mexico's

Below: The Mk I Jaguar saloon of Albrecht and Christine Haase tackling the treacherous Mil Cumbres section up between Querétaro and Morelia. **Opposite:** A Mercedes-Benz 300SL, which took part in the 1955 event.

ribbon of blacktop made a vital contribution to the network of roads that run for 16,000 miles (25,760km) between Alaska and Tierra del Fuego.

The first Carrera Panamericana began on 5 May 1950. The concept was simple: a flat-out, border-to-border race along 2,000 miles (3,200km) of the newly completed super-road. The regulations were equally straightforward, if a little curious when viewed from a European racing perspective, for only large-scale series production cars with at least five seats were permitted to enter. Of course this suited homegrown American machinery perfectly, and those huge, brightly coloured Cadillacs, Lincolns and Oldsmobiles that competed made an impressive if rather ungainly spectacle.

That first year the Carrera started in the northern border town of Ciudad Juárez. Sister to the Texan

town of El Paso, the two frontiers lie on opposite banks of the famous Rio Grande river. Leaving Juárez in the rearview mirror, the route then headed southbound on the Pan-Am Highway, stretching for 2,096 miles (3,375km) to the finish in El Ocotal, close to Mexico's southern border with Guatemala.

Though a great success in is inaugural year, subsequent Carreras ran in the opposite direction, starting in Tuxtla Gutiérrez before spearing northwest back to Ciudad Juárez. It was a smart move, for finishing close to the US border ensured more people witnessed the climax of the race, which would in turn generate more publicity. With it came more high-profile teams from North America and Europe, whose exhausted personnel would doubtless appreciate the added convenience of finishing 2,000 miles (3,200km) closer to home!

As the race matured, so too did the regulations, initially by opening the entries to more specialized Sport as well as Production cars, then by further sub-division of these primary classes into those for small and large engine capacities. Entries flourished and the competition intensified as each year passed.

Though it ran just five times – from 1950 to 1954 – the Carrera firmly established itself as one of the all-time great road races. Then, as now, the American market was vital for every major car-maker. A strong showing in the Carrera would undoubtedly boost showroom sales; a fact evidenced by works entries from the most famous European and US manufacturers. Teams from Alfa Romeo, Ferrari, Jaguar, Lancia, Maserati, Mercedes-Benz and Porsche all travelled down Mexico way to lock horns with US giants Chrysler, Ford and General Motors. With them came the greatest drivers of their day: the likes of Juan Manuel Fangio, Karl Kling, Alberto Ascari and Phil Hill all risking life and limb to rise to the challenge of the Carrera.

The Great Road Races

Above: At 18,848ft (5,747m), the permanently snow-capped Pico de Orizaba, an extinct volcano, is the highest peak in Mexico.
Opposite: A Mercedez-Benz 300SL from 1955.

Above: Carrera Panamericana hero Ak Miller in his *Caballo di Hiero* (Iron Horse) outside his garage shortly before setting off for Mexico in 1954. The Mexicans loved the way Miller and Doug Harrison gave the expensive European cars such a hard time in their odd-looking machine, which had cost all of $1,300.

Even by the carefree safety standards of the 1950s, the Carrera was a perilous race. Scant regard was paid to crowd control, and crash barriers were conspicuous by their absence, even on the many vertiginous mountain passes. The sheer mileage involved (twice that of Italy's Mille Miglia) and sustained high speeds, not to mention a diversity of terrain that saw competitors tackling everything from breathless 10,000ft (3,000m) mountain climbs to flat-out charges across searing desert plains, regularly saw man and machine pushed to the limits of endurance.

To this day driving the route of the Carrera is a challenge not to be taken lightly. For starters, it's not immediately apparent which route to take, for following the Pan-American Highway isn't like following, say the Stuart Highway in Australia or, on a more prosaic level, the M1 in England. All you can do is take a dot-to-dot approach, using each of the start/finish points of the Carrera's eight timed legs as your way-points. Following the 1950 route therefore, you'd start in Juarez and head for Chihuahua, then Durango, Leon, Mexico City, Puebla, Oaxaca, Tuxtla Gutiérrez and finally El Ocotal. For subsequent Carreras simply start in Tuxtla and work your way 2,000 miles (3,200km) north towards Juárez.

The distances are huge, but even they pale into insignificance compared to the challenge of Mexico itself. While package holidays are increasingly popular, staying in one of the many resorts is a far cry from inland Mexico. As in most Latin American countries, life away from the tourist traps is edgy and visceral, with many people living in extreme poverty. Scratch through Ciudad Juárez's thin tourist-friendly veneer and you'll find a gritty frontier town, heaving with traffic and troubled by armed street crime. At the other end of the country, in El Ocotal and Tuxtla, skirmishes between armed guerrilla factions, the army and drug trafficking gangs working their way up from Central America are not uncommon.

'**Scant regard was paid** to crowd control, and crash barriers were conspicuous by **their absence'**

Above: The 'official' Mercedes team portrait in Mexico, 1952. Left to right: Hermann Lang, Erwin Grupp, Hans Klenk, Karl Kling, John Fitch and Eugen Geiger.

Thankfully, between the two troubled border zones lie some of the most breathtaking scenery and most thrilling driving roads in the world. From the humid, tropical south with its ancient Mayan ruins and the craggy majesty of the Sierra Madre mountain range near Durango, to the arid central plateau of Chihuahua, the Pan-American Highway scribes a relentless path through the wilderness. Against this kind of backdrop, is it any wonder the Carrera forged such a formidable reputation?

Thinking back to 1952, we can only marvel at what an adventure it must have been for the Mercedes-Benz team as they embarked on the long journey from Stuttgart to Tuxtla in search of global glory. Coming at the end of a tremendous year of European success at Le Mans, the Nürburgring and the Mille Miglia, Mercedes knew that the Carrera was both the richest prize and the toughest challenge yet for their dominant driver line-up and advanced 300SL racing prototypes.

Just getting to Mexico was a trial in itself. Although the race wasn't scheduled to start until 19 November, the trio of 300SLs, together with the team's support vehicles and service crew, were required to leave Hamburg at the beginning of October on a two-week Atlantic crossing bound for the Mexican port of Veracruz. Team boss Alfred Neubauer together with his driver and co-driver pairings of Karl Kling/Hans Klenk and Herman

Lang/Erwin Grupp followed them at the end of October, this time from Stuttgart on a KLM DC6 aircraft. Though much quicker than a sea crossing, the journey still took two days, flying via Amsterdam, Gander, Montréal and Monterrey. How times have changed.

By the time the team re-convened in Mexico just three weeks of preparation time remained before the arduous race was due to commence. The drivers completed a full recce of the route, with their co-drivers – Klenk in particular – making a rudimentary record of what they saw. As they were using a rather sedate Mercedes 300 Saloon and as the route comprised literally thousands of bends and assorted hazards it was hardly definitive, but Klenk's 'Prayer Book' of pace notes would give advanced warning of most of the dangers the Carrera had in store for them.

Some 90 cars took the start (29 Sport and 61 Production), each separated by one-minute intervals, the first car powering away from the line at 6.30am. By modern standards the 300SLs weren't especially powerful – their 3-litre straight-six engines developing a modest 180bhp – but they were light and extremely aerodynamic. This enabled them to reach a top speed of 150mph (240kph), a velocity the drivers hit with alarming regularity on the endless straights of the Pan-American Highway.

Left: The Saab 96 of Swedish duo Nicolina Hübert and Anna Sörrensson on the Jalcomulco stage near Tehuacan in 2006.

Above: An eagle soars above the Highway. **Right:** A Lincoln Capri in 2006. The 5.2-litre car was hugely successful in the 1953 race, taking the first four places in the stock car category.

It was on one of these sections, during the first day of the race, that Kling and Klenk had an all-too-close encounter with a buzzard, which they struck at what was conservatively estimated at 120mph (193kph). The hapless bird, which had a wingspan of at least 4ft (1.2m) and, according to the stunned duo, 'weighed as much as five fattened geese', came through the windscreen, striking Klenk in the face and knocking him briefly unconscious. On regaining his wits, Klenk heroically shouted at Kling to 'get going!' and waited until the first scheduled roadside pit stop to remove fragments of glass, feathers (and worse) from his face! The team replaced the windscreen and bolted eight vertical 'buzzard bars' across it as rudimentary protection against further bird strikes. It was an act of inspired improvization that immediately passed into Carrera folklore.

Freed from the rigours of flat-out competition you could spend weeks covering the Carrera route, but in 1952 the crews had just five days to devour 2,000 miles (3,200km) of Mexico. The logistics, both for teams and the Carrera's organizers, were astonishing. Some 40,000 soldiers were enlisted to police the route, together with 3,000 medics and 600 race officials. So great were the distances covered each day by the race cars that a fleet of 65 aircraft were required to transport team personnel and materials from one stage to the next.

For the teams on the ground the Carrera posed other unique challenges. Pit stops were carried out at the roadside, often quite literally in the middle of nowhere. The gruelling conditions, abrasive tarmac and rough road surfaces were incredibly hard on the cars, and mechanics had to be poised to replace anything from worn tyres to broken shock absorbers, crumpled body panels to smoking clutches. With the change in topography they also had to change spark plugs and transmission ratios, for the thin air and sinuous roads found in the high-altitude mountain regions placed very different demands on the car from the endless desert straights, some of which ran for 40 miles (64km) or more.

At the start of the last day, Kling and Klenk were lying in fourth position, but a drive of chilling commitment over the final stage (and the retirement of the leading Ferrari) saw the battered duo snatch victory. Such was their astonishing pace they even outran team boss Neubauer, who was flying in a chartered DC3 Dakota, and their eventual finishing time of 18 hours, 51 minutes and 19 seconds set a new course record. Their average speed? A scarcely believable 103mph (166kph).

It seems impossible to conceive of such extraordinary exploits occurring in the mollycoddled 21st century, but such is the Carrera's enduring appeal that it was revived as a classic rally in 1988. While far from the death-defying challenge of the original Carrera, competitors in this modern re-creation still attack the wild and gnarly roads of Mexico, some in those same Cadillacs and Oldsmobiles. Their booming V8 engines, vivid liveries and occasional but spectacularly huge accidents provide poignant echoes of La Carrera Panamericana's past glories.

MILLE MIGLIA

DISTANCE: 1,000 MILES (1,600KM) FIRST RACE: 1927 LOCATION: ITALY

Has any race won the heart of a nation so completely as the Mille Miglia? A thousand-mile (1,600km) lap of Italy through packed city streets, thronged town squares and sleepy villages, the race – and its distinctive 'Red Arrow' logo – soon came to symbolize Italy's love affair with the car.

The Mille Miglia was the inspired vision of two young Italian aristocrats, Aymo Maggi and Franco Mazzotti. Both were keen drivers and both found great sport in regularly racing the train from their home town of Brescia to the city of Milan in their Bugatti and Fraschini cars. Together with fellow Brescian Renzo Castagneto and motoring journalist Giovanni Canestrini, they decided to create a race that would stretch the limits of man and machinery, and place their beloved Brescia at the very heart of the action.

To this end they devised a truly spectacular route. Starting in Brescia and heading east towards Padova, it then turned south to Rovigo, continuing through Ferrara and Ravenna before hugging the Adriatic coastline and spearing through the seaside towns of Rimini, Ancona and Pescara. Turning inland, the route then passed through awesome mountain scenery at L'Aquila before eventually reaching the Italian capital of Rome.

From here began the long slog north, taking in the distinctive rolling terrain of Tuscany, followed by the more rugged Futa and Raticosa passes. Beyond them lay Bologna and the flat, fertile plains of Modena and the Po valley before the route made its triumphant return to Brescia.

Rain plagued the first running of the Mille Miglia, in March 1927. Torrential and unrelenting, it made

an already gruelling race a raw test of survival. The roads – often rudimentary and always pockmarked – became cratered, flooded and rock-strewn, jarring the crews and tearing tyres to shreds. Tyre changes were inevitable, but some competitors reportedly chewed through as many as half a dozen sets. By the end of the race both the crews and crowds were drenched and muddied, but such was the magic of the Mille Miglia that all were dreaming of 'next year' before their clothes were dry.

Although the route essentially remained the same throughout its history, the Mille Miglia's heyday was undoubtedly the post-war years, from 1947 to 1957, when the finest drivers of the day were employed by the most prestigious manufacturers to grasp at glory on the open roads of Italy. Perhaps

the most celebrated of those golden years was the 1955 event, when Mercedes-Benz and the British crew of Stirling Moss and journalist Denis Jenkinson triumphed over Ferrari in an all-consuming 10-hour battle.

More often than not co-drivers in the Mille Miglia were little more than fleshy ballast: brave men tasked with ensuring the car was correctly checked-in and out of each time control station. Mainly though, they were required simply to sit still and keep quiet. In an effort to level the playing field against a raft of Italian drivers who knew every inch of the route, Moss and Jenkinson made an accurate recce of the course, details of which Jenks painstakingly noted down on a 'Roller-Map'. This odd-looking wooden box, complete with a window

Left: The view over Brescia at sunset. **Right:** A pre-war Alfa Romeo taking part in a recent running of the Mille Miglia.

Some superb classic cars such as this Ferrari 250GT LWB Berlinetta Zagato **(left)** and this Jaguar XK120 **(above)** can still be seen taking part in the legendary race.

through which to read the notes, proved an invaluable aid, enabling Jenks to tell Moss of approaching corners and hazards by means of a simple series of hand signals. It's a testament to Jenks' resolve and steely nerve that Moss could decipher anything useful from such signals, for put in Jenks' shoes most of us would have curled into a tight, quivering ball and let Moss get on with it.

These were road racing's most thrilling years, thanks to the tremendous pace of the cars and the bravado of the drivers. In those heady days spectacle took priority over safety, and as a consequence triumph was often shadowed by tragedy. And so it proved with the Mille Miglia, for just two years after Moss and Jenks' euphoric victory, Ferrari driver Alfonso de Portago, his co-driver Edmund Nelson and nine hapless spectators died when the duo's Ferrari suffered a puncture at around 150mph (242kph) and flew into the unprotected crowd just 30 miles (48km) from the finish. Coming so soon after the 1955 Le Mans disaster, in which 83 spectators were killed, it was inevitable that 'the most beautiful race in the world' also fell victim to Portago's terrible accident.

Such tales of extraordinary success and sacrifice charge the Mille Miglia with a special kind of magnetism. It's this abiding fascination that draws car enthusiasts to Brescia from around the world, and what makes it the perfect place to embark on a 1,000-mile (1,600km) pilgrimage to follow in the tyre-tracks of Moss, Fangio and other racing heroes.

It also provided the impetus for a Mille Miglia revival some 20 years after the ill-fated 1957 race,

Left: The Mille Miglia takes in some truly stunning Italian scenery: this is the route through San Marino

1954-1957 Route
2007 Route

'it must have taken huge reserves of courage and confidence to keep the throttle pinned along the unrelenting straights'

this time not as a round of the World Sportscar Championship, but as a series of time trials, open to cars that did or could have competed in the original Mille Miglia. While far from the death-defying battle through Italy it once was, this modern event is still a sensation, the roads thronged by ecstatic spectators, the air filled with animalistic engine notes and the heady tang of exhaust fumes.

With the local police on hand to clear a path through troublesome traffic, it's still possible to see these fabulous, priceless old racing cars driven in anger. If you're bold and equipped with a suitably potent road car, you can even try following the priceless cavalcade, although your chances of keeping up are slim, to say the least.

The imposing Piazza Vittoria is an appropriately grand location for the Mille Miglia's hundreds of cars and competitors to gather. Flanked by towering architecture – a legacy of Italy's Fascist era – it's hard to imagine that this vast civic square could possibly be crammed to capacity, but every year it was, with busy team personnel, stressed race officials, nervous drivers and excited spectators, all craning to catch a glimpse of the fabulous racing cars being primed for action. Visit Brescia in May for the start of the modern Mille Miglia and you'll see it with your own eyes, like pictures from a history book made real.

From the piazza it's a short drive through cobbled backstreets to the start ramp on the Viale Venezia. Wide, straight and lined with grand houses and proud chestnut trees, it's a strangely suburban scene, given the scale of the race that started here. One thing's for certain: it's not the place to enjoy putting your car through its paces. But then if you're a student of the Mille Miglia's history, simply knowing that men like Nuvolari, Fangio, Moss and Von Trips would have powered away from the start and been touching 160mph (258kph) or more

Above left: Brescia town square, the starting point for the race.
Left: A 1929 Bentley Speed Six Le Mans preparing to take part in a recent event. **Opposite:** The route runs right through many of Italy's ancient towns and cities.

within the first few miles is enough to send a shiver down your spine.

As you leave Brescia it's an easy job to trace the route. Simply take a map and head for Verona, then Vicenza, Padova and Rovigo, making sure you avoid the autostrada. Leave early, preferably at dawn on a Sunday morning, and you stand a chance of some clear stretches of road, but likely as not you'll be stuck behind a lorry for some of the way. The truth is, unless you're totally committed you're unlikely to follow the route religiously, for the traffic soon becomes tedious. Better to cherry-pick the key sections of the route and bypass the busiest stretches by hopping onto the excellent autostrada network, which often runs close to the original old roads but is much, much quicker.

The route's first major change in character comes at Ravenna, where the road turns to hug the Adriatic coast. Set far enough inland to make glimpses of the sea fleeting, to say the least, the road compensates by running almost arrow-straight, with only the occasional level crossing to deflect you from your trajectory. This is where the Mille Miglia got really serious, and where the quickest cars could really stretch their legs.

What the racers and co-drivers must have experienced defies even the most vivid imagination. Ducked behind a Perspex bubble screen, deafened by the barely silenced roar of the engine, choked by fumes and seared by the hot exhausts and beating sun, it must have been close to unbearable. With only rival competitors to share the road, it would have taken huge reserves of courage and confidence to keep the throttle pinned along the unrelenting straights. To make matters worse, the occasional zigzag around railway huts or electricity sub-stations could be hidden in the heat haze. Even at normal road speeds these hazards can take you unawares. Careering along at more than 170mph (274kph), the crews' hearts must have been pounding and their eyes out on stalks.

There's no doubt that's an astonishing speed for the 1950s, but one that has paled a little with the

A BMW 328 **(above)** and a Fiat 1100S **(right)** along the route.

advent of the 250mph (403kph) supercar. However, one figure that still has the power to shock is 107mph (172kph), for that's the speed the fastest crews *averaged* all the way from Brescia to Rome. That equates to a journey time of just five hours, including pit stops, the twisty inland run to L'Aquila and onwards to the capital itself. For some added perspective, read a modern tourist guidebook and it will recommend allowing up to two hours just to get from L'Aquila to Rome!

There goes a saying that whoever leads at Rome will not win the Mille Miglia. That certainly proved the case for English hero Peter Collins, who was also driving for Ferrari in the ill-fated '57 race. All the way to Rome he delivered a virtuoso drive from behind the wheel of his V12-engined sports car. In fact he was devouring the route so fast he was threatening the outright race record of 10 hours and 7 minutes, famously set by Moss and Jenkinson in 1955. Collins's pace was all the more remarkable given he was accompanied by the photographer Louis Klemantaski, who was documenting the race from the best seat in the house (see panel page 31).

As they powered north from Rome, through the beautiful Val D'Orcia in Tuscany, their lead extended. Collins was revelling in his command of the fearsome Ferrari and relishing the prospect of attacking the Futa and Raticosa passes, which lay just north of Florence. Drive them today and you can share his enthusiasm, for the relentlessly sinuous SS65 that snakes its way through the densely wooded Appenine foothills is a driver's paradise.

The mountains are as stern a test of technique now as then, and provide a golden opportunity to experience the road just as racers like Collins would have done. While the last 50 years or so have seen Armco barrier sprout at the fringes of the biggest drops, enough of the corners remain lined by low walls, the unyielding trunk of a century old tree or sometimes just fresh air. It's a daunting but inspiring place, somewhere to get the best from whatever car you're driving. It's quiet too, thanks to the autostrada taking the bulk of the traffic, leaving this magical road to you and a smattering of locals.

As you pass through the small towns and villages that dot this section of the route take the time to stop for a coffee and a bite to eat, for you're sure to find a restaurant proudly displaying grainy old photographs taken when the Mille Miglia roared through. It's at moments like this you appreciate what it means to the people of a country when a race literally passes by their doorstep.

For Collins and Klemantaski their valiant effort was about to grind to a halt. A crunching noise from the back axle had developed as they fought their way through countless first and second gear hairpins in rain and driving sleet. Despite this they survived the mountains, but cruelly, with just 100 relatively straightforward miles (160km) between them and victorious return to Brescia the ailing transmission failed, denying them a historic win. That honour would fall to another Ferrari driver – Piero Taruffi – a 51-year-old veteran who won after more than a dozen failed attempts. He then retired on the spot: a wise decision, for he lived to see his eighties, unlike so many of his contemporaries, who gave their lives to the sport they loved.

LOUIS KLEMANTASKI

Modern motorsport photographers rely on huge zoom lenses to get themselves close to the action. For Louis Klemantaski, pioneering motor racing photographer, capturing breathtaking images required a more direct approach. Often standing inches from the trackside, sometimes even riding alongside the drivers during races, his exceptional work remains unsurpassed to this day.

Like many people born at the turn of the 20th century, Klemantaski's life was rich in experience and achievement. Born in Manchuria in 1921 to a Russian mother and Dutch father, Klemantaski travelled to England aged 16 to complete his education. After graduating from King's College, London, Klemantaski shunned a career in the City to indulge his passion for cars, and spent the 1930s racing supercharged single-seaters at Brooklands, and working as a mechanic. To supplement his income he also took photographs of the cars and drivers.

After suffering an accident in 1933, which permanently damaged his leg, he remained close to racing by taking the position as Secretary of the Junior Racing Drivers Club. During this time he is credited with starting the first racing driver-training scheme in the world. He also continued to nurture his love of photography.

By the time war broke out he was an action photographer of some note. It was his knowledge and skill at capturing images of objects travelling at high-speed that saw him working for the Department of Miscellaneous Weapons Development, where he was involved in the development of Barnes Wallis's dam-busting bouncing bomb.

After the war he became a full-time photographer and rekindled his interest in motor racing. He was fascinated by the dynamics of a moving car, and took the unprecedented step of entering races and rallies to increase his understanding. The most famous and fruitful of these hands-on adventures are his participation in five Mille Miglias.

Of these, Klemantaski's greatest images came while sitting alongside Ferrari driver Peter Collins (left and above). In 1956 the pairing finished the race in second position, and came tantalisingly close to outright victory the following year (see main text). The photos he took – while travelling at incredible speeds and ultimately risking his life – give a uniquely intimate perspective of a racing driver at work, and are rightly regarded as the most inspirational motorsport studies ever taken.

Klemantaski retired in 1982, and sadly passed away in June 2001. However, his work lives on thanks to Peter G Sachs and the world-renowned Klemantaski Collection. Containing some 60,000 of Klemantaski's pictures – together with the combined works of a number of other noted motorsport photographers totalling some 500,000 images – the Klemantaski Collection sells high-quality photographic prints to order. Log on to www.klemcoll.com for more information.

TARGA FLORIO

DISTANCE: 44.6 MILES (71.8KM) **FIRST RACE:** 1906 **LOCATION:** SICILY, ITALY

For budding vulcanologists, Sicily is the simmering seat of Mount Etna. For fans of the Godfather movie trilogy, Sicily is the birthplace of Don Corleone. For car enthusiasts, this small, sun-baked island perched just off the toe of Italy is the home of perhaps the greatest road race of them: the Targa Florio.

The Targa can trace its origins right the way back to 1906. The vision of wealthy Sicilian Vincenzo Florio, the race to which he gave his name was held on a 92-mile (148km) course that traversed the rugged island. Held on what can only be described

as basic roads and tracks, the Targa was as much a test of man as machine, with unforgiving mountainous terrain, unpredictable weather, wild animals and even bandits to contend with.

A three-lap race of some 277 miles (446km), the event was contested by just ten cars, but as Florio had introduced the very first car to Sicily only a handful of years before, attracting ten cars to the island for a race was deemed a great success. Unsurprisingly many of those cars succumbed before the finish, including the unfortunate Florio himself. However, after nine hours of racing,

Alessandro Cagno won the inaugural Targa Florio, at an average speed of 29mph (47kph).

Despite the modest entry, that first event captured the island's imagination, and a second Targa was planned for the following year. This time 50 cars entered, including early Fiats, Lancias and a host of long-since disappeared French manufacturers, including Darracq. Even in these formative days of the automobile, the importance of motorsport success was growing, and with it flourished the legend of the Targa.

World War I resulted in a four-year hiatus, but in 1919 the Targa was revived, and indeed revised, with the original 92-mile (148km) course shortened to 67 miles (108km). However, the number of laps was increased from three to four, maintaining the race distance at a fearsome 268 miles (431km). The new race was notable for two things: the weather, which was atrocious, and the entry of a certain Enzo Ferrari, who was driving a Lancia in his first major race.

By the early 1920s, the Targa Florio attracted the first full works racing teams. Alfa Romeo, Fiat and Mercedes fought fearlessly through the Madonie mountains, while the likes of Tazio Nuvolari and Achille Varzi – drivers who would soon go on to become Grand Prix stars of the 1930s – honed their dazzling skills.

Once again, global conflict brought a halt to the Targa, but it soon recovered time lost to World War II, and by 1955 had become a round of the World Sportscar Championship. Earlier that year,

Left: Spectators lining the route during the 1970 Targa, as Jonathan Williams passes in his Alfa Romeo T33/2. **Opposite:** The Targa Florio remains a hugely popular event for enthusiasts: the sight of classic cars like this Alfa Romeo GTA rushing through Sicillian streets is a thrilling spectacle.

'The true spirit of the Targa is to be found behind the wheel of your car, on the road that winds into the Madonie mountains'

Classic Lancias like the Aurelia (**left**) and Fulvia (**right**) can still be seen heading for the depths of the Sicillian countryside.

Mercedes were involved in a disastrous crash at Le Mans. It was, and remains, the worst incident in racing history, and led the German manufacturer to withdraw from motorsport at the end of the season.

However, competitive to the end, Mercedes still wanted to steal the championship from Ferrari, and made a Herculean effort at the '55 Targa, entering no fewer than five 300SLRs (the Audi R10 of their day) with an awesome driver line-up, including GP stars Juan Manuel Fangio, Stirling Moss, Karl Kling and Peter Collins. It was the most fiercely contested Targa in the great road race's history.

The course, now in its third and final incarnation and known as the Piccolo Madonie circuit, measured 44.64 miles (71.83km) of closed public road, but the number of laps had increased to 13, bringing the Targa Florio to a total of 580 flat-out miles (934km).

It seems incredible now, but back in 1955, practice for the Targa was held while the roads were still open to the public, so in addition to the challenge of keeping their fiercely quick racing cars on the narrow, bumpy tarmac, drivers also had to contend with oncoming traffic, pedestrians and herds of livestock. Surprisingly, not only did the Mercedes team survive the perils of practice but the Moss/Collins car went on to win the race, and the championship for the team, despite two car-damaging accidents along the way. Once again the Targa had delivered an epic race.

A vast and impressive autostrada now runs the length of Sicily, just inland from the north coast. Spearing through the countryside and spanning huge ravines, it creates a high-speed link between the port of Messina, close to the Italian mainland, and the island's capital of Palermo. Stray from the modern motorway however, and it's easy to imagine the Sicily of half a century ago. Back then Targa time would have meant a snaking procession of brightly coloured race trucks working their way along the tight rural back roads towards the start line, paddock and pit garages built at Cerda, some two thirds of the way from Messina to Palermo and a few miles inland. It must have been quite a convoy.

Today's journey to Cerda is stimulating enough, for Sicily's scenery is diverse and spectacular, but as you head inland, you eventually round a tight left-hand bend to catch sight of the still-imposing start line complex. Derelict but still regularly used as a backdrop for new car launches and the annual Targa Florio revival meeting, the stark concrete buildings wear an incongruous coat of whitewash. Mercifully, areas of the original concrete remain, and you can still see the flaking, fading evidence of old advertising. It's an evocative setting, but the true spirit of the Targa is to be found behind the wheel of your car, on the road that winds into the mountains. Just the thought of it makes your pulse quicken with anticipation.

It doesn't matter what you're driving as you pull away from the ghostly grandstands, for whether it's a rental Fiat or a priceless Ferrari, the relentless twists and turns demand your complete attention. The repeated action of hot summer sunshine bakes the road surface to a hard shine, while dust from the fields adds to their slippery nature. Away from the small villages punctuating the course, traffic is light. In fact there are times when you feel like

The Great Road Races

Right: The ramshackle buildings on the outskirts of some Sicillian towns provide a contrasting backdrop to the speed and excitement of the Targa.

you're the only person on the island, with only the sound of the blood pumping around your head, and the distant straining of a decrepit Vespa moped to break the silence.

By the 1970s, speeds had risen to such extreme levels that the Targa's days as a World Championship venue were numbered. Safety concerns, though still laughably relaxed by the standards of today, were forcing organizers to make efforts to protect competitors and spectators, but with as many as 700,000 Sicilians camped out around a 44-mile (71km) route, the task was hopeless. Teams and drivers were becoming increasingly edgy about racing their 500bhp, half-ton projectiles between the people, trees and stone walls that lined much of the lap, but still the challenge of beating each other, and the course itself, proved irresistible.

One man in particular relished the trials of the Targa. His name was Nino Vaccarella. A headmaster at a private school on the island for most of the year, when it came to the Targa Florio he was a master of the Piccolo Madonie road circuit. A former winner of the race, he was a favourite of the crowd, and also of Ferrari and Alfa Romeo, who regularly enlisted his services at Targa time.

Everyone knew that the 1973 Targa would be its last as a top-flight World Championship round. Understandably home favourites Alfa Romeo and Ferrari both wanted to win desperately, and with Porsche bringing a pair of road-based 911 racers in place of the purpose-built 908s, it looked as though the last 'real' Targa would be an Italian benefit. Just as in 1955, all the stops were pulled out, with Alfa and Ferrari fighting tooth and nail during qualifying. Records tumbled each time a car took to the track. Vaccarella didn't set the fastest time, but his Ferrari teammate Arturo Mezario did, lapping the tortuous

Right: A fruit and vegetable stand in one of the many market towns along the Targa route.

Far right: Serious subsidence along part of the route – a result of heavy rain.

44-mile (71km) course in 33min 38.5sec. The scene was set for an unforgettable battle.

For Vaccarella the pressure must have been unbearable, for every time he drove he carried with him the hopes of all Sicily. Look at old photographs of races from the early 70s and you'll spot his name, or more often a distinctive double V for Viva Vaccarella, or 'VN' for Viva Nino daubed on trees, walls, houses, even the road he knew so intimately. In fact you can still see remnants of that passionate graffiti some three decades later.

Inspiring clues to the island's recent but spectacular past, the doodles also provide you with evidence that you're following in Nino's wheeltracks. In truth, once you've picked your way inland to Cerda, the remainder of the Piccolo Madonie course is easy to follow. With so few roads, and armed with the names of classic Targa waypoints, such as the remote mountain town of Caltavuturo (the most southerly point on the course), Scillato, Collesano and Campofelice, you really can't go wrong.

You spot Caltavuturo from miles away, perched high on a craggy sun-bleached rockface, buzzards wheeling high above on warm currents of air. It's a dramatic landmark, but one that comes less than halfway into the relentlessly challenging course. As a visitor it's the perfect place to go in search of a fine rustic lunch of delicious dried meats or pasta, but for the drivers it would have barely warranted a second glance, for with some 700 corners packed into each 44-mile (71km) lap, the slightest distraction could spell disaster.

With dozens of cars on the circuit the race soon became hard to follow; many of the quicker cars were stuck behind the smaller, slower machinery. The verges were littered with Fiat 500s abandoned by spectators and the edges of the track defined by low stone walls, ditches, trees or craggy rock faces, so that negotiating slower traffic was one of the major hazards of the race.

Imagine the frustration as you close in on a gaggle of road-based cars in your works Ferrari, knowing that no matter how much of their mirrors you fill with scarlet paintwork they simply refuse to let you pass. But when you put yourself in the slower car's position it's easy to see that it was often impossible to move over without putting your own race – your own life – in jeopardy. No wonder many a front-runner fell victim to hidden stone mile markers or other unforgiving road furniture as they attempted to squeeze through non-existent gaps.

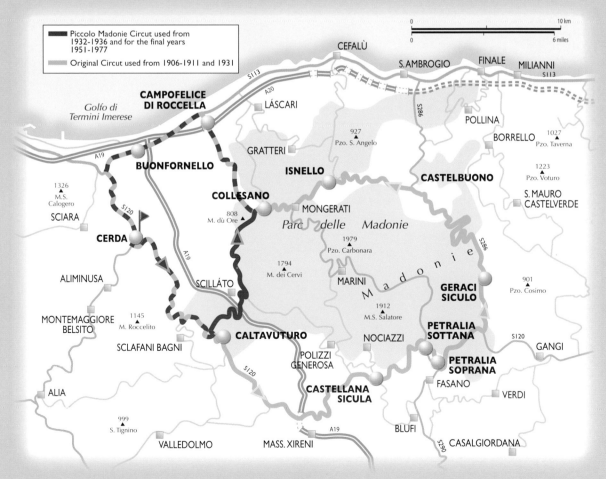

VIC ELFORD

Nino Vaccarella may have carried the hopes of Sicily with him when he raced the Targa Florio course, but even the local Madonie maestro concedes that when it came to knowing the circuit – and he means *really* knowing the circuit – only one man could claim to have all 44 miles (71km) committed to memory. That man's name is Vic Elford.

Speak to Vic and he attributes his unrivalled knowledge of the circuit to his rallying background. So conditioned was he to making pace notes with his co-driver, David Stone, that even when he was driving solo, as he did in the many sports prototypes he drove for Porsche in the Targa, that on his first practice laps he was making a mental note of every bump and crest, corner and camber change that could affect the trajectory of his flying Porsche.

Of course it helps that Vic also believes he has a photographic memory, but unfair genetic advantage or not, there's something remarkable about Vic's extraordinary record in this most intense road race of all. Of his six visits to the island Vic failed to be the fastest driver only once.

Of those visits his greatest drive – many say the greatest Targa drive of all – was in 1968, when he won at the wheel of a Porsche 907 (right). Having been forced to stop twice during the first lap with wheel and tyre problems he fell 18mins behind the leader. By the end of the race Elford had set a new lap record (a whole minute faster than the previous record!) and led the field home by 3min.

At that time Porsche had a tradition of producing posters to celebrate each victory. All feature the winning car in action, except that marking the 1968 Targa victory, which features Vic, smiling, just moments after crossing the line to win. Later, when asked why they had chosen to feature Vic instead of his 907, they said they did it because, for once, it wasn't Porsche that had won, it was the driver.

Some respite came on the long Campofelice straight, which runs parallel with the coast and a railway line. How the drivers must have longed for, then dreaded, the endless charge: relieved that they could capitalize on their superior power but paranoid that the unrelenting punishment dished out by the Piccolo Madonie circuit would lead to a mechanical failure that would pitch them to oblivion at 190mph (306kph).

As the battle between Ferrari and Alfa intensified the fans were whipped into a frenzy. Just as in

practice the pace was unrelenting, and just as in practice mistakes and mechanical maladies began to claim the home favourites. Vaccarella's teammate suffered a puncture early in the race, and in managing to get the car back to the pits terminal damage had been done to the transmission. Shortly after Nino took over, the Ferrari's gearbox failed, robbing him of another victory.

The attrition continued as one by one the Italian teams managed to snatch defeat from the jaws of victory. For the Porsche 911 crews, who were hopelessly outpaced at the start, the unthinkable suddenly appeared within their reach. According to Helmut Markko, the loss of the Italian pace-setters was the best news, for prior to that point both he and his teammate had simply decided to 'drive like hell' in an effort to remain in contention. Now free from the need to push themselves and their outgunned Porsche beyond the limit they could afford to take less risks and steal a legendary win.

Doubtless heartbroken by the failure of the Italian team, the crowd were facing a greater disappointment, for the '73 Targa was the last to count as a World Championship event.

Though the glory days are over, so long as there's a road through the Madonie mountains, the Targa's magnetism remains as strong as ever.

Above: The familiar shape of a Porsche 911 rushing through the Madonie mountains.

TARGA TASMANIA

DISTANCE: 1,336 MILES (2,150KM) **FIRST RACE:** 1992 **LOCATION:** TASMANIA, AUSTRALIA

Sicily and Tasmania. Two islands, half a world apart, united by a shared passion for motorsport and one evocative word: Targa. Though it's Sicily that enjoys the higher profile amongst car enthusiasts, Tasmania is also steeped in motorsport history. From 1953 to 1968 car and motorcycle races – including the 1959 and 1965 Australian Grand Prix – were held on the Longford road circuit, just inland of Launceston on the island's northern coast.

Known as 'the Reims of the South Pacific', Longford was an extremely fast and treacherous 4.5-mile (7.2km) circuit, with a series of long hedge- and tree-lined straights linked by four tight corners. Highlights included a Flying Mile, a high-speed jump over a railway crossing, a scary kink beneath a brick viaduct and an extremely popular pub situated on the outside of the right-hander in Longford's town centre.

As you can imagine, there was something of a party atmosphere during race weekends, and one of Longford's many colourful legends has it that a racer by the name of Lex Davison once crashed into the pub and retired from the race. Upon jumping out of his car he headed straight for the bar, where the locals bought him a commiseratory drink!

Despite its huge popularity, the highest level of competition, and a hall of fame that included great names such as Jim Clark, Jack Brabham, Jackie Stewart and Bruce McLaren, Longford eventually went the way of so many great road circuits, the organizers deeming it too dangerous to continue. Perhaps they did have a point, for sports cars were regularly exceeding 180mph (290kph) along the Flying Mile, while Chris Amon's Longford lap record-setting average speed of 121mph (195kph) remained an Australian record from 1968 until the 1996 Formula One GP in Melbourne.

Longford's glory days left some unique memories and enduring records, but it was another, more prosaic legacy that would play a part in the creation of Tasmania's very own Targa-style road race. When the Longford circuit was first proposed back in the 1950s, legislation was required to permit the closure of public roads for racing purposes. Some 25 years after the last race in 1968, this same legislation would once again enable cars to race on the roads of Australia's island state.

Much had changed in that intervening quarter of a century. Cars had got faster and more specialized and the sport had become commercialized, while race organizers and local authorities were even less willing to take responsibility for wheel-to-wheel racing on public roads. And yet, just as Vincenzo Florio's vision and passion provided the impetus to create a Sicilian road race at a time when few Sicilians had even seen a car, let alone driven or owned one, so Tasmanian-born businessman John Large and Australian motoring journalist Max Stahl's dream of reviving the island's racing heritage came to fruition.

Below: Stephen Rochester and Don Milner navigate their 1959 Triumph TR3A through the early morning mist. **Right:** The Mini Cooper of Syd Jenkins tackling the Tasmanian roads during the 2001 event.

CompAir
Howard Instruments
CompAir
CompAir
WEBSTER
T01 416

Inspired by Florio and driven by raw enthusiasm, the duo conceived an event that would capture the rugged spirit of the Targa Florio and the all-encompassing national fervour of the Mille Miglia, while taking modern demands and sensibilities into consideration. It was a long and complex gestation, but the end result – the Targa Tasmania – would put the island back on the motorsport map.

In the beginning, Large and Stahl were adamant that the event should principally be for classic sporting cars and keen amateur owner-drivers, rather than highly specialized modern racing machinery. To this end they operated the inaugural Targa Tasmania on an invitation-only basis. Using Stahl's network of contacts and encyclopedic knowledge the entrants were divided into three principle classes: a Thoroughbred

Division, for road cars manufactured before the end of 1960, the Classic Division, for cars built between 1961 and 1976, and the Contemporary Exotic Division, for cars built from 1977 onwards.

Despite early concerns that they would struggle to generate enough entries to make the event financially viable, almost 200 crews entered the 1992 Targa, among them a certain Stirling Moss, who drove his own Shelby Mustang with his wife, Suzy, co-driving alongside him.

The route was also planned in meticulous fashion, and designed to ensure the greatest challenge for the crews and maximum exposure for Tasmania's World Heritage-standard scenery. Starting in Launceston and finishing in Hobart on Tasmania's southern coast, that first Targa course covered some 1,250 miles (2,012km) over five days, with more than a quarter of this mileage run as closed, competitive stages: a format that remains essentially the same to this day.

Left: An overhead shot just after the start of the Bonnet Hill stage, which journeys into the Huon Valley area south of Hobart. The vantage point is the 48m-high (157ft) Shot Tower, built in 1870.

'In almost every respect that matters the Targa Tasmania is a glorious throwback to the epic days of road racing'

While the stage-by-stage format where cars are released individually at regular intervals is more akin to rallying than pure road races such as the Targa Florio, the sheer scale of the Targa Tasmania infuses it with the same essential thrill and challenge. In almost every respect that matters the Targa Tasmania is a glorious throwback to the epic days of road racing.

It's a mark of the first event's popularity that of Tasmania's half a million or so inhabitants, an estimated 150,000 lined the route during its five days. That first Targa had a bewitching effect on all involved, including Sir Stirling Moss, who described it as 'one of the greatest driving experiences of my life.' Coming from one of the most celebrated racing drivers of all time, that's quite a eulogy.

With feedback like that it didn't take long for the Targa to gain a must-do reputation amongst the keenest competitive drivers. Nor did the world's car manufacturers waste any time in recognizing the kudos and credibility that a successful assault on the Targa would bring. As its profile grew so the entry list featured more and more professional

Below: Ray Julian and Michael Helmers in their 1995 BMW M3 south of Hobart. **Below right:** Scott and Leigh Kent in their 1965 Ford Mustang coupe.

drivers in well-prepared factory machinery. This could have signalled the end for the Targa Tasmania as an event that anyone, from rank amateur to former F1 or rally World Champion, could enter. However, displaying the healthy pragmatism that created the event in the first place, the Targa organizers allowed the race to evolve while preserving the interests of those enthusiastic amateurs who were there from the beginning.

A variety of non-competitive classes were introduced to enable the less committed but no less enthusiastic drivers to enjoy the Targa, while the influx of professional teams and drivers brought new pace and drama to the event. And, although this meant that the quickest guys often found themselves in the quickest cars – drivers like Australian touring-car heroes Jim Richards and the late Peter Brock – the burgeoning talents of local amateur crews soon resulted in some giant-slaying performances. On the Targa, reputation counts for little.

In 1994, Australian F1 legend Sir Jack Brabham learned this first hand, when he misjudged a fast corner, lost control of his BMW M3 and slid off the road. Mercifully both he and his co-driver emerged with nothing more than bruised egos, which is more than can be said for their BMW, which came to rest on its side hard against a tree.

Above: Steve Glenney in his 2002 Subaru Impreza WRX STi during the 2006 event. **Right:** Paul Stuart and Michael Herrod in their 2003 Porsche 911 GT3 RS competing in the same year.

Once you've seen Tasmania's scenery and the roads that pass through it, you can appreciate why even the best are easily wrong-footed. The roads are fast, narrow, and dotted with deceptive corners and unsettling blind crests. Stretches that appear straightforward often conceal wicked sections to catch out the unwary or just plain unlucky. Through the many wooded sections, lethal patches of moss can lie at the fringes of the tarmac, leaving minimal room for error. Drivers rely heavily on their co-drivers, and on their powers of self-restraint, for a completely open stretch of road viewed through the windscreen of a Lamborghini or a Porsche is a tantalizing sight. In the Targa it pays to remember that those who get carried away behind the wheel often get carried away by the recovery truck before the event is out.

The key to the Targa's epic nature is Tasmania itself. Some 75 per cent larger than Sicily, yet burdened with just a tenth of its population, Tasmania is blessed with vast tracts of unspoiled wilderness. Some of the oldest and tallest eucalyptus trees on earth can be seen in the island's subtropical rainforests, while Tasmanian Devils – the somewhat milder-mannered incarnations of the whizzing, snarling, pesky-wabbit-eating Looney Tunes cartoon character – are also native to Tasmania's remote forests and lush plains.

With the tremendous diversity of roads and scenery comes a fabulous mix of stages. Three of these – Mount Arrowsmith, Cethana and The Sideling – are rated amongst the finest competitive tarmac stages anywhere in the world. From short sprints of just over a mile to marathon tests of mental and mechanical stamina, the Targa throws everything at the crews. Mother Nature also tends to do her bit. In fact, there has never been a

completely dry Targa, and for the last two years snow has fallen on the Mount Arrowsmith stage, adding an extra hazard to this already extraordinary 30-mile (48km) stage.

Perhaps as a consequence of the unpredictable weather and the tortuous nature of some of the stages, all-wheel drive cars are becoming more and more popular in the Modern Competition category. Naturally there are some Subaru Imprezas and Mitsubishi Evos amongst them, but there are also an increasing number of genuine supercars, including the Lamborghini Gallardo, Nissan Skyline GT-R and Porsche 911 Turbo.

As the race has grown in stature, and the cars have grown in pace and quality, so the calibre and commitment of the crews has increased. True to the spirit of the Targa, local heroes often mix it with seasoned professionals. Inevitably this leads to some classic battles, the fiercest of which always seem to centre around Australian pro-racer Jim Richards. With seven Targa wins to his name, Richards is the unofficial King of Tasmania, but local nephew-and-uncle team of Jason and John White are threatening his supremacy.

After their first win in 2005, aboard a Nissan Skyline R34 GT-R, the Whites changed to a Lamborghini Gallardo for 2006 in an effort to maintain their advantage over Richards, who prefers the unique challenge presented by a Porsche 911. The Whites took the '06 Targa title for back-to-back

wins, but the supremely talented Richards remains a constant threat. His ability to completely demoralize his rivals with wet-weather pace to humble even the quickest all-wheel drive crews is the stuff of Targa legend, yet the man himself remains humble and quick to share the glory with his co-driver, Barry Oliver.

Although the Targa Tasmania lacks World Championship status, such intense rivalry between the likes of the Whites and Richards is as old as motorsport itself, for they are pushing themselves and their cars to the absolute limit, on public roads in the fastest (road) cars of the day. In the 21st century, nothing comes closer to emulating the character of those great road races of the past.

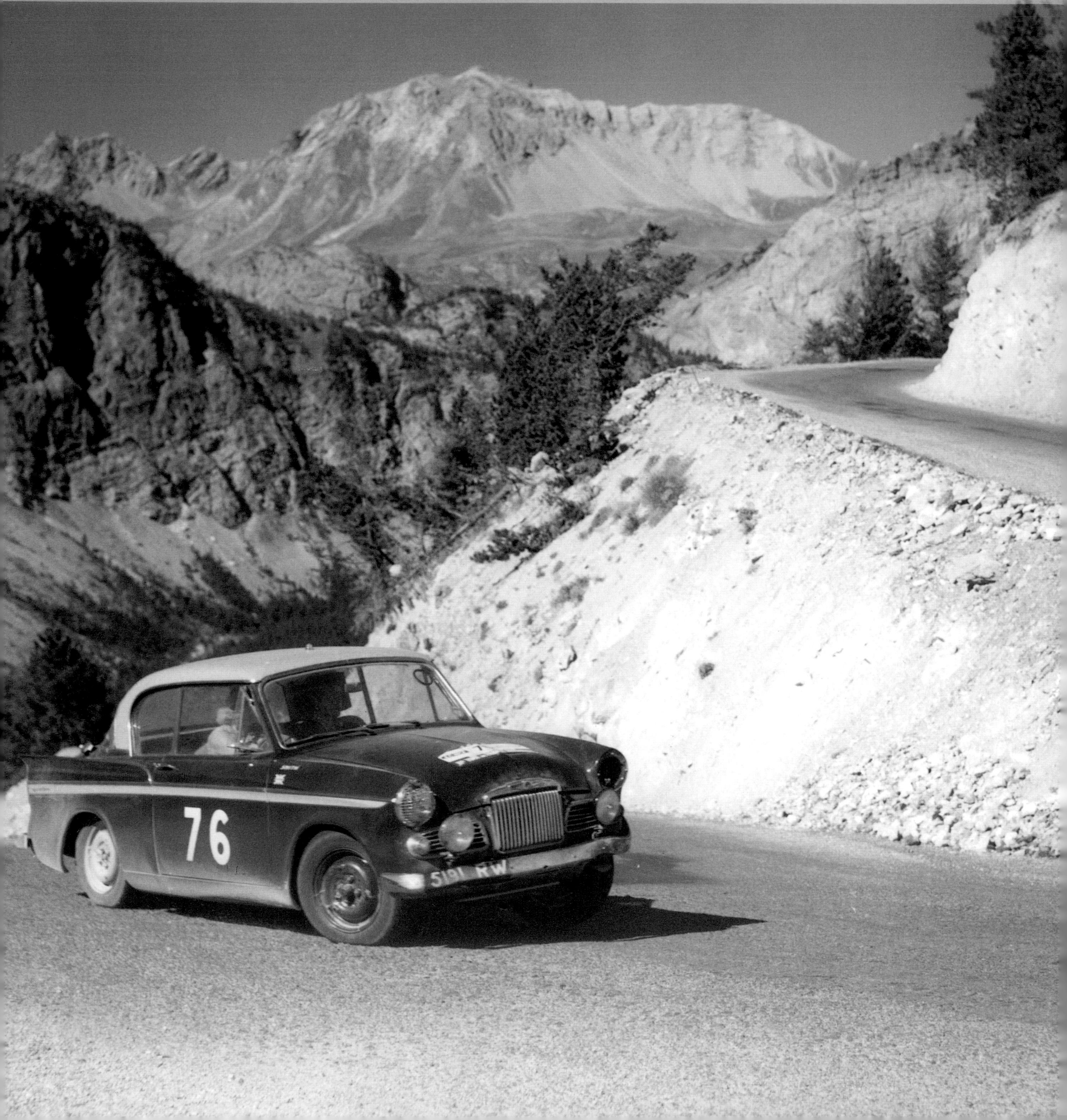
76

TOUR DE FRANCE AUTOMOBILE

DISTANCE: 2,500 MILES (4,025KM) **FIRST RACE:** 1889 **LOCATION:** FRANCE

Overshadowed by its pedal-powered namesake, the petrol-powered Tour de France, or Tour Auto as it eventually became known, was first held more than a century ago. Yet despite maturing into a unique multi-discipline event, combining circuit racing with hillclimbs and extensive road mileage, the Tour never quite attained the legendary status of the Mille Miglia and Targa Florio. However, to those who love the notion of full-blooded racing cars driving the length of France on public roads and closed racetracks, the Tour Auto remains one of motorsport history's gems.

Looking back, it was an incredibly ambitious move by the fledgling Automobile Club de France (ACF) to stage a competitive driving event at the end of the 19th century, at the very dawn of the automobile age. Yet the ACF continued undaunted and successfully held its first Tour. Proof of how different motoring was back then comes in the truly arcane rules to which the Tour was run. Open to four-wheel vehicles (cars), three-wheelers (motorcycles) and 'others' – whatever that meant – it was also a requirement that at least one of the crew in each vehicle was a member of the ACF, and that they weigh a minimum of 70kg (154lb)!

In those pioneering days the Tour de France was more a test of endurance than a pure test of speed. Cars were frail and relatively slow, the roads poor and weather protection for the crews rudimentary, to say the least. Covering up to 2,500 miles (4,025km), the Tour may not have been a race in

the modern sense, but it was certainly an adventure for the first generation of car enthusiasts and a huge challenge for the car makers of the day.

It would be another seven years before the second Tour was held. Such interruptions, it seems, soon became an integral part of the Tour's patchy history, with lengthy pauses for both world wars and other assorted political and financial crises. Having ceased in 1937, it wasn't until 1951 that the event hit its stride once more. By this time it had matured into a major motorsport event, with prestigious makes and famous drivers taking part. While still including considerable road mileage, the Tour's format featured more and more racetracks, hillclimbs and other closed-road sections, making it one of the most complete competitive tests of a car and driver ever held.

Thanks to a lack of funding there was another break in proceedings from 1965, but when the Tour returned in 1969 it was to enjoy what many regard as the event's golden era, thanks to the efforts of five-times Tour de France winner, Bernard Consten. Not only did he attract the necessary sponsors back to the event – which he re-branded 'Tour Auto' to avoid confusion with the cycling event – but he also created an unrivalled spectacle by inviting sports prototypes to compete.

Aside from Formula One cars, these machines were the quickest and most exciting of their day, designed to compete in endurance circuit races such as the Le Mans 24 Hours and Spa 1000kms. French team Matra entered its beautiful racing blue MS650 racer, while a privateer Ferrari 512S and Ford GT40 made a race of it.

Both the Matra and Ferrari were powered by fabulous V12 engines: the big-bore 5.0-litre Italian motor developing a mighty 550bhp at a wailing 8000rpm, the lighter Matra using a detuned version

of its 3.0-litre F1 engine, which kicked-out a less muscular 420bhp but at an even more vocal 9500rpm. Both of these spectacular open-topped cars were capable of 200mph (322kph), and together with the thunderous V8-engined Ford – not to mention the rest of the Tour's substantial entry – must have made for a truly incredible sight as they popped, banged and roared along the public roads.

Left: The Sunbeam Rapier of Rosemary Smith and Rosemary Seers in the 1962 Tour de France Auto. The pair went on to win the Coupe des Dames award – the highest award for women in motorsport.
Right: Jacques Cochin at the wheel of his Porsche 910 between Sarlat and Albi.

'Seemingly the only thing consistent about the Tour Auto's route and competitive stages was it's glorious inconsistency'

In a country as fiercely proud as France it was inevitable that the Matra would be the crowd favourite. How could they resist, when the team fielded an all-French driver line-up, comprising F1 heroes Patrick Depailler and Jean-Pierre Beltoise, and a certain Jean Todt. So you can imagine the euphoria when the trio drove to victory in the 1970 Tour, beating the Ferrari into second place. When Matra repeated the feat the following year the place must have gone crazy.

After such heady success it seems inconceivable that the event should have hit more problems, but thanks to the global oil crisis the Tour Auto suffered more fallow years in the late 1970s. It was a hiatus from which the event never fully recovered, and with funding and entries fading, the 1986 event – the 50th running of the Tour – proved to be the last true competitive event.

It's hard to fathom why the Tour's history should be so fraught with problems, especially as its size and spectacle was a match for any motor racing event held before or since. Perhaps it was the Tour's unusual and constantly changing route that made it hard to embrace. Rather than a pure lights to flag road race on a closed-road course, the Tour Auto was a five-day journey, stopping in a different town

or city every night and using a public road route to get competing cars and crews between some of the France's finest racetracks and hillclimbs.

In 1970, for example, the Tour started in Bandol, a small coastal town on the Côte d'Azur between Marseilles and Toulon. Why Bandol? Because it's a stone's throw from the Paul Ricard circuit, where the Tour Auto's entrants would take part in the first race of that year's event. From there the route headed inland to Albi, some 50 miles (80km) northeast of Toulouse, where another competitive element was held, then Pau – close to the Pyrenees mountain range and the nearby glamour of Biarritz – where another race would take place. And so it went on, heading north as far as the Grand Prix circuit at Rouen (just north of Paris), before heading southwards once more, via Dijon, Le Mont Dore and Aix Les Bains, before finally arriving in Nice to a rapturous reception for the grand finish.

You only need to look to the following year's itinerary to appreciate why the Tour Auto was a unique challenge that the drivers relished, but the public found difficult to take to their hearts. Instead of Bandol, the Tour started and finished in Nice, following a completely different route that even managed to include forays into Germany – to race

Above: The Ferrari 250GT of Olivier Gendebien and Lucien Bianchi in 1958. The pair went on to win the race.

at the Nürburgring – and Spain to complete at the Montjuich Park circuit on the outskirts of Barcelona. Seemingly the only thing consistent about the Tour Auto's route and competitive stages was it's glorious inconsistency.

It was a recipe that was successfully revived in 1992 by Patrick Peter, who, with the help of several other racing enthusiasts, decided to bring the Tour Auto back as a historic event, much like the hugely successful Mille Miglia revival. This time however, the Tour Auto's eclectic mix of road route, racetrack and hillclimbs was a positive strength. The combination of driving through some of the most picturesque regions of France, competing at legendary racing venues and enjoying stopovers in fine hotels transformed the Tour Auto from a gruelling marathon into a high-octane social occasion. Unsurprisingly it proved irresistible to the owners of classic road and race cars made between 1951 and 1973, some of which actually competed in the original Tour Auto.

How do you follow the route of the Tour Auto? The simple answer is you don't. Well, not as you

Left: A 1963 AC Cobra, between Sarlat and Albi. **Above:** A 1970 Porsche 911 ST.

would an old Grand Prix circuit or the Targa Florio. But in many ways that's the beauty of the Tour, for whether you're chasing the modern retrospective event, or merely looking for a more stimulating passage through France, all you need to capture the spirit of the Tour is a list of the towns and circuits through which the race passed on a particular year, a detailed road atlas of France and a handful of days to kill. The rest is up to you. In fact, given that the Tour Auto has included classic stand alone venues such as Le Mans, Le Mont Ventoux, the Nürburgring Nordschleife, Pau, Reims and Spa-Francorchamps, you could cover many of the routes in this book under the Tour Auto banner.

For the true Tour Auto experience you really should chase the event itself, for you'll meet more great people and get closer to more mouth-watering classic road and race cars than you'd ever believe possible. Traditionally held in late April, it involves more than 200 cars, some entered in the Competition class, while others choose the less frenetic but no less competitive Regularity class. Whatever the category, you're sure to see these magnificent cars being driven in the way their makers intended!

Whether you opt to follow the Tour in its entirety, or simply grab a glimpse of the action, the start is a must-see. The modern Tour has established a tradition for gathering in the centre of Paris, and certainly knows how to put on a show. Every April a glittering array of the world's most desirable road and racing cars is gathered around the beautiful Trocadero in the shadow of the Eiffel Tower. Those same cars are then coaxed into roaring life, checked through a time control at short intervals before being waved off into the mêlée of a mid-morning Champs-Elysées, escorted by dedicated outriders from the French Gendarmerie. It's enough to bring even the most frantic Parisian rush hour to an awestuck standstill and a car enthusiast go weak at the knees.

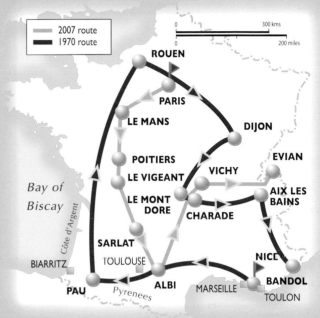

Each leg of the Tour will take anywhere between 150- and 300-mile (241–483km) bites out of the total route distance, and is likely to include one or possibly two different race venues each day. Although the competitors and crews have their accommodation arranged for them by the Tour's organizers, the route is available well in advance, so even if you're not lucky enough to be directly taking part you can plan your overnight stops to mirror those of the Tour. For the most comprehensive details of each Tour Auto you're best advised to visit www.tourauto.com.

With no shortage of competing cars (or their support crews) to latch onto, it's possible to get swept along the road sections with your windscreen full of a Ferrari 250 GTO's curvaceous £10-million rump and your mirrors equally brimmed with the unmistakable snout of a Porsche 911 RSR. This could happen anywhere from the centre of Paris to a fabulous mountain road in the Pyrenees or Alpes-Maritimes. As a way to experience the best roads France has to offer, chasing the Tour has no peer.

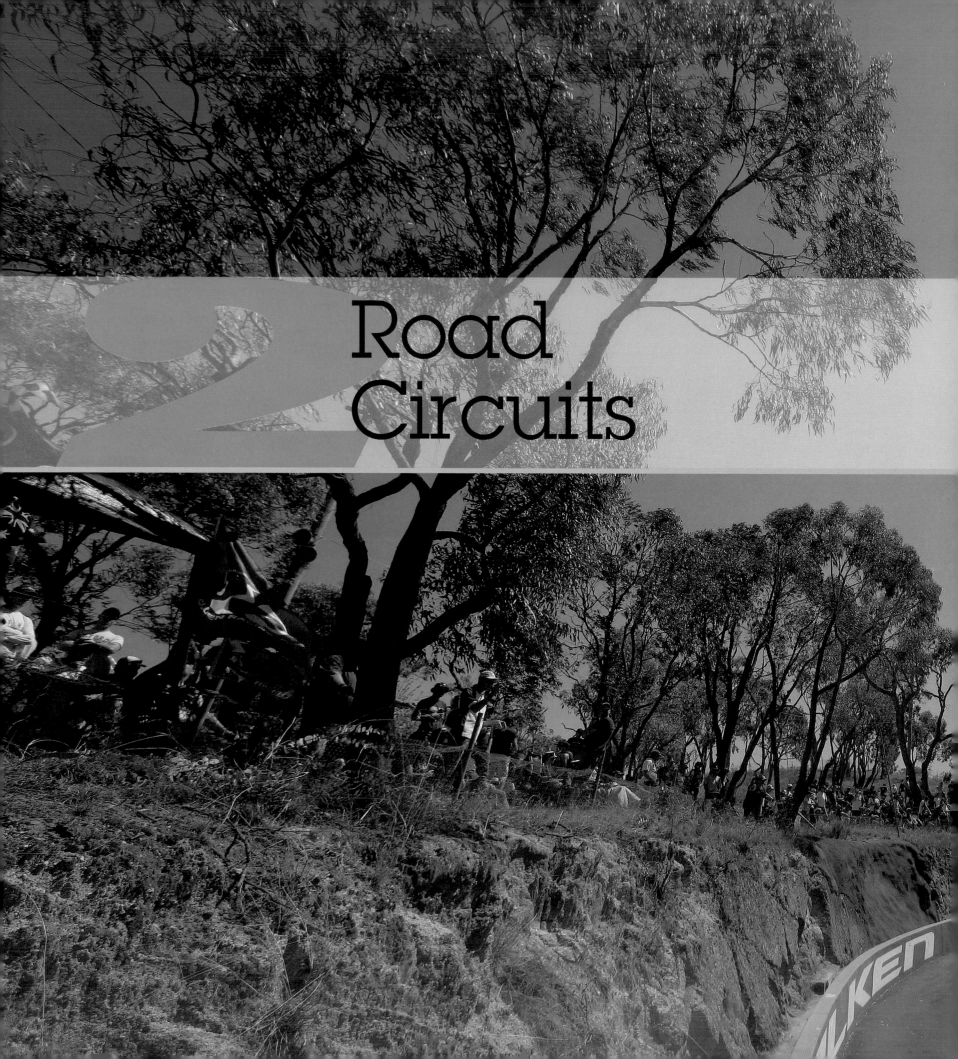

2 Road Circuits

The Holden Commodore VZ of Steve Owen and Tony Longhurst
during the Supercheap Auto 1000 at Mount Panorama, Bathurst in 2006

ISLE OF MAN TT COURSE

DISTANCE: 37.73 MILES (60.7KM) **FIRST RACE:** 1907 **LOCATION:** ISLE OF MAN

The painted kerbstones tell the story. Like a length of black-and-white boundary rope they line the edges of town streets and village lanes, passing by pubs and post offices, driveways, schools, telephone boxes and countless front doorsteps. For 48 weeks of the year they are nothing but a curiosity, but come the end of May and the middle of August this endless monochrome spool defines the fringes of what anyone with a drop of petrol in their veins regards as the last great road circuit. Welcome to the Isle of Man: The Road Racing Capital of the World.

The story of how the Isle of Man came to be synonymous with road racing can be traced way back to the turn of the 20th century. While France and Italy embraced the new and exciting spectacle of automobile racing, the obvious risks and regular fatalities prompted the British and German governments to pass legislation that prohibited the closure of public roads for racing purposes.

In an indirect way we have the son of a Scottish-born, US-domiciled publishing magnate to thank for the Isle of Man's proud racing heritage. His name was James Gordon-Bennett. Born into a life of wealth and privilege, he was a notorious playboy. Fortunately his wild and extravagant behaviour was tempered by his generous charitable donations, and his ceaseless funding of polar expeditions and events that fostered sporting endeavour.

One such event was the Gordon-Bennett Cup, a race conceived to determine which nation built the best motorcar. The first Trial took place in 1900, and was contested by French, German and Belgian teams on a 350-mile (563km) course between Paris

and Lyon. By 1902 a number of English enthusiasts had expressed serious interest in competing, and an English driver by the name of S F Edge won that year's G-B Cup driving a Napier. By the terms of the competition, the winning nation was to host the Cup the following year, but as racing wasn't possible on the UK mainland the 1903 race was eventually held in County Kildare, Ireland. The contingency was made possible because the official name of British motorsport's governing body was the Automobile Club of Great Britain and Ireland.

Edge failed to successfully defend his title, but national pride in the British automobile industry was growing, as was frustration at the lack of a suitable circuit on which to test and develop all-British racing machinery. Once again offshore help

was at hand, thanks to some aristocratic nepotism between the Secretary of the Automobile Club of Great Britain and Ireland, Julian Orde, and His Excellency The Right Honourable George Fitzroy Henry, who was Governor of the Isle of Man and – handily – Orde's cousin. The Governor, Tynwald (the Manx Parliament) and the Manx people embraced the idea of road racing on their island, and Britain soon had a new road racing venue.

Describing the 227sq mile (588sq km) island's minimal 50-mile (80km) network of unsurfaced and badly rutted tracks as 'roads' was stretching the point a little, but most were utilized in the quest to create a complete test of what were then cutting-edge machines, but are now classified as veteran cars. The course looped through Man's diverse

Motorcycles screaming through the peaceful villages of the Isle of Man are a unique sight; here are Jeremy Toye **(opposite)** and Martin Finnigan **(right)** during the 2006 event.

'it really is impossible to imagine what it must be like to see, or better still ride, a motorcycle down here at as **much as 170mph'**

topography, from lush meadows and open grazing to foggy mountain crags and broad coastal vistas, and provided an almost insurmountable test of engines, transmissions, brakes, tyres and drivers.

With the course defined, the Isle of Man played host to the first Gordon-Bennett Elimination Trial in May 1904. As the name suggests, it was a national competition designed to select the cars and drivers that would go on to represent Britain in that year's Gordon-Bennett Cup. The event was repeated the following year, with an additional day's competition arranged for motorcycles, which was a reflection of the growth in motorcycle sales and British desire to be at the forefront of two-wheel design and manufacturing. It would also point to the island's racing future.

During the 1905 Trial rumours had begun circulating that Gordon-Bennett was going to withdraw support for his eponymous cup the following year. This could have put paid to the island's aspirations, but such was the Isle of Man's passion for racing that it had already made plans for another motor race in 1905 to attract more visitors. Initially held as a race for cars only, the motorcycling fraternity soon followed suit, holding their own copycat meeting in May 1907. The Tourist Trophy was born.

Left: A picture of concentration: Cameron Donald and Davy Morgan in the 2006 event. **Below:** David Jefferies in 2002

Fast-forward to 2007 and the racing cars have long-since disappeared, but come the month of May the island is thronged with motorcyclists from across the globe, present to witness or compete in the world-famous Isle of Man TT races. Truer to the original concept now than ever, the Tourist Trophy has turned the island into motorcycle mecca.

There's a certain charm about travelling to the Isle of Man. Yes, of course you can catch a flight and rent a car on arrival, but for many a Manx adventure starts with a sea crossing on the Steam Packet Company's ferries. During TT fortnight these ferries carry more than 35,000 people and 13,000 motorcycles, but at other times of the year deck space is at less of a premium, making travelling to the island extremely simple.

On arrival at the main port of Douglas you're just a few minutes from the start of the TT's famous Mountain Course. Drive along the seafront, perhaps stopping for some fish and chips along the way, turn onto Broadway, then, as the road splits, take the right fork onto Ballaquayle Road before taking the next main right onto Glencrutchery Road.

Once there the first thing you'll notice is the grandstand and vast lap time and race positions board. This enormous black edifice is as much a part of the TT as any stretch of tarmac. Shunning the digital age, the scoreboard relies on timings taken by officials at the start/finish line, which are then relayed to a team of markers, who paint the lap times onto black boards, which are then taken to the back of the scoreboard by 'runners' from the local boy scout troop, who then hand them to officials who put the times in the correct position. There was a move to replace this old-fashioned method with modern computer-controlled electronic timing screens, but when the computers crashed and the timing screens went blank, the boy scouts saved the day!

From the start the first major challenge was Bray Hill. A picture of suburban normality – and subject to urban speed limits – it really is impossible to imagine what it must be like to see, or better still ride, a motorcycle down here at as much as 170mph (274kph). Racers regularly complain that

ISLE OF MAN

the right side of their bike's fairing scrapes on the road through the compression at the bottom of the descent. Then, as they crest the rise they have to fight the bike's desire to buck and rear onto its back wheel like an unbroken horse.

Clearly it takes a certain kind of courage to race here. Many of the corners – Drinkwater's, Handley's Corner and Birkin's Bend to name a few – are named after riders who lost their lives on the circuit. Back in the days of Barry Sheene the TT used to be a part of the World Championship, and though very few riders of the day refused to race on the Isle of Man, many entered the TT silently wondering if they would survive to see another race. Even from the safety of your car, you can see why.

Inevitably the TT lost its World Championship status on safety grounds, and the world's best riders were no longer compelled to race on the island. Though this dented the TT's lofty profile, the Mountain Course maintained its reputation as the most challenging and exciting race venue in the world. Brutal and dangerous though it is, the IOM continues to provide a showcase for speed and bravery. Riders know that the TT also offers an unsurpassed thrill, and that success here forges an enviable reputation. Riders such as Carl Fogerty and Steve Hislop made their names on the island before progressing to the safer and more commercial confines of circuit racing in the World Superbike and Grand Prix categories. Others, such as the late and much-loved Joey Dunlop, who won no less than 26 TT titles, preferred the unique challenge of road racing to the fame and potential fortune of mainstream bike racing.

As you continue along from the roller-coaster start of Bray Hill towards Quarter Bridge you can appreciate why for some nothing else comes close to racing here. The stone walls, houses and telegraph poles give way to a line of trees, which merge into a green tunnel of leaves at racing speed.

The bumps, kerbs and white lines, all barely noticeable at legal speeds, upset the racing bikes as they brake hard for the first real corner. A tight right-hander formed by a white-painted mini roundabout, the racers cut inside it on their way to the village of Union Mills.

The road begins to widen, with glimpses of open countryside, but as you enter Union Mills it narrows again. Houses are built right up tight against the tarmac. For the racers, the first 8 miles (13km) or so are pretty much flat out, but for law-abiding drivers the first quarter of the course is characterized by 30 and 40mph (48 and 64kph) limits. For the racers this suspension of reality, and the opportunity to flash through villages at five or six times the posted 30mph (48kph) speed limit, is what makes the TT unique.

Road racing throws other unique hazards at competitors. Take Ballaugh Bridge for instance, a narrow hump-backed bridge positioned on a slight corner. It comes at the end of a typically fast section, where the quickest bike racers will be touching 150mph (240kph) or more, and requires them to brake down hard to less than 30mph (48kph), before being thrown briefly airborne as they take the bridge.

For visitors to the island, these sections are fascinating but also frustrating, for it isn't until the wide open stretches which lead up and over Snaefell that the Isle of Man's famous speed limit-free sections of open road can be enjoyed to the full, for where you see a national speed limit sign you can go as fast as you like. Be warned though: the police will stop you if you're deemed to be driving in a reckless manner.

Applying common sense doesn't mean you have to deny yourself some fun, and you'll notice that once you get beyond Ramsey, and round the tight left-hand hairpin to begin the climb onto the mountain road, most Manx drivers don't tend to hang about. The sense of freedom given by the liberal road traffic laws, few vehicles and the brooding mountain and moorland terrain makes driving here an invigorating experience.

By the time you return -- breathless no doubt -- to Douglas and negotiate the tight turn over Governors Bridge, the end of this magnificent 37.73-mile (60.7km) course is almost within sight. If you've stopped to admire the views, or for refreshment at one of the many pubs and restaurants along the way, it may have taken most of a morning or afternoon to complete your lap. During the 2007 TT, rider John McGuinness set a new outright TT lap record at an average speed of 130.35mph (209.78kph). Bikers are indeed a different breed...

Above: William Dunlop, nephew of TT legend Joey Dunlop, during his first TT in 2006

LE MANS

DISTANCE: 8.5 MILES (13.5KM) **FIRST RACE:** 1923 **LOCATION:** FRANCE

The locals call it Les Hunaudieres. Most of us call it the Mulsanne. Road maps refer to it as the N138. None of these are the most evocative designations for a 3-mile (5km) stretch of public road that lives a double life as the most famous straight in motor racing. But then at Le Mans action has always spoken louder than words.

There are races with more glamour; there are races that also run twice around the clock, but no race has embedded itself so deeply into motorsport history, and the hearts of enthusiasts, as the Le Mans 24 Hours. Bentley, Alfa Romeo, Jaguar, Ferrari, Ford, Porsche and, most recently, Audi have

all discovered the unrivalled halo effect that comes with repeated success at Le Mans, while the drivers who master its gruelling challenge are worshipped as heroes. Even Hollywood actor and hopeless petrolhead Steve McQueen made a film about the race. It nearly ruined him, and got duff reviews at the time, but *Le Mans* now enjoys a cult following.

The roads around the town of Le Mans first hosted a motor race in 1906 – the very first French Grand Prix, in fact – but it wasn't until 1923 that the first 24 Heures du Mans was held, on a revised configuration of public roads to make a 10.8-mile (17.4km) course. That first road circuit remained

unchanged for six years, during which time the British Bentley team was the first to become synonymous with Le Mans success, winning in 1924, '27 and '28.

The expansion of the town of Le Mans led to the first in a long line of circuit changes, with the Automobile Club de l'Ouest (ACO, the race organizing body) constructing a link road to avoid Le Mans' suburban fringes on safety grounds. Just half a mile (1km) shorter in length, the essential character of the course remained the same, as did Bentley's dominance, with Bentley Boy – the heroically named Woolf Barnato – continuing where he'd left off in 1928, sharing the winning car in 1929 and 1930 to become the first man to score a Le Mans hat trick. Almost 80 years later, only a few have managed to equal his achievement.

The revised configuration was to be short-lived, for the circuit was once again changed in 1932, when a new purpose-built section was added to link the end of the pits straight with the new Tertre Rouge corner, which rejoined the Mulsanne straight. Now cut to approximately 8.5 miles (13.5km), it was the start of Le Mans' shift from old-school road circuit to the mix of permanent circuit and public roads it is today.

While the circuit had become shorter, the change in character and the advances in engineering saw average lap speeds increasing. In 1928 the winning Bentley averaged just under 70mph (113kph) for the duration of the race. In 1931 the victorious Alfa Romeo 8C's race average had risen to 75mph

Left: The Porsche Turbo RSR of Gijs van Lennep and Herbert Müller in the 1974 race. **Opposite:** Pedro Rodriguez and Jackie Oliver (Porsche 917 LH) lead Gerard Larrousse and Vic Elford (Porsche 917 LH), Mark Donohue and David Hobbs (Ferrari 512M), and Jo Siffert and Derek Bell (Porsche 917 LH) during the 1971 event.

Above: An Audi R10 heads down the Mulsanne in 2006. **Opposite:** The Ferrari 550 Maranello of Darren Turner, Colin McRae and Rickard Rydell in 2004.

(121kph), while by 1955 the winning Jaguar D-type's race average had leapt to a fraction under 108mph (174kph).

After the disastrous 1955 disastrous crash involving Pierre Levegh and Lance Macklin on the narrow pit straight, in which Levegh and 80 spectators lost their lives, the pit straight was widened, and the pit lane was eventually separated from the pit straight by a wall. The famous Le Mans start, where drivers would run across the straight to their car, was another anachronism to be lost in the march for increased safety.

Despite the aftermath of what remains the worst accident in the history of motorsport, the circuit retained a large proportion of public roads right into the late 1960s. Stretching from Tertre Rouge at the start of the Mulsanne right the way back round to beginning of the pit straight, it was narrow with little or no run-off areas. With trees and houses lining much of the circuit from Mulsanne to Maison Blanche (named after the white house which was

just inches from the Armco) the circuit was becoming increasingly unsuitable for the immensely powerful cars, such as the Ford GT40, that were now competing in the 24 Hours.

Inevitably the track began to bypass original elements, such as Maison Blanche, and although the character changed with it, the ACO effected the changes intelligently, creating sections such as the Ford Chicane and Porsche Curves, which have now become unmistakable landmarks of their own.

A big part of Le Mans' enduring magic is that while the circuit has incorporated more and more permanent sections for racing only, many of the old road sections have reverted back to their original role, which means that you can drive the same stretches of tarmac as the Le Mans pioneers like Woolf Barnato. Even adhering to the posted speed limits, there are few more evocative journeys to make.

As you join the N138 and see the 100-year-old poplar trees approaching on your left, a quick glance to the right will reveal the point at which the

racing cars leave the purpose-built part of the circuit and merge with the Mulsanne straight. Triple-height layers of Armco are a graphic illustration of the dangers to be found along here during a race, and are in stark contrast to the leafy suburban scene to be glimpsed beyond the barriers and debris fencing.

As you continue along the straight, your mind will fill with images and thoughts of Jaguar D-types, Ford GT40s and Porsche 917s streaking into the darkness. A mile or so in you'll note that as the road continues straight there's a finger of tarmac that curves abruptly away to the right, then merges back after 50m (55 yards) or so. Blocked by barriers when the N138 is doing its day job, this is the entry to the first of the two modern chicanes, which were installed in 1990 amid much protest.

Possibly the most controversial revisions in the circuit's history, they chopped the legendary Mulsanne straight from one daunting and majestic run into three distinct sections, to bring it in line with the FIA's (the governing body of motorsport) ruling on the maximum-permitted length of uninterrupted straight. While the cars were still reaching speeds of 200mph (322kph) between the chicanes, it undoubtedly emasculated one of Le Mans' unique features, as 1988 Le Mans-winner and Jaguar team driver Andy Wallace laments:

'There was nothing quite like the old Mulsanne, especially in the Jaguar XJR-9 I drove in '88. The speeds were huge, but because the Jag only had a five-speed gearbox you had this real sense of conflicting information. We'd shift from fourth to fifth at around 180mph (290kph), but because the Jag was geared to hit 240mph (386kph) the engine noise would drop from frantic in fourth to a laid-back note in fifth as it gradually began to pull that tall gear.

'The scenery would be flashing past the windows like crazy but the engine noise just didn't match the

'I can remember aiming for gaps
between cars that would close to almost nothing by the time
I got there'

picture. Then the speed would build and build and build relentlessly until the engine noise and speed blur got back in sync. Then you'd be left with little else to do but keep one eye on the road ahead and the other on the rear tyre pressure warning lights, dreading the moment when one might start glowing. The team had fitted them to try and warn us of an impending blow-out, because with the rear wheels enclosed by aerodynamic covers, a rear-tyre failure would rip the bodywork apart and destroy the rear wing, at which point you'd probably fly into the trees…'

In addition to the fear of a mechanical failure, the X-rated Mulsanne amplified the enormous speed differential between the quickest and slowest cars. As Wallace explains, this often led to some hair-raising situations.

Left: The spectacular sight of the Le Mans pits at night.
Below: The Jaguar XJR 9LM of John Watson, Raul Boesel and Henri Pescarolo in 1988.

'In a car like the Jaguar you'd always be dealing with slower traffic. Sometimes you'd come onto the Mulsanne and see two sets of tail lights in the distance. You'd pray it wasn't a pair of 911s or something, because they'd be totally absorbed in their own race and probably not notice me steaming down on them at maybe 70mph (113kph) or quicker. At that sort of speed you're totally committed, and I can remember aiming for gaps between cars that would close to almost nothing by the time I got there. Every lap I'd scream at myself for taking such a risk, but every lap something similar would happen. When you mix classes of car it's all part and parcel of endurance racing.'

As you drive along the Mulsanne you'll notice a roadside restaurant on your left-hand side called Auberge des Hunaudieres. It is one of the great Le Mans landmarks, for it remains open throughout the duration of the 24-hour race. Although its terrace is now protected by deep layers of Armco and cloaked in debris fencing, you can still sit and

Above: The Prodrive Aston Martin DBR9 of David Brabham, Darren Turner and Stephane Sarrazin in 2005. **Right:** Jean-Marc Luco at the wheel of his Porsche 917.

eat with racing cars travelling at more than 200mph (322kph) passing just a few feet from your plate of steak and *frites*. It certainly brings new meaning to the phrase fast food.

After the rush of the Mulsanne, complete with the daunting kink and deceptive crest, which was re-profiled after Mark Webber and Peter Dumbreck both spectacularly flipped their Mercedes CLK-GTRs, you brake for Mulsanne corner. You'll probably be disappointed to find that this famous corner is actually defined by a mini roundabout in regular use.

To follow the direction of the circuit you turn right onto the D140, which takes you on what would undoubtedly be another flat-out charge towards Indianapolis, the section which many drivers say is the scariest part of the lap. Once again speeds will be above 200mph (322kph), with narrow strips of grass and trees either side of the circuit, and a golf course beyond the barriers.

Indianapolis funnels the cars into the slow right-left-right at Arnage. This is a great place to watch during the dawn stint of the race, as you really get to see who's sharp and who's tiring – the slow but technical nature of the road often reveals a driver's lack of concentration. The exit of Arnage is actually a T-junction, so you'll have to stop before turning right and continuing along the D139, which is another of the oldest parts of the course.

This is the fast run towards Maison Blanche. Once again it's characterized by the clear potential

for enormous speed in a racing car, the broad sweeping curves taking you towards the site of the famous old white house. Just as at Tertre Rouge and the Mulsanne chicanes, you can see where the new circuit parts company with the old road section, veering right into the concrete canyon of the Porsche Curves.

Shortly after this point you'll arrive at a roundabout. Turning left will take you into the village of Arnage. Although never part of the Le Mans course, Arnage has become a traditional haunt of race fans – particularly Brits – who want to take a break from the action and go in search of a cold beer or two.

Continuing straight on will take you along the Boulevard des Italiens, which runs parallel with the new circuit and follows the path of the original 1923 course to the location of the old Pontlieue hairpin. At this point the original circuit hooked tight right back onto the N138 to commence a much longer run down the Mulsanne.

However, once you get close to the track's main entrance you may want to stop and spend a few hours in the nearby Musée Automobile de la Sarthe. Containing past veterans of the 24-hour race, including local favourites the Matra 670B from 1974 and Peugeot's 1992 winning 905, you'll also find other race-winners such as the Ford GT40, Porsche 917, Jaguar XJR-9 and Mazda 787B.

After driving most of the circuit on which these fabulous cars raced, you'll never be in a better position to sit and reflect on what it took to master this unique race, and why for many the 24 Heures du Mans is the greatest motorsport event in the world.

PORSCHE – LEGENDS OF LE MANS

Forget Audi's recent dominance of the Le Mans 24 Hours, for it pales when compared to Porsche's supremacy in the greatest endurance race of them all.

Since 1970 the Stuttgart manufacturer has won Le Mans no fewer than 17 times, with an extraordinary period of dominance between 1976 and 1987 when its cars took 10 victories from 12 starts, the last seven of which were consecutive wins.

Unsurprisingly this success has made heroes of the winning drivers and icons of the cars they drove. Jacky Ickx and Derek Bell scored four wins each in Porsches, Al Holbert scored three, while Hans Stuck and Klaus Ludwig grabbed a pair of wins each.

Of all Porsche's Le Mans-winning machines, the awe-inspiring 917 remains the most famous, although it was one of Porsche's less successful cars at Le Mans. Of course all things are relative, and the 917's pair of wins in 1970 and '71 came after fierce competition from the works Ferrari 512s. That they are still remembered for their tremendous pace – they were attaining speeds of 230mph (370kph) on the Hunaudieres straight – and spectacular looks (especially in pale blue-and-orange Gulf livery) is testament to the enormous impression they must have made in their day.

Then, as now, Porsche's commitment to endurance racing wasn't just at the top level. Road-based 911s also dominated the lower classes. Evidence of this comes no clearer than the results table for the 1971 race, when 10 Porsches (two 917s, a solitary 907 and no fewer than seven 911 Ss) appeared in the first 13 places. By far the most successful Porsche at Le Mans was the 956, which later evolved into the 962. Best remembered wearing the blue-, white-and-red livery of the Rothmans tobacco brand, the 956 changed the face of endurance racing, combining massive performance with impregnable reliability and, when compared with the animalistic 917s, extremely driver-friendly handling. Including the 936/81, which was the direct predecessor of the 956, Porsche won every Le Mans from 1981 to 1987.

It was during this purple patch that Derek Bell forged his legendary Le Mans career. Driving with Jacky Ickx he shared the spoils in 1981 and '82, and finished third in '83. He then finished third again in the 962's Le Mans debut in 1985 with Ickx and Hans Stuck, before winning in '86 and '87 with Stuck and Al Holbert. In 1988 he was the first Porsche home, in second place. Although he would continue to drive for the marque, this was his last podium finish in a Porsche.

MOUNT PANORAMA BATHURST

DISTANCE: 4 MILES (6.5KM) FIRST RACE: 1938 LOCATION: AUSTRALIA

It's not often that a motor race becomes a national institution, but the Bathurst 1000 is a glorious exception. Held each October on the spectacular Mount Panorama circuit in New South Wales, the 'Great Race' is where the bitter rivalry between Ford and Holden reaches fever pitch. Not only is it the biggest race in the Australian V8 Supercar Championship, but the racing at Bathurst means far more to the average Australian race fan than the Formula One Grand Prix in Melbourne.

Mount Panorama is on the outskirts of Bathurst, a town lying some 120 miles (193km) west of Sydney. Discovered by William Evans in 1813, Bathurst is the oldest inland settlement in Australia. Whether the indigenous Wiradjuri Aboriginal tribe would agree with this 'discovery' is doubtful, as they had used the Mount Panorama as a vantage point from which to watch over their lands for millennia.

The region has many claims to fame: it was the first place in Australia to yield gold, and also became the first place in the country to embark on the large-scale cultivation of grapes for wine. The great botanist Charles Darwin came to Bathurst in 1836, and Queen Elizabeth II made two visits to the town. Sadly the records don't reveal whether Her Majesty is a Ford or Holden fan.

With the greatest respect to Bathurst's esteemed visitors, the most important man in the region's history was undoubtedly Mayor Martin Griffin. Together with the Bathurst City Council, Griffin worked on an idea to construct a scenic road to the crest of the Bald Hills, of which Mount Panorama is part, in an effort to create employment during the Great Depression of the 1930s.

Convinced of the plan's merits, and at ease with Griffin's thinly veiled ulterior motive to create a new and challenging motor racing circuit under the guise of this 'scenic road', the state government provided a grant to fund the work scheme. There followed an intensive period of consultation between the Council and the NSW Light Car Club, during which the layout of the circuit was decided. After a huge road-building programme the 4-mile (6.5km), dirt-surfaced Mount Panorama Scenic Drive was opened, on 17 March 1938.

Mayor Griffin didn't waste any time in putting the road to good use, as on 16 April that same year he opened the racing circuit for the Australian Tourist Trophy motorcycle race. Two days later Mount Panorama held its first car race – the Australian Grand Prix, no less – which was contested over 38 laps. An Englishman by the name of Peter Whitehead won the race, and confirmed many an Australian's suspicions about mad Poms by donning full evening dress for the duration of the two-and-a-half hour race, but refusing to wear a crash helmet.

The outbreak of the World War II brought a temporary halt to proceedings, but the racers returned in 1946, and have been back every year since. Back then the circuit was fraught with dangers. The surface – still unmetalled – was bumpy as hell, while trees, ditches and wire fences

Left: The view from inside a Holden Monaro on the Mount Panorama course. **Right:** Craig Lowndes and Glenn Seton in their Ford Falcon in the 2004 Bathurst 1000.

'The surface - still unmetalled - was bumpy as hell, while trees, ditches and wire fences lined the circuit'

lined the circuit. Facilities were also basic in the extreme, with temporary tented pit and administrative 'buildings' erected before each race meeting. Although permanent pit buildings and proper crash barriers were introduced in the 1960s, it was still possible at certain sections of the circuit for unlucky drivers to crash unimpeded into trees as late as the 1980s.

Even today the Mount Panorama circuit remains one of the last great 'no-prisoners' venues at which to race. It's still the only motor racing circuit in Australia that is a genuine public road between race meetings, and as such has become a must-drive road for racing drivers and fans from around the world.

You don't have to try hard to find it: simply head towards the town of Bathurst on the A32. Once in the centre of town look for signs for Mount Panorama, and within a couple of miles you should catch sight of the circuit, stark black against the lush green foothills. Be prepared to feel a little odd as you first set your tyres on the hallowed tarmac, for although it is 100 per cent public road, you'll be fighting the feeling that you must have missed a security gate or simply stumbled onto the track. Imagine taking a turning off the A43 in Northamptonshire and finding yourself on Silverstone's Hangar Straight and you've got some idea of how this unique road makes you feel.

This feeling of doing something illicit is intensified by the total absence of white centre lines, despite the road being open to two-way traffic, and the proliferation of advertising hoardings, brightly painted kerbs, high concrete and steel barriers and the small matter of the permanent pit lane complex and control tower.

Unfortunately, despite Mount Panorama's impeccable racing pedigree, it's not granted any dispensation from Australia's draconian speed limits, and the whole circuit is covered by a blanket 37mph (60kph) limit. In truth you don't need to speed to appreciate the drama of this place. Simply being here, on the track where Australian heroes

like Peter Brock enthralled 100,000 spectators is enough. And what history doesn't give you, Mother Nature provides, for short of the Nürburgring Nordschleife in Germany few circuits drape themselves over more spectacular topography to greater effect.

Unlike the flat and sterile familiarity of racetracks designed in the modern era, Mount Panorama is a real roller-coaster ride. You can divide it into three distinct sections, the first of which starts with the short sprint along the start/finish straight. Bizarrely the start line is 320 yards (293m) closer to the first corner than the finish line is, in order to ensure the 161-lap Bathurst 1000 race runs to exactly 1,000km (621.5 miles). This measure also gives a little more space for the starting grid, which prevents the assembled competitors from stretching too far round the final corner and hence being unsighted for the start.

Hell Corner is the somewhat unsettling name for Turn 1. This tight left-hander is often the scene of some robust moves during the first few laps of any race, which frequently lead to accidents. Once the

Left: The Holden Monaro CV8 of Nathan Pretty, Steven Richards, Cameron McConville and Garth Tander in the 2003 Bathurst 24 Hours.
Right: Dusk at the 2003 event.

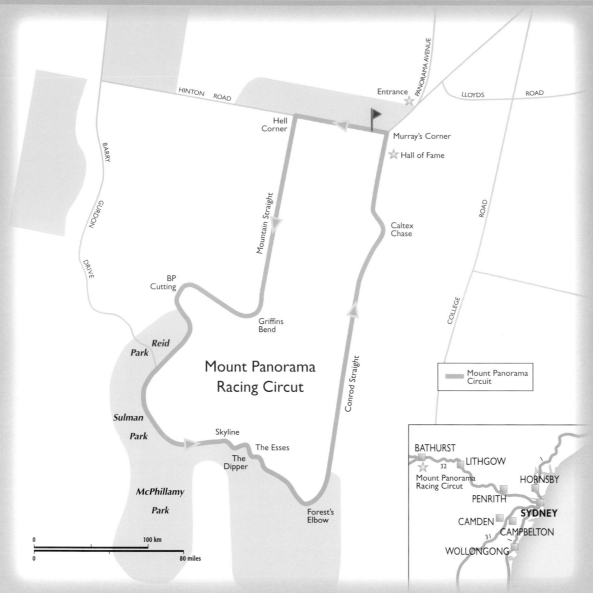

Mount Panorama
Racing Circut

Mount Panorama
Circuit

BATHURST
LITHGOW
32
Mount Panorama
Racing Circuit
HORNSBY
PENRITH
CAMDEN
SYDNEY
CAMPBELTON
31
WOLLONGONG

race has settled down drivers focus all their energy on getting the best possible exit from Hell Corner as it leads directly onto the Mountain Straight, which begins the long, speed-sapping 1-in-6 climb towards Griffin's Bend, named after Bathurst's inspirational mayor and father of the Mount Panorama circuit.

You'll notice the deceptively awkward negative camber on this corner, which threatens to push the racing cars wide on the exit and run the risk of clouting the wall. Assuming you don't fall prey to this tricky turn there's just a short run into the claustrophobic Cutting, which, as its name suggests, is a steep-sided man-made chute through the hillside. There's no room for error here, with substantial concrete walls built right at the edges of the track. Steep and tight, the Cutting's pair of left-hand turns take you through Reid Park, then down a steep drop and through a climbing left-hander before you reach the highest point of the circuit at Sulman Park.

From here the track drops downhill once more, into the section known as McPhillamy Park, after the family who donated the area of land for public amenity use prior to the construction of the Mount Panorama Scenic Drive. Traditionally for the Bathurst 1000 race this tranquil area becomes home to a large group of feral, beer-fuelled race fans known as the 'McPhillamy Mob.' It's doubtful old man McPhillamy would approve, but the carnage is somehow part of the Great Race's character and nobody seems to mind too much.

One of the scariest sections of the course is Brock's Skyline, so called because as you make the steep climb towards the corner your windscreen is filled with nothing but clear blue sky. It could equally be called Robert's Skyline, for it was during the 1970 Bathurst 500 that Tony Roberts lost control of his Ford Falcon and was launched

Right: Craig Lowndes and Jamie Whincup on their way to victory in their Ford Falcon BA at the 2006 Bathurst 1000.

PETER BROCK – KING OF THE MOUNTAIN

Australia has produced countless great racing drivers, but none enjoyed the hero worship reserved for Peter Brock. His nicknames included Peter Perfect and Brocky, but the most revealing is The King of the Mountain, in recognition of his unique tally of 10 victories on the Mount Panorama circuit.

Born on 26 February 1945 in the state of Victoria, Brock's driving career began in the unlikely form of an Austin 7, which he reputedly bought for the princely sum of £5. Like many of Brock's early cars it was a mongrel machine. The most famous of these was a blue Austin A30 fitted with an oversized Holden six-cylinder engine, which he raced with no little success.

Brock's fame and adulation came from his uncanny ability to extract speed from Australia's hugely popular V8 touring cars. This branch of the sport is particularly close

to the Australian fans' hearts, thanks to a fierce rivalry between car manufacturers Holden and Ford. Brocky was a Holden man through and through, and scored all 10 of his record-breaking Bathurst victories in the Australian manufacturer's cars. Such was his zeal for the brand that he reputedly claimed he'd prefer to throw up than back a Ford down his driveway.

Brock was a passionate road safety campaigner, and from the mid-1970s his racing cars famously bore the number 05 as a nod to the 0.05 per cent blood alcohol limit in his home state of Victoria.

Like many great racing drivers Brock retired a number of times from top-flight competition, the first announcement coming in 1997. However, he was to make a several of returns to Bathurst, the most notable being a shared drive in a 24-hour endurance race. He and his three team mates won, driving – yes, you guessed it – a Holden Monaro.

Although he did eventually step back from full-time professional racing, Brock's passion for driving continued to play a big part in his life. Some of his most high-profile appearances were on the Targa Tasmania (see page 40), where he shared his car with his stepson, James. It was on a similar road race event – the Targa West – near Perth in Western Australia that Brock was to have the accident that claimed his life, when he lost control of his Daytona Coupe and collided with a tree.

His death saddened the entire nation, and he was given a state funeral on 19 September 2006. His memory lives on through the Peter Brock Foundation, a charity he founded to provide help to individuals and community groups in need of support, but for race fans the most fitting memorial to Brock is the Mount Panorama circuit itself.

backwards over the abyss before clattering down the hillside.

Never are you more aware of the Mountain's tortuous character than when you exit Brock's Skyline and power into a series of four linked corners known as The Esses. Lined with concrete barriers and relentlessly twisty, it has the effect of a tarmac toboggan run, reaching a crescendo at the aptly named Dipper, which has such a pronounced drop-off to the inside that race cars often tip onto two wheels as they get thrown into the tight left-hander.

From this point you're really aware of descending back down to the flat plains that surround Bathurst. With speed building all the time you can imagine racers taking one last deep breath as they set their car up for Forrest's Elbow, a medium quick left-hand curve that leads onto Mount Panorama's sensational Conrod Straight. It pays not to be thinking too hard about Conrod before you've negotiated the Elbow, however, for this all-important corner has a habit of claiming the unwary or overly ambitious. The most spectacular example of this came in 1983, when a hard-charging Dick Johnson ran wide on his qualifying lap, clipped a tyre wall and went for a terrifying ride through a grove of trees. His Ford Falcon was totally destroyed but Johnson emerged miraculously unscathed.

Undulating like a roller-coaster for almost a mile and a half (2.5km), Conrod is one of the most awe-inspiring straights in motor racing. Unsurprisingly it's the fastest section of the Mount Panorama circuit, with the V8 Supercars that contest the Bathurst 1000 routinely hitting 185mph (298kph). As a consequence the Conrod Straight is also the most dangerous part of the circuit. Hauntingly it wasn't a violent accident but natural causes that were to blame for the death of 1967 F1 World Champion, Denny Hulme: the 56-year old New Zealander suffered a heart attack while racing along the straight in a BMW M3 in the 1992 Bathurst 1000.

After the first rush of Conrod, drivers experience the thrill of The Chase. A three-turn complex, the initial peel in from the Conrod is the fastest corner in Australian motor racing. You are then required to brake hard to complete the slower left and then right, which feeds you back onto the remainder of the Conrod Straight for the final charge towards the last corner.

Before The Chase was added the mighty Conrod Straight ran uninterrupted. Quite what it must have been like, careering over the blind crests, knowing that ahead of you lay the 90-degree left-hand Murray's Corner, is hard to imagine. Now, thanks to The Chase, which was introduced in 1987 to comply with FIA regulations, the approach to Murray's isn't quite so terrifying, but still allows for some classic braking duels as drivers fight for an opportunity to steal one last position before the finish line, which as you'll remember arrives 320 yards (293m) before the start line.

It takes just a single lap at sensible speeds to understand why this breathtaking place has been an integral part of Australian car culture for almost 80 years, and why Mayor Griffin's vision for the home of Australian motor racing continues to produce a terrific spectacle.

Any racing driver worth their salt loves it, the fans love it and if you ever get the chance to make the 120-mile (193km) drive out from Sydney to try it for yourself, you'll love it too. A road circuit like no other in a location like no other, the reality of Mount Panorama more than lives up to its legendary billing.

Left: The Holden Commodore of Greg Murphy and Rick Kelly – winners of the 2004 Bathurst 1000. **Right:** The 2003 24 Hour race.

PAU

DISTANCE: 1.7 MILES (2.8KM) **FIRST RACE:** 1901 **LOCATION:** FRANCE

Imagine Grand Prix cars racing through narrow city streets and you immediately think of Monaco. Couldn't be anywhere else, right? Wrong. The streets of Monte Carlo may host the most glamorous race in today's Formula One calendar, but there's a city in southwestern France with an even greater motor racing history. Its name is Pau.

Halfway between Biarritz and Toulouse, in the foothills of the Pyrenees mountain range separating France from Spain, Pau (pronounced Poh) is a beautiful and historic city, which – aside from the obvious street racing connection – bears an uncanny physical resemblance to Monte Carlo.

Though lacking the drama of Monaco's coastal setting, Pau compensates with a dramatic view of the jagged Pyrenean range. Endowed with not one but two cathedrals, Pau's centre has surprising scale, while a casino, imposing chateau, tranquil park and hilly streets lined with palm trees bring classic grandeur and a dignified ambience to the old centre.

Pau can trace its racing roots back as far as 1901, when it hosted the very first motor race to be called a Grand Prix. That was followed by a three-decade gap in the action, but in 1930 Pau had the honour of staging the French Grand Prix, on an out-of-town circuit not dissimilar in character to that of Le Mans, made up of 10 miles (16km) of fast and

sinuous country roads. A race dominated by the entry of no fewer than 16 waspish Bugatti Type 35s, it was also notable for the heroic efforts of Sir Henry 'Tim' Birkin, one of the famous 'Bentley Boys', who wrestled his cumbersome Blower Bentley to a wholly unexpected second place.

In 1933 the Pau GP course moved once again, this time to within the confines of the city for the first time. One final circuit revision was made in 1935. Amazingly, it is this configuration that's in use today. Not only does this make Pau's street circuit layout the least changed of its kind in the world, but it also presents today's up-and-coming racing drivers with the age-old pre-war challenges of commitment, bravery and total concentration. In this age of sanitized greenfield racetracks, such an unsuitable venue would never get the go-ahead.

The long shadow of World War II brought racing to a close in 1939, but not before Mercedes-Benz had made its mark on Pau's record books. Traditionally the Pau race was held early in the year, and this fact plus its non-championship status meant some teams used Pau's streets as a last-minute shakedown for the season proper. Typically competitive, Mercedes did just that in 1938, and were naturally expected to win. So you can imagine the delight when French hero René Dreyfus in a Delahaye beat the all-conquering Germans into second place. Galvanized by the defeat, Mercedes returned to Pau the following year with three cars, and although Caracciola retired, Lang and von Brauchitsch claimed the first two places.

After the war, top-flight racing soon returned to Pau, but despite the excellent circuit and keen

Left: The Lotus 32-Cosworth of Jim Clark at the 1964 Pau Grand Prix.
Opposite: The Signature Plus Dallara of Fabio Carbone in the 2003 Formula 3 Grand Prix.

'established Grand Prix drivers would happily enter the F2 race and mix it with the sport's young lions'

competition the Pau GP was never to attain full Formula One World Championship status. Fortunately that didn't stop the finest drivers of the day coming to Pau to race in Formula One and Formula Two events throughout the 1960s and 70s. It was the F2 events that really captured people's imaginations, as much for the fact that established Grand Prix drivers would happily enter the F2 race and mix it with the sport's young lions as for the spectacle of the cars themselves.

As F1 got more and more commercialized, and its star drivers grew increasingly reluctant to risk their

Left: Christian Bakkerud (Carlin Motorsport) leads Mike Conway (Räikkönen Robertson Racing) in the 2006 British Formula 3 race.
Below: The 2006 British and French GT Championship.

hard-won reputations in the less lucrative lower formula, F2 gradually lost its appeal, and Pau's GP organizers were driven to attract a fresh category to the circuit. In 1985 the new F3000 series obliged, opening an exciting chapter in Pau's long and varied history.

By the late 90s F3000 was also a fading force. Once again, though, Pau's enduring appeal attracted a fresh spectacle in the form of the prestigious European Formula 3 Championship, which continues to bring the unique challenge of Pau's unforgiving kerb-lined streets to a new generation of budding World Champions. With former Pau GP winners including Nuvolari, Fangio, Ascari, Brabham, Clark, Rindt, Laffite, Alesi, Montoya and F1's most recent star, Lewis Hamilton, there's no question Pau is an accurate barometer of true driving genius.

With the massive popularity of Goodwood's Festival of Speed and Revival meetings, Pau recognized that its rich heritage deserved to be celebrated, and the Pau Grand Prix Historique was born. Held since 2000, usually towards the end of May or in early June, this fabulous event sees a host of full-blooded races, including those for classic F1, F2 and F3 single-seaters, along with other classes for sports cars, GTs and thunderous sports prototypes.

To see and hear such a diverse selection of priceless machinery driven flat out through these splendid city streets is a unique experience, and one that brings Pau's glorious sporting history vividly to life. Unlike Goodwood's retrospective events, apart from Pau's grandstand seating areas, you can watch the action for free. What better backdrop to enjoy a tasty sandwich and refreshing glass of wine?

There is another way to appreciate Pau's century of motor racing, and that's to get in your car and experience the twists and turns first hand. Of course, as it's a street circuit you're guaranteed not to have the opportunity to emulate the speedy exploits of yesterday's heroes, and whatever you're driving is unlikely to replicate the ferocity of a pre-war Silver Arrow or the agility of Jim Clark's Lotus.

However, as you nudge out into the traffic on the Avenue Lacoste you'll have to try hard to suppress the frisson of excitement as the realization dawns that you're travelling along Pau's start/finish straight, driving between the deep layers of Armco and brightly painted red-and-white kerbs.

The quickest racing cars can hit 160mph (258kph) along here, flashing past the pits and through what must be a very daunting right-hand kink. Then, before you know it, the Virage de la Gare, or Station Hairpin, is filling your windscreen with steel-grey barriers and more red and white paint. It's one of the trickiest parts of the circuit, and one that puts the drivers under huge pressure to brake as late as they dare.

The Station Hairpin begins the long climb up between an avenue of mature tress towards Pont Oscar, a nasty and deceptive left-hander, which dives beneath the bridge that passes high overhead. After the more open nature of the pit straight, this section immediately feels more confined, as you're dwarfed by the trees and massive arched spans of the viaduct that runs along the left-hand side of the circuit.

No sooner has Pont Oscar receded in the mirrors than you're having to deal with an even nastier corner: the Lycée Hairpin. The scene of many a

The 2006 British Formula 3 Championship event at Pau. James Jakes (Hitech Racing, **above**) and Juho Annala (performance Racing Europe, **right**).

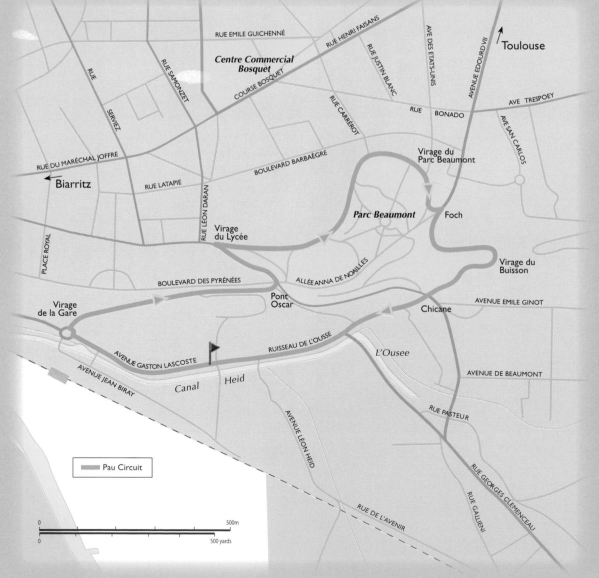

The following labels appear on the circuit map:

RUE EMILE GUICHENNÉ
RUE HENRI FAISANS
AVE DES ETATS-UNIS
AVENUE EDOURD VII
→ Toulouse
Centre Commercial Bosquet
RUE JUSTIN BLANC
RUE
RUE SAHONZET
COURSE BOSQUET
RUE CARRÉROT
AVE TRESPOEY
RUE BONADO
SERVIEZ
AVE SAN CARLOS
RUE DU MARÉCHAL JOFFRE
BOULEVARD BARBAÈGRE
Virage du Parc Beaumont
← Biarritz
RUE LATAPIE
RUE LÉON DARAN
Parc Beaumont
Foch
PLACE ROYAL
Virage du Lycée
Virage du Buisson
BOULEVARD DES PYRÉNÉES
ALLÉE ANNA DE NOAILLES
Virage de la Gare
Pont Oscar
Chicane
AVENUE EMILE GINOT
AVENUE GASTON LASCOSTE
RUISSEAU DE L'OUSSE
L'Ousee
AVENUE JEAN BIRAY
Canal Heid
AVENUE DE BEAUMONT
AVENUE LÉON HEID
RUE PASTEUR
RUE DE L'AVENIR
RUE GEORGES CLEMENCEAU
RUE GALLIENI

| Pau Circuit |

0   500m
0   500 yards

first-lap tangle, this corner is so incredibly tight it's a wonder today's F3 cars can get around in anything less than a three-point turn!

Your reward for successfully clearing Lycée is the fast, endless courage-testing left-hand sweep that runs alongside the impressive Palais Beaumont Casino. This is followed immediately by a long looping right-hander, which passes around the fringes of the leafy and normally peaceful Parc Beaumont and the Jardin Anglais. The trees and three layers of Armco make this sinuous run almost blind, even in a road car. The sense of speed you would get from the cockpit of an F3 car, glued to the tarmac thanks to the adhesive qualities of slick tyres and downforce-generating wings, must be incredible.

The rush continues as you pass the spectacular new Hotel Beaumont and jink through the Virage Foch, which curves around a sizeable stone monument dedicated to Ferdinand Foch, Marshal of France and the supreme commander of the Allied armies for the final phase of World War I. By this stage the circuit becomes little more than a steel-and-tarmac chute, tumbling downhill in a hypnotic rhythm of interconnected corners until another tight hairpin snaps you out of your trance.

As if the proximity of the barriers and the high kerbs isn't enough to cope with, the last chicane has some evil camber changes. Although not so unsettling when you have to remain on the correct side of the road, taking a ruthless racing line must send your car pitching off the road's pronounced crown like a waterskier crossing a speed boat's wake. It's another section of the circuit that demands courage and commitment, for any loss of nerve here leaves you vulnerable to attack as you rejoin the

Above: Jamie Green (ASM) in action in the 2003 Pau Grand Prix.

Avenue Lacoste and charge across the line and on towards the Station Hairpin, for another lap of what is rightly regarded as the thinking-person's Monaco.

If this spectacular street circuit isn't enough for you and you're willing to venture 15 miles (24km) or so to the west of the city on the D945 – no hardship as the scenery is breathtaking – Pau has another surprise in store for keen drivers, in the shape of the Circuit Pau Arnos.

Set in magnificent rolling countryside, Pau Arnos (www.circuit-pau-arnos.com) is a privately owned purpose-built racetrack, with a lap length of just under 2 miles (3.2km). The owner (who lives at the circuit in a wonderful old farmhouse) says he was inspired to create his beautiful racetrack after a visit to Brands Hatch in the UK. The rural setting is certainly every bit as special, and the undulating site has the familiar feel of a natural amphitheatre, but you only have to take in the view from the elevated pit lane to appreciate Pau Arnos is so much more than a French facsimile of the famous Kentish circuit.

If you've ever been to Brands Hatch, Cadwell Park in Lincolnshire or Oulton Park in Cheshire you'd feel right at home here. It shares their spacious, parkland feel, but also musters a sense of intimacy you simply don't get at classic British airfield circuits such as Silverstone or Snetterton. Best of all, with the owner living on site, there's a reasonable chance that, should your visit not coincide with an organized event, a polite request and an offer of some euros will secure you an informal lap or two (maybe more if you're in an interesting car).

If you do happen to meet Pau Arnos's owner, Monsieur Canavesio, be sure to be at your most persuasive, for just like its illustrious urban forebear, this gem of a circuit is one of the best kept driving secrets in Europe.

ULSTER TT

DISTANCE: 7.4 MILES (11.9KM) **FIRST RACE:** 1950 **LOCATION:** NORTHERN IRELAND

There are few more significant letters in the lexicon of motor racing than TT. Perhaps most readily associated with the Isle of Man, where the Tourist Trophy concept originated and continues in two-wheeled form (see page 52), it's a lesser-known fact that though short-lived on the Isle of Man, the four-wheeled TT enjoyed an extensive and action-packed history on two terrific road racing circuits in Northern Ireland.

The earliest of these is the Ards course, a 13.5-mile (21.5km) circuit situated within sight of Stormont Castle, home of Northern Ireland's government, and encompassing open country roads and small town streets. Used from 1928 until 1936, the Ards circuit saw some exceptional racing between Alfa Romeo, Bugatti and Mercedes-Benz, as well as illustrious British makes like Aston Martin (winners in 1934), MG (winners in 1933), Lea-Francis (winners in 1928), Singer and Riley.

Racing on the Ards course was stopped after the 1936 race, during which eight spectators were killed and many more injured when a car crashed into a lamppost and ricocheted into the crowd. The race subsequently found a temporary home at Donington in England before World War II brought racing to a close once more.

It wasn't until 1950 that the TT returned to the roads of Northern Ireland, on a shorter and narrower course to the west of Belfast. Called Dundrod, the TT's new home was entirely on country roads. As it was more remote there was less chance of spectators lining the kerbs, but the

rugged nature of the roads made it far less forgiving of driver error or mechanical failure.

As with most road racing circuits of the 1950s, when you look back through their history, one man's name comes to the fore: Stirling Moss. He may never have won a Formula One World Championship, but Moss was without question the finest road racer the world has ever seen. Arguably his greatest season came in 1955 while driving for the illustrious Mercedes-Benz factory team in a 300SLR. Moss scored epic wins in the Targa Florio (see page 32), Mille Miglia (page 22) and Tourist Trophy races, and he also stood a fine chance of winning the 1955 Le Mans 24 Hours before fate intervened and the team withdrew.

Moss formed an instant bond with Dundrod, winning the circuit's inaugural TT race in 1950, on

the eve of his 21st birthday, at the wheel of an alloy-bodied Jaguar XK120. His second (partnered by Tony Rolt) came the following year in a works Jaguar C-type. Few doubt he would have gone on to complete a hat-trick of victories had the 1952 event not been cancelled because of the bemusing lack of interest from international teams.

By 1955, however, road racing was at its peak and there was certainly no shortage of international competitors in that year's Tourist Trophy. Reading through Dundrod's entry list is like a who's who of 1950s motor racing: Stirling Moss, Mike Hawthorn, Peter Collins, Tony Brooks, Juan Manuel Fangio and Karl Kling, to name but a few legendary drivers. Imagine a sports car race with Michael Schumacher, Kimi Räikkönen, Fernando Alonso and Jenson Button amongst the entries – all piloting the fastest

Opposite: The Jaguar D-types of Robert Berry and Mike Hawthorn lead the way at the start of the 1955 Tourist Trophy at Dundrod.
Right: Stirling Moss taking the chequered flag in his Jaguar XK120 at the 1950 event.

'The scenery is blissfully

pastoral, with the rolling green fields so typical of the

Emerald Isle'

Opposite and right: Dundrod today. A Porsche Boxster S is put through its paces along the course. **Above:** Peter Walker in the Jaguar C-type he shared with Stirling Moss in the 1953 TT.

sports cars of the day – and you've got some idea of the magnitude of the 1955 TT. And to think it was all taking place on 7.4 miles (11.9km) of country road just a short distance from Belfast.

Perhaps more extraordinary is the fact that despite the Dundrod circuit being deemed too dangerous to use as car racing venue in the immediate aftermath of the 1955 TT, the world's best road racing motorcyclists continue to take their lives – literally - in their hands around the same perilously rapid roads in the annual Ulster Grand Prix.

Hold that fact, and make a trip to Dundrod, for you'll never see a more graphic illustration of the difference in attitudes between modern car and bike racers. Such is the circuit's perfectly 'natural' state that unless you join the route at the start/finish area, where the makeshift paddock and grandstands are located, you could drive most of the lap without any inkling that you're on one of the fastest road race circuits in the world.

The scenery is blissfully pastoral, with the rolling green fields so typical of the Emerald Isle. The road is narrow, bumpy and bordered by established hedgerows and mature trees. Telegraph poles, gateposts, and barbed-wire fences are as close as Dundrod comes to providing any kind of barriers, and where these assorted items of road furniture are absent, ditches and hefty earth banks line the road instead. As a racing venue it's as raw and unforgiving as they come.

Shocking proof of this came soon after the start of the 1955 race. With an estimated 60,000 people lining the circuit, Dundrod was buzzing with the anticipation of seeing Jaguar's solitary D-type (driven by the dashing Mike Hawthorn and his teammate, the young Ulsterman Desmond Titterington) do battle against Hawthorn's friend, Peter Collins, and Tony Brooks in an Aston Martin, together with a trio of Mercedes 300SLRs with Moss, Kling and Fangio amongst their glittering driver line-up.

As the race started the crowd's loyalties must have been divided between the patriotic combinations of Hawthorn in the Jaguar and Collins in the Aston, and the almost unbeatable Moss and his spectacular Silver Arrow, shared on this occasion by the American racer John Fitch. True to form, TT expert Moss was leading from Hawthorn after the first lap,

but as the field charged towards the dauntingly fast Deer's Leap on the far side of the circuit, a driver by the name of Jim Mayers lost control of his Cooper as he attempted to pass another Mercedes, driven by the Vicomte De Barry. Mayers collided with a stone gatepost and was killed instantly.

His car, now ablaze, was flung back into the middle of the track. In the melee five other cars were engulfed in the fiery chaos. One of these was Bill Smyth, who had no chance of avoiding the wreckage and smashed into the hulk of Mayers' Cooper. He too died from his injuries at the scene. It's a mark of the age that such a terrible incident didn't stop the race – as it undoubtedly would today – but then nor did a third fatality, which came

on lap 35, when Dick Mainwaring overturned his Elva-Climax at the tricky Tornagrough right-hander and was trapped beneath it as it caught fire.

In hindsight, the deaths were as much to do with the lack of safety equipment (roll-cages, fire extinguisher systems, safety fuel cells, proper full-face helmets and fireproof overalls were all absent in this era) and the cars' terrifying propensity to ignite. Racing them on a brutal circuit like Dundrod was a potentially lethal activity, but then in those days death was a very real part of motor racing. Just like today's bike racers, all the drivers understood the risks. The very best – men like Moss and the up-and-coming Tony Brooks – revelled in them, as they revealed when reflecting on their experiences in the Northern Irish TT race.

'I enjoyed Dundrod greatly', said Brooks, 'although it was the year of the dreadful accident there. What with Le Mans and then the Deer's Leap tragedy in the TT I had something of a baptism of fire, which really brought home to me the fact that motor racing was dangerous, but I took it in my stride. The thing I learned most at Dundrod was what fantastic fun real road racing was. I got so much more satisfaction out of driving there than on the many British circuits, which were almost exclusively aerodrome-based. I thoroughly enjoyed racing there, although it was frankly quite narrow in parts. But going through brick bridges with only a few inches to spare, I thought, fantastic! Mind you, today's drivers wouldn't even warm up their engines at Dundrod, let alone put the thing in gear…'

Moss' view is less effusive, his sentiment more hard-nosed, but the message is equally unequivocal. 'Danger was an important ingredient [of road racing]…You are gambling, and you are gambling to try to beat somebody. To me, I must say, if it had not been dangerous, I would not have enjoyed it so much.'

When you see just how narrow and uneven the roads are around Dundrod, and how close the rocky banks are as they flash through your peripheral vision and the minuscule margin for error they leave, you can't help thinking Brooks, Moss, Hawthorn and company must have been insane to race wheel-to-wheel around this place. But then you feel the flow of the road, sense its rhythm and see the lines, and you begin to understand how seductive – and addictive – it must have been to drive what were the very fastest racing cars of their day on what were and remain very obviously real public roads.

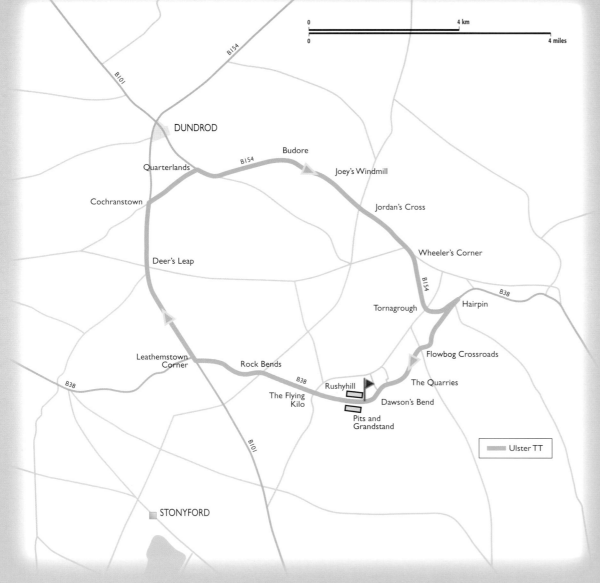

Above: The Mercedes-Benz 300SLR of Juan Manuel Fangio and Karl Kling leading the Cooper T39-Climax of Ivor Bueb and MGH McDowell in the 1955 Tourist Trophy at Dundrod.

As you round Dawson's Bend and start to accelerate across the gently curving start/finish line you are immediately confronted with one of the fastest parts of the circuit. Now called 'The Flying Kilo', this arrow-straight but horribly confined stretch charges down the aptly named Rusheyhill, some sharp-edged bumps grabbing your attention as you brake before peeling into Rock Bends.

After a fraught race in which the Moss/Fitch Merc and Hawthorn/Titterington Jag repeatedly swapped the lead, it was as Moss was crossing the line to start the final lap that he grabbed his chance and slipstreamed past Hawthorn at 170mph (274kph) for the lead. A few miles later Hawthorn's misery was compounded when the Jag's engine seized and spun him – fortunately – up a side road. He strolled back to the pits as Mercedes scored a crushing 1-2-3 finish.

Exiting Leathemstown Corner, the road opens onto another long, bumpy and undulating straight. At racing speeds in a train of flat-out sports cars the numerous blind crests must have been mouth-parching tests of nerve. On a 21st century superbike it's one of Dundrod's three 190mph (306kph) bucking-bronco rides.

Only after the super-fast right-hander at Cochranstown and the short straight to Quarterlands does the pace drop appreciably, with a sinuous left-right-left sequence at Ireland's Corner that's one of the few technical sections of the lap. Another perilously fast right – Budore - takes you past Joey's Windmill and Jordan's Cross on another

hair-raising charge through Wheeler's Corner and the deceptive Tornagrough, where poor Mainwaring perished in '55.

The Hairpin really rushes up at you, and is made doubly deceptive – at least when the roads aren't closed for racing – because you actually have to turn right off the main road and skirt around a small grass promontory before joining the road that takes you across the Flowbag Crossroads. Almost immediately you enter the testing Quarries Esses before peeling into Dawson's once more, passing the Joey Dunlop Memorial Grandstand to complete the lap.

To complete your education about what road racing at Dundrod is all about, come back in August when the Ulster GP riders are in action. As those 60,000 who witnessed the last Dundrod TT would testify, the speed and spectacle will blow your mind.

3 Rallies

Tommi Mäkinen in action during the 2000 Tour de Corse, Corsica.

CIRCUIT OF IRELAND

DISTANCE: VARIES FIRST RACE: 1931 LOCATION: IRELAND

For petrolheads of a certain age in the UK, just seeing the name Circuit of Ireland is enough to bring back fond memories of Saturday afternoons spent glued to BBC *Grandstand's* rally coverage. Those dynamic images of Jimmy McRae, Russell Brookes and Tony Pond battling local heroes like Bertie Fisher and Billie Coleman along the bumpy and ultra-fast Irish lanes were unforgettable, and with good reason, for those hard-fought Circuits of the 1980s are now regarded as the golden years of this great Irish rallying institution.

Below: David Llewellin's MG Metro 6R4 in action at the Circuit of Ireland in 1986. **Opposite:** A Ford Zephyr at the 1953 Circuit of Ireland Trial

The very first Circuit of Ireland was held in 1956, but the origins of the rally can be traced back to 1931, when the Ulster Automobile Club held the Ulster Motor Rally. This event continued for five years before evolving into the highly popular Circuit of Ireland Trial, which ran until 1955, before being renamed and repackaged as the Circuit of Ireland Rally.

Although its format has changed in the last decade or so, the Circuit of Ireland retains a reputation for maximizing the amount of competitive stage mileage, and for being one of the toughest events for the crews to master. In mileage terms, however, the modern Circuit is a pale imitation of the old-school event, which was a genuine lap of Ireland following the coastline from

Dublin via Cork, Killarney, Galway, Donegal and Derry before completing the loop in Belfast.

When the Circuit first started it was a gruelling navigational event rather than a speed-orientated special stage rally. Ireland in the 1950s and 60s was a very different place to the prosperous country it has developed into. The roads were rough and narrow, and detailed mapping was almost non-existent, which often made even finding the end of the stages extremely difficult. The roads weren't closed to public traffic either, which sounds lethally irresponsible, but actually caused few problems, thanks to Ireland's minimal traffic and the remoteness of the country roads used.

Unsurprisingly on the warren-like lanes of rural Ireland, local crews came to the fore, with one man in particular – a certain Patrick Hopkirk – shining brighter than most. Having won the 1958 Circuit in a Triumph TR3A and the '61 event in a Sunbeam Rapier, he was soon picked up by the works BMC team and notched up another pair of wins in '65 and '67 at the wheel of a Mini Cooper S. Although Hopkirk enjoyed the highest profile, countless homegrown drivers honed their skills on the Circuit.

In those apparently carefree days the Circuit was an extremely tough event, which lasted five days and included a significant amount of night driving. When special stages were introduced in 1964, the Circuit placed even tougher demands on the crews, who now had to contend with timed flat-out stages on closed roads as well as the fatiguing effects of covering large distances with little sleep.

As the Circuit grew in stature and significance – becoming a round of the British Rally Championship – so the size and calibre of the entry list grew. During the late 1960s and throughout the 70s and 80s, Britain's best crews pitted themselves

'A shimmering palette of rustic greens
and golds with a thin squiggle of black tarmac meandering
towards the horizon'

against each other and Ireland's wickedly fast roads in everything from RS1800 Escorts and Porsche 911s to the fabulously exciting Opel Manta 400 and Metro 6R4 Group B cars.

As the competition intensified, so the Circuit built its reputation, and some of the stages attained classic status. Sally Gap, Moll's Gap, Hamilton's Folly, Torr Head and the Healy Pass are but a few of the names etched on the minds of crews and spectators alike, their breathtaking scale and searing speed commending them as some of the toughest and most spectacular tarmac stages anywhere in the world.

Thanks to its length you're unlikely to retrace the Circuit's looping route in its entirety. There's no real reason to do so either, for you can learn everything you need to know about the rally by cherry-picking two of its signature stages: Sally Gap in County Wicklow and the Healy Pass on the Beara Peninsula in County Cork.

The former couldn't be more conveniently sited, for Sally Gap is in the heart of the Wicklow Mountains, which, unlikely though it sounds, are just an hour or so from the middle of Dublin. At the point where it passes over Sally Gap itself, the R115 is the highest public road in Ireland, at 1,673ft (510m) above sea level. Some 25 miles (40km) in length, the R115 crosses the beautiful heather-covered moorland and mossy bogs that characterize the Wicklow region and forms the major portion of the Military Road: a historic route built to open up the county's mountainous region to the British Army in an effort to contain the last

Above: An Opel Manta 400 competing in the 1983 British Rally Championship at the Circuit of Ireland. **Opposite:** Sunrise over the rugged mountains of Moll's Gap in Killarney.

few remaining rebels who'd gone to ground after the 1798 Irish uprising.

Taking nine years to complete and stretching for 43 miles (69km), from Rathfarnham in County Dublin to Aughavannagh in County Wicklow, the road was used to transport troops, horses and cannon to the numerous barracks constructed along the route. Records show the road cost £43,587, or just over £1,000 per mile. The mind boggles at what such a road would cost to construct today, given the rigours of the wilderness and harsh weather the Highland Regiment's men must have endured while building the road.

Incredibly, despite the primitive nature of the Military Road's original macadam surface, it remained largely unchanged until the 1950s, but is now thankfully surfaced in modern bitumen-based tarmac. What remains unchanged since the day it was laid is the path the road takes, which explains its tortuously organic nature as it skirts the many natural obstacles on its way to Sally Gap. They didn't know it at the time, but the Army were building what would come to be appreciated as one of the great driving roads a whole century before the motor car was invented.

Even at the speed Jimmy McRae and company came steaming through here, the scenery must have been terribly distracting. A shimmering palette of

rustic greens and golds with a thin squiggle of black tarmac meandering towards the horizon, the undulating moorland approach to Sally Gap is mesmerizing and thrilling in equal measure.

Visibility is good and the road is wide enough to enjoy, while the lack of kerbs and other road furniture enhance the feeling of unconfined space. Occasional stone walls and the odd wind-gnarled tree lie in wait for the unwary, but with little traffic (assuming you avoid weekends) and fast, sweeping corners this section of the stage is hugely satisfying.

As you begin the climb to Sally Gap, the road gets narrower and bumpier, with solid stone walls lining the drops. After the open, flowing approach the road writhes its way up the mountain in an effort to minimize the gradient, but you're still aware of the inexorable climb to the summit. Once there the views across the Wicklow Range to Mount Kippure are very special indeed.

If you want to experience the Healy Pass you're in for quite a drive, for it's to be found on the Beara Peninsula, which forms the southwesternmost tip of

the island. With views over Bantry Bay, the peninsula itself straddles the counties of Cork and Kerry, while the pass – built in the 1920s at the insistence of Tim Healy, the first Governor General of the Irish Free State, as a means of creating employment in the area – is regarded as the most desolate and scenic road in Ireland.

There's a curiously alpine look and feel to the road, with classic sequences of smooth, sinuous switchbacks that can be admired from the top of the pass. If it wasn't for the lack of altitude and the all-

Far left: An Austin Healey Sprite in the 1962 Circuit of Ireland Rally.
Left: The Triumph 2000 of Roy Fidler in 1965. **Opposite:** The steep and winding Healy Pass on the Beara Peninsula.

pervading greenness of the scenery you could easily be fooled into thinking you were driving one of the great mainland European cols. Although some of the towns and villages in the vicinity are a bit tacky, the pass itself is blissfully free of tourist traps and shamrock-encrusted souvenir shops. Traffic is generally thin on the ground, especially if you avoid peak holiday periods, leaving you alone to enjoy what is without doubt the most extraordinary driving road most people have never heard of.

When you're immersed in the thrill of driving a road like the Healy Pass it's easy to see why the Circuit of Ireland had such a fearsome reputation. Driving roads like this at the very limit of your ability in a state-of-the-art rally car for days on end must have been physically and mentally draining, but also hugely exciting. It's certainly no wonder that those overseas drivers who did venture across the Irish Sea are reported to have left Ireland with a great deal more respect for its roads than they came with.

The biggest blow to the Circuit of Ireland came in the early 1990s, when it lost its British Rally Championship status. While it has continued as a round of the Irish Tarmac Championship, the local crews miss the opportunity to compete against top international crews from the British and European mainland. Despite this setback the Circuit of Ireland remained the longest tarmac rally in the world for a few more years, even eclipsing the sealed-surface rounds of the World Rally Championship.

It seems hard to accept that this magnificent rally should have lost its leading role in British rallying, but it has been slowly in decline since the 90s. While it has done its best to change with the times, the Circuit has struggled to make the transition from the long and intensive tests of yore to an age when rallies have to be more efficient, both in terms of time, resources and even environmental impact. Sadly the concept of the all-encompassing circuit-style rally doesn't fit with the needs of modern-day competition, but efforts to evolve have resulted in erosion of the unique identity of the Circuit of Ireland.

Perhaps as a consequence the Circuit has been beset with funding and organizational wrangles in recent years, which have threatened its long-term survival. Indeed, thanks to a spat between the Ulster Automobile Club and the Circuit's title sponsor, the venerable Circuit of Ireland name was dropped from 2007's traditional Easter extravaganza of top-quality Irish tarmac rallying.

For die-hard fans of the Circuit, these problems, and the threat posed by the advent of a high-profile Irish round of the World Rally Championship are doubtless traumatic. But though its long-term future remains uncertain, its legacy and memory is secure, thanks to roads like Sally Gap and the Healy Pass. It's in these roads that the spirit of the Circuit of Ireland lives on.

Sally Gap Stage

Glencree River
Wicklow Mountains
R759
Cloghoge River
Lough Tay
GLENCREE
Military Road
Cloghoge Brook
Lough Dan
R115
Long Brav Lower
Long Bray Upper
Sally Gap
Wicklow National Park
752 Kippure
Cloghoge River
4 km
2 miles
Military Road
River
R115
647 Corrig Mountain
R759
River Liffey
Inchavore
Lough Ovier
816

Healy Pass Stage

Clashduff River
R572
Glanrastel River
R574
ADRIGOLE
Adrigole Harbour
Caha Mountains
R572
Adrigole Mountain
412 Stookeennnalaokarecha
412 Ballaghscart
389 Knockastumpa
Caha Mountains
Healy Pass
R574
366 Derreen
LAURAGH
Glanmore Lake
R571
2 km
2 miles

JIM CLARK RALLY

The origins of the Jim Clark Rally are simple and heartfelt. It's not overstating things to say that when Jim Clark was killed in 1968, the world mourned his loss. From London to Los Angeles, Sydney to Stockholm, racing enthusiasts were numbed by the news that he had died while competing in an insignificant Formula Two race at Hockenheim in Germany. Even his friends and rivals from F1, hardened and fatalistic after years in a sport where deaths were frequent, were shaken to the core. If it could happen to Jimmy, they reasoned, it could easily happen to them.

By the time of Clark's death he was a superstar, but he had remained humble and understated throughout his career: a man who clearly had no intention of forgetting his rural roots. Born in Fife but raised from the age of six on a farm in Edington Mains, near the small Scottish Borders village of Duns, Clark's rise from farmer's son to F1 World Champion began on the roads around his home, and on the local airfield circuits – Winfield and Charterhall - which had been created after the war.

Competing against his parents' wishes (and initially without their knowledge) in his humble Sunbeam-Talbot, his promise was spotted by the Border Reivers, a local racing team. They provided him with faster and faster machinery in which to hone his skills. He revelled in the divergent demands of the Reivers' Porsche 356 and Jaguar D-type, and soon developed his legendary skill of finding a way to drive around a car's inherent flaws to extract winning speed from less-than-winning combinations. It was while driving a Lotus Elite in 1958 that he met Colin Chapman. Indeed Clark

Left: The Subaru Impreza of Derek McGarrity at the Jim Clark Rally, 2006 British Rally Championship.

hadn't just met him, but had finished second to Chapman in a Lotus Elite. The Lotus boss was so impressed by young Clark's performance that he invited him to race one of his Formula Junior single-seaters. It was the opportunity Clark's talent had been waiting for.

By 1960 he was travelling the world driving for Colin Chapman's Team Lotus, competing in the Formula One World Championship. By 1963 he had won his first F1 Driver's title, following with another in 1965. Clark was at his peak, and had the single-seater world at his feet. Yet such was his love of driving that he would often race saloons and sports cars when the F1 calendar permitted, grabbing the opportunity to drive something interesting with both hands (while applying some opposite lock, naturally).

Clark lived in the days before racing drivers specialized in racing a specific genre of car, and consequently his career encompassed outings in a huge assortment of machinery, including Aston Martin and Lotus sports cars, Ford saloon cars and even Indy and NASCARs in the USA, all in addition to his F1 commitments. It's a mark of Clark's rare versatility that one of his finest moments came not at a racetrack, but on gravel tracks, behind the wheel of a Lotus Cortina in the 1966 RAC Rally.

Imagine Fernando Alonso driving in Rally Spain at the height of his F1 career and you've got some idea of what it meant to have Jim Clark (F1 World Champion in 1963 and 1965) competing in the RAC. His co-driver was Brian Melia, who remains in awe of Clark's performance even after 40 years, as he explained in an interview for *Motor Sport* magazine.

'I knew he'd be good, but he far exceeded my expectations. He adapted so quickly, especially when you consider he'd had just one day of testing in a Kent woodland. We had a few close shaves, but

that was to be expected for someone so inexperienced. All would be fine until we came across something unexpected, something beyond his knowledge. But then he'd use his reactions and technique to get out of the situation.

'He drove how I'd always wanted to. I'd always believed there was a perfect balance to be struck between Roger Clark's very sideways technique and Vic Elford's pointier style, and Jimmy proved it existed.'

Comfortably inside the top ten by the halfway point in the rally, Clark made a misjudgement and clouted a rock on a Scottish stage. He incurred time penalties but kept going, despite the crab-like progress of his car. Eventually, though, he was caught out again, rolling the car three or four times and retiring from the rally.

'He was disappointed', says Melia. 'He'd loved the event and insisted we went to some stages to spectate. The team loved him for his spirit, enthusiasm and attitude. He was a potential rally champion.'

He hadn't won. In fact he hadn't even finished, but in those three fastest stage times Clark had proved his genius to be just as great on gravel as it was on tarmac. A man so clearly born to drive, it made his fatal crash less than two years later all the more painful for the sport and his fans.

To those who knew him, and others who lived in and around his home it was clear that some kind of memorial to Jim was needed. After some consideration the Berwick and District Motor Club (of which Clark was president) decided that there was no better way for a region so rich in motorsport history to celebrate the life of its most famous son than to create a competitive event in his memory. The seeds of the Jim Clark Rally had been sown.

'The team loved him
for his spirit, enthusiasm and attitude. He was a potential
rally champion'

Left: Floors Castle during the 2006 Jim Clark Rally. **Above:** Jonny Milner at the Rally in 2004.

Apart from the unspoiled scenery and some fabulous fishing on the river Tweed, the Scottish Borders' most abundant resource is its wonderful assortment of roads. Frustratingly, the law prevented the organizers from closing some of the roads for the rally, but such was the desire to make the event happen that it was held on private roads and tracks for more than 20 years.

A major breakthrough came in 1996, when the Scottish Borders Council approved an application from the rally organizers to use the roads around Duns for special stage rallying, and the resulting 'Scottish Borders Council (Jim Clark Memorial Rally) Order 1996' enabled them to run the only closed-road rally on the British mainland. News that the Jim Clark Rally could now be held on the public roads thrust the event from a low-key club rally right to the top of British rallying's must-do events.

Now firmly established as a round of the British Rally Championship, the Jim Clark Rally is a unique challenge for the crews and a golden opportunity for motorsport fans to watch as rally cars are driven flat out on the British mainland's public roads.

And what glorious roads they are. The Borders have a magical air of unspoiled isolation about them that you won't find anywhere else in Britain. Brooding hills, rolling fields, serene stretches of river and the quietest, most absorbing, engaging and exciting country roads you could ever wish to drive.

If you're a student of Clark's career, or simply a motorsport enthusiast with a broad appreciation of his uncanny skill and brilliant achievements, you can't help but feel the tingle of adrenaline in your bloodstream as you cross the Tweed Bridge at Coldstream. Picking up signs for Duns, it's now that you realize you're driving on some of his favourite and most familiar roads.

Appropriately, although the rally's base is in the market town of Kelso, the heart of the Jim Clark Rally is Duns, for it's here that you should head if you want to immerse yourself in both the rally's many stages and the life and career of Clark himself.

To experience the rally in its most concentrated and intense form, you should head first for the 3-mile (5km) Langton stage. It's easy enough to find. Once you've made your way to the centre of Duns, follow the A6105 west towards Greenlaw, passing the Jim Clark Room on your right. Resist the urge to stop – there'll be plenty of time to look around later

– and continue for a short distance until you see a turning on your left at Clockmill. From here you almost immediately enter the Langton stage: a short loop that drops into a small valley. With the fields forming a green bowl around you, this short, narrow and bumpy road throws everything at you, from a handful of tight 90-degree lefts and rights to a watersplash and a couple of jumps for good measure. Unsurprisingly, it's a crowd favourite, as it is often run at dusk and in fully dark conditions, which only adds to the drama.

The rest of the stages are longer and faster, if less spectator-friendly, and all are within 20 minutes' drive of Duns. The Edrom stage is perhaps the most poignant, for it is the stage that passes closest to Edington Mains, where Clark grew up, and the village of Chirnside, where he is buried. To find the start of the Edrom stage, head east out of Duns on the A6105 to Chirnside then join the B6355 towards Ayton. Approximately halfway to Ayton you'll see a small turning to the left, which is where the stage starts. From this point a detailed map is essential, for the stage zigzags its way on the most minor roads back towards Edrom, crossing the B6355 at one point before diving back onto the tiny lanes through Edrom and Buxley before reaching the finish at Preston. Like most of the lanes around here, you'll doubtless think you're lost forever, until you eventually emerge from the warren at a main road junction.

A good navigational rule of thumb is, if in doubt head for Duns. It's the perfect place to find a cup of tea, and also to spend an hour or two exploring the charming Jim Clark Room. Well signed and easy to spot, the Room is in an attractive stone house in the middle of Duns, and contains a fabulous collection of mementos from Clark's career. From crash helmets and overalls – which reveal his diminutive stature – to a glittering array of trophies, the Jim Clark Room is a warm and intimate museum that enables you to gain a real feel for his achievements.

Most revealing are the countless photographs, taken from the very earliest days of Clark's career competing in autotests, sprints and races at Winfield and Charterhall right through to his finest moments in Formula One, and in America where he became the first driver to win the Indy 500 in a rear-engined car. If you look closely you'll even find some pictures of his hard-charging efforts in the '66 RAC Rally: vivid proof, if any were needed, that the Jim Clark Rally is the perfect way to remember a great and much-loved man.

Right: Simon Hughes in a Renault Clio at the Jim Clark Rally in 2004

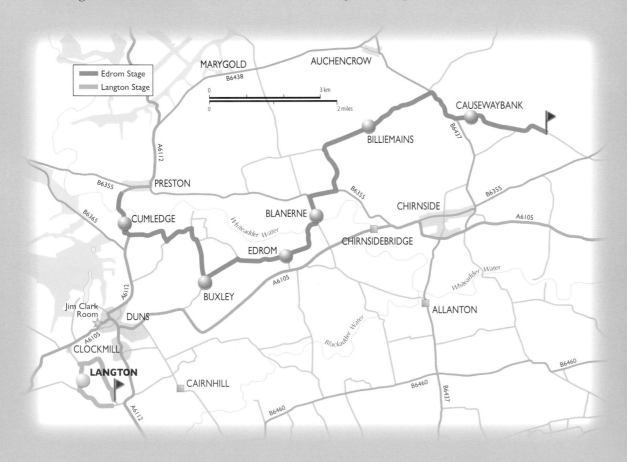

MANX RALLY

DISTANCE: VARIES **FIRST RACE:** 1963 **LOCATION:** ISLE OF MAN

'Flat left over crest maybe…': five of the most daunting words in rallying, yet some of the most commonly read pace notes on the Manx Rally. While there's no place for faint hearts during the rally, the Isle of Man's web of minor roads are a driver's paradise and memorable evidence that you don't have to be a motorcyclist to be drawn to the island.

Below: The perfect vantage point? A Nissan Almera GTi flashes past a pub window in the 2002 Manx Rally. **Opposite:** The 2006 race.

Understandably, the island's century-old love affair with the TT has somewhat overshadowed its rich rallying heritage. But there have been closed-road competitive rallies held on the island since 1963 when the first Manx Trophy Rally was contested by 75 cars in front of huge crowds. The rally has since become a favourite fixture of the British Rally Championship, growing in scale and stature to the point where it is regarded as one of the fastest and most challenging tarmac rallies in the world.

Many great drivers have shone here over the years, with home-grown heroes Russell Brookes, Jimmy McRae and Tony Pond all scoring victories in a variety of fabulously charismatic cars, including the Ford Escort RS1800, Opel Manta 400, Truimph TR8, MG Metro 6R4 and Sierra RS Cosworth during the 70s and 80s. Overseas drivers have also risen to the island's challenge, among the most memorable were the hard-charging Ari Vatanen and the Belgian tarmac ace Patrick Snijers, who won in 1988.

It says a great deal for the diversity of roads on the Isle of Man that the Manx Rally uses only a tiny section of the island's legendary 37.7-mile (60.6km) Mountain Course, preferring instead to use the tangle of narrow and bumpy 'yellow' roads that criss-cross the island. With ultra-fast moorland stages and even a blast through one the island's most historic towns, the Manx is as diverse a challenge as any rally driver can face on tarmac. Which is why following the path of some of its signature stages is the perfect way to explore this fascinating self-governing satellite of the British Isles.

A detailed map of the island is essential if you're to find your way to some of the narrower and more remote stages, but once suitably equipped, most are easy to find. Getting to them also gives you the perfect excuse to combine your exploration of the Manx Rally with a taste of the TT circuit, for many

of our selected stages lead directly from the main roads that form the TT loop.

As the Isle of Man is just 32 miles (51km) long and anything between 8 and 15 miles (13–24km) wide, it doesn't take too long to get around, especially if you rely on the main A roads that connect all the island's main towns. Even so, it pays to plan your route in advance, for some of the stages are long and can take you virtually the full width of the island without touching a main road.

The nature of rallying means that many of the Manx stages can be run in slightly different configurations and combinations, which means the rally tends to change from year to year. However, if you want to experience the full breadth of the island's roads then the following four stages provide a perfect snapshot of rallying Manx-style.

Assuming you are starting from Douglas, the best direction to head is north, following the TT circuit out of town on the A1 through Union Mills, Glen Vine and Crosby before bearing right onto the A3 and starting the northward climb up the island, past Cronk-y-Voddy and Kirk Michael before finally turning left off the TT course at Ballaugh onto the A10.

When you get to the amusingly named The Cronk, turn right onto a minor road, and then almost immediately right again towards Ballacoraige. This is 'The Curraghs' and is one of the tightest and bumpiest stages in the whole rally. As you leave Ballacoraige behind you and head for Kella at the other end of the stage, via a left turn, you won't believe how confined the roads are, nor how you could possibly hurl a rally car along a lane with grass growing down the middle of it!

With trees, ditches, high earth banks and car-killing solid stone walls rushing past the side windows, the sensation of speed is magnified

'he only has time to say 'Woah!' before looking up to see that his side of the car is on a perfect collision course with a hefty gatepost'

Above and opposite: Andreas Mikkelsen in his Ford Focus during the 2006 event.

immensely. During the rally, both driver and co-driver are pummelled by the violent bumps and dips, the latter struggling to keep pace with the notes, the former struggling to hear over the thwack of branches against the door mirrors, and stones clattering in the wheel arches. Despite the ultra-tight roads the rally cars really carry speed through here, but the slightest misjudgement will almost always result in a collision with a tree, wall or one of the many sturdy gateposts, which seem to sit on the outside of every tricky-to-read 90-degree left- or right-hand bend. Wise (and popular) is the farmer who leaves his gates open when the rally's on!

As you emerge from the tight confines of The Curraghs into the small village of Kella at the end of the stage you've got just enough time to catch your breath before you turn right onto the Sulby Straight section of the TT Course. You're effectively going against the direction of the circuit for a quarter of a mile or so (0.5km) before turning left onto the A14 just after the school in the centre of Sulby.

This is one of the most famous stages of the Manx Rally, thanks mainly to some spectacular in-car footage from Ari Vatanen's Opel Manta on the 1983 Manx International Rally (more of which in a moment).

The A14 starts in the quaint village surroundings, but soon breaks out into open countryside. Following the course of the Sulby River, the stage road skirts the slopes of Mount Karrin, squeezing between the steep mountainside and rushing river valley as it climbs towards the huge forestry plantation of Tholt-e-Will, which is approximately halfway to the finish and gives the stage its name.

You don't need to be driving a full-blown rally car to appreciate that the road leaving Sulby forms one of the all-time classic Manx stages. Even when speed limits prevent you from driving in a manner that befits its rallying pedigree, you can see how fast it would be if you were lucky enough to find yourself competing in the rally itself.

However, it's doubtful that even in your wildest dreams you would imagine just how quick this stage is, even through sections where there's barely a car-and-a-half's width between the drystone walls. All of which brings us neatly back to one of the most famous sequences of in-car footage in rallying: Ari Vatanen and co-driver Terry Harryman's 'Dear God!' moment on the climb to Tholt-e-Will.

The road is wet and greasy as the pair power away from Sulby. Sideways through the village they accelerate hard along the valley road, Harryman's measured pace notes providing a serene vocal accompaniment to Vatanen's finest thrash metal as he steers his Manta 400 along a rushing tunnel of trees and stone while flat in fifth gear. As the pace reaches its dizzying peak Harryman remains impassive, guiding Vatanen impeccably through

Below: Eugene Donnelly at the wheel of a Toyota Corolla WRC during the 2006 race.

the stage with his distinctive, staccato Irish tones: 'Flat left over brow… flat right maybe… seventy flat left into absolute right, one-fifty unseen early right, fifty early left…'

As Vatanen nudges their charging Opel into the early left he makes the smallest of misjudgements and thumps the stone wall with the left-hand front wheel, throwing them sideways in fourth gear at what must be a good 80mph (129kph). Harryman is still immersed in the notes, but as he feels the car slew he only has time to say 'Woah!' before looking up to see that his side of the car is on a perfect collision course with a hefty gatepost.

What follows is two seconds of sheer, silent terror as Harryman stares death in the face while Vatanen manfully winds on the perfect amount of opposite lock. Just as a sickening impact looks inevitable, Vatanen flicks the car straight and the Manta scythes between the gateposts and across the cattle grid, while Harryman utters the immortal words 'Dear

God!' before continuing seamlessly with his notes, '…brow one-fifty, flat right maybe…'

As you rumble across the grid you can spare a thought for the steely-nerved Harryman, for he and Vatanen completed the remainder of the stage at what appears to be unabated speed, despite the impact having punctured the left-front tyre. The speed on this last open moorland section is even more sustained, and while the sense of space is increased, it's worth noting that the stone walls have been replaced by barbed wire fences and fresh air drops on the climb towards Snaefell, the highest point on the island.

It's said you can see six kingdoms from Snaefell's summit: those of Man, Scotland, England, Ireland, Wales and Heaven. Unfortunately the reality is that, thanks to the fog that usually swirls around these parts, far from seeing six kingdoms, you're often lucky if you can see the end of your car's bonnet. However, if the weather's on your side, there's

another classic stage to explore just a few moments from the end of Tholt-e-Will.

Rejoin the TT circuit at Bungalow Station, turn right and follow the circuit to Hailwood's Height, before turning right onto the B10. This road is another ultra-fast moorland road, peppered with flat-out jumps and the occasional slippery cattle grid to keep you awake. It's an epic run that makes a distinct change in pace and character at the Manx landmark, Brandywell Cottage, for you need to take a sharp hairpin right onto a minor road, followed immediately by a hairpin left to join the bumpy and much narrower road to Druidale. This road actually cuts around the far side of the Tholt-e-Will plantation, eventually bringing you back out onto the TT circuit at Ballaugh, which is pretty much where our adventure began.

If you've had enough of the high-speed moorland roads and fancy a complete contrast, instead of driving the Brandywell stage take a drive along the remainder of the TT circuit to Douglas. Not only will you then have completed a full 37.7-mile (60.6km) lap, but you're also perfectly placed to continue south towards the picturesque Castletown harbour. You will find it the perfect spot to stop and enjoy the national dish of 'spuds and herrin' – a simple plate of boiled potatoes and herring – and the delights of locally caught queen scallops, but you can take a leisurely drive through the town, following the path of the stage and passing the castle and monument before teetering along the edge of the harbour wall.

If you visit immediately after the Manx International Rally has taken place (usually the middle of May) you'll still be able to see dark stripes of racing rubber smeared around seemingly every corner, the unmistakable evidence of this spectacular and unique motorsport event.

MONTE CARLO RALLY

DISTANCE: VARIES **FIRST RACE:** 1911 **LOCATION:** MONACO/FRANCE

Grit and glamour are not a common combination, but come January the two fuse together to spectacular effect in the form of the Monte Carlo Rally.

Created by two men – Gabriel Vialon and Anthony Noghes – and organized by the Automobile Club de Monaco (the same body responsible for the even more glitzy Monaco Grand Prix), the Monte Carlo Rally is a motorsport institution. First run in 1911, with the blessing of Monaco's then-ruler Prince Albert I, the primary motivation for holding a rally in the principality was commercial rather than sporting, as the Monagasque community was looking for a way to draw wealthy and sophisticated clientele away from the attractions of neighbouring city Nice – just along the Côte d'Azur – and into its own lavish hotels and casinos.

Vialon and Noghes decided the most effective way to achieve this was to organize an automobile rally.

Below: The Porsche 911T of Vic Elford and David Stone in the 1968 race. **Opposite:** The mountains of the famous Col de Turini stage.

Their concept mirrored that of an existing Italian cycle race, and required competitors to converge on Monaco from a variety of starting points in far-flung European cities, including Berlin, Vienna and Brussels, as well as the rather closer Paris. Open to any type of motor car – 23 machines entered the inaugural event – and run to a relaxed set of rules, competitors could choose when and from which city they started, and had a maximum of seven days to reach Monaco. On arrival in the principality they gathered for, of all things, a fête.

Prizes took into account speed, distance, the number of people carried, the car's comfort and its state on arriving in Monaco. Amusingly, many of the cars were actually driven by chauffeurs, not the owners, who clearly preferred to travel in style. Whether the winner of the immense £400 prize money, Henri Rougier, who started from Paris and completed the 570-mile (918km) journey in a little over 28 hours, was actually driving or not isn't recorded.

The scattered format, long distances, mountainous terrain and changeable weather made the Monte Carlo Rally one of the toughest tests of reliability and durability, but it was precisely because of this gruelling nature that it became an ideal means of testing the most advanced cars of the day. Sometimes simply getting to Monaco was an achievement. Finishing the rally was a major accomplishment, while winning brought invaluable prestige and publicity, and forged the reputations of cars and drivers alike.

As rallying evolved, so too did the Monte. While the far-flung start points remained well into the 1960s – can you believe in some years competitors started from as far afield as Glasgow, Athens, Stockholm and Tallinn? – the emphasis of the competition gradually shifted from the navigational

and reliability challenges, handicaps and unfathomable 'indices of performance' to a combination of navigation and flat-out, closed-road special stage sections, which were introduced in 1961. Eventually the rally adopted the modern recipe of a series of closed-road special stages linked by strictly controlled road sections: a format that remains largely unchanged to this day.

Since 1973, the Monte Carlo has been the World Rally Championship's season-opener, but even before the creation of the global rally series it had long been regarded as the blue riband of rallying. A double-whammy of fiendish mountain roads and unpredictable winter weather, 'The Monte' is renowned for serving-up anything from snow and ice to rain and low cloud or bright sunshine and dry tarmac, often in the space of the same rally, and sometimes in the space of one stage. Some drivers thrive on the unpredictability and high-stakes tyre choices, while others detest the ever-changing road conditions and the ever-present risk of being caught on the wrong rubber.

The odd thing about the Monte Carlo Rally is that although it starts amid unrivalled pomp and ceremony in Monaco's famous Casino Square, no sooner do the cars drive slowly off the start ramp than they hightail it out of the crowded tax haven and up into the isolated mountain roads of southern France. There have been time trials held on the Grand Prix street circuit (indeed the 2007 Monte made a popular return to the GP circuit), but it's up in the mountains, amongst the baying fans and honking air horns, that the real rally begins, and where the fun starts if you want to explore some of the highlights of this epic route.

There are many great stages from which to choose, but four in particular stand out: the mighty Sisteron, with its huge change in elevation from

'the Col de Turini

stands head and shoulders above the lot, both

physically and metaphorically'

start to finish; St Auban, with its river-cut canyon and claustrophobic overhanging rocks; the remote and relentlessly twitsy Loda to Luceram stage; and finally the Monte Carlo's most famous stage of all, the Col de Turini.

If you have a couple of days to spare, doing all four is no problem, for Sisteron and St Auban are close to one another – to the northwest of Monaco – while Loda–Luceram and the Col de Turini are also adjacent to one another and much closer to Monaco. Where you're based and whether you've driven south from France or flown to Nice and then rented a car will dictate which stages you tackle first, but as Sisteron is a good 80 miles (129km) from either Monaco or Nice as the crow flies (further if you take all the twists and turns of even the main roads into account), it makes sense to drive the Sisteron and St Auban regions first.

The Sisteron stage is a 23-mile (37km) classic and certainly worth the drive, encapsulating the problems every rally crew and tyre technician face on the rally proper. If you're sensible you'll time your trip for June or July, when you can enjoy 25–30°C (77–86°F) sunshine, cloudless azure skies and the constant chirruping of crickets in the roadside verges as you make the ascent from lush low-lying alpine pastures to the pale 4,200ft (1,277m) crags of the Alpes de Haute-Provence. In January, by contrast, the rally drivers have to contend with the fickle mood swings of Mother Nature, and roads that demand nothing more than a set of lightly cut slicks at the start of the stage to studded ice and snow tyres at the top.

The road's changing character ensures an almost theatrical crescendo of speed and drama. The first ten gently climbing miles (16km) are comprised of fast and often clearly sighted third-gear corners. The road is wide(ish) and the tarmac relatively smooth, but as the incline steepens and the vegetation begins to fade, bent and battered Armco signals you're now being protected from some seriously unnerving drops. The road is bleached by sun and cracked by frost, broken by the rigours of baking

summers and freezing winters. By the time the road plateaus and you glance across the yawning valleys to the adjacent peaks you feel on top of the world and high on adrenaline.

On the descent, the Sisteron stage changes character once more, knotting and tangling itself into a nightmare of narrow, blind corners and dark pine forests. This section is not a place to enjoy when on-coming traffic could be hidden around every corner, but it's certainly a place to come and enjoy the peace and isolation, and to contemplate what it took to drive a fire-spitting Group B car down here with snow and ice rather than warm, grippy tarmac under your tyres.

The confines of these wooded turns are a fitting prelude for the frankly claustrophobic roads of St Auban. One of the most challenging areas of France for practitioners of the extreme sport of canyoning (where climbers swim, slide and clamber their way through sheer-faced gorges and white-water rapids), the road to St Auban is literally carved into the rock face. The rock forms a ragged ceiling over your head, making driving along the road feel like surfing through an arched wave of stone. On the open side a low wall and barrier are all that's between you and a sheer drop into the roaring river gorge.

The road is narrow and surprisingly busy, so you really need to be cautious, especially around some of the tighter corners, which are blind. The bonus – apart from the mesmerizing drama of such spectacular geology – is that the tunnel effect makes for some awesome sound effects if your car has a fruity exhaust note. TVR owners take note: this road could have been built with you in mind!

The Loda–Luceram stage is less well known, but it has played a pivotal role in shaping the results. In 1986 it was the Monte's final stage, and provided Audi's Walter Röhrl with the ideal opportunity to put his mark on the event. Poised for a win early in the rally, a puncture had put paid to his challenge, but this didn't prevent him from humiliating the opposition, and having fought his way back to fourth place with a series of five fastest stage times, and the 10-mile (16km) Loda–Luceram stage would be his finest hour.

Left: The Skoda Fabia WRC of Alexandre Bengue during the 2005 Monte Carlo Rally.

Remote and unrelenting in its intensity, this comparatively understated stage lacks the vertiginous drama of Sisteron, but the roads are easier to read and more suited to cutting loose. In fact, it's so far away from any towns or villages that for the bulk of the stage you're in blissful isolation: just you, your car and road ahead. Röhrl was fastest through here, of course, but just how much faster beggared belief, completing the icy stage a sensational 50 seconds faster than the next quickest driver, who just so happened to be his teammate, Hannu Mikkola. It was a fitting swansong for the fearsome 500bhp Group B Audi Sport Quattro, and a reminder that Röhrl was still one of the all-time Monte masters.

However, even he would agree that of all the Monte's many great stages, the Col de Turini stands head and shoulders above the lot, both physically and metaphorically. Running from La Bollène to Sospel, this larger-than-life 20-mile (32km) stage passes over the 5,271ft (1,607m) summit of the most famous mountain in rallying.

Heading from Sospel, the stage begins on the D2566, with some long and fast straights. At Notre-Dame de la Ménour you'll get your first taster of the feats of hairpins to come, with a small tangle of switchbacks. A long straight of more than a mile and half (2.5km) – where the rally cars will top 115mph (185kph) – ends with a trio of hairpins before climbing through a dark, almost impenetrable pine forest. At 3,838ft (1,170m) the road climbs out of the Valley of Bévéra and the ascent of the Turini begins in earnest.

As you crest the summit the road flattens and you emerge into a cluster of rustic chalets, restaurants and hotels. In the summer it makes an ideal spot to stop and admire the view, but during the rally this place is transformed into a cauldron of riotous celebrations and, every now and again, acts of partisan skullduggery.

Right: Marcus Grönholm tackling one of the many mountainous switchbacks of the Monte Carlo Rally during the 2006 event.

If there's snow – as there almost always is at this altitude in January – the fans are happy, but if the icy precipitation shows signs of wearing thin on the

road they'll invariably kick and throw what snow they can find into the path of the rally cars, in an effort to trip up the drivers. In 1979 they placed more than snow on the road, as the leader, Bjorn Waldegård, discovered when his path was blocked by two huge boulders. He lost 30 seconds while negotiating the improvised roadblock, while the Lancia Stratos of Frenchman Bernard Darniche ripped through unimpeded to win the rally by 6 seconds. It's just one of the many great Monte Carlo scandals (see box).

During the 1970s, 80s and even into the 90s, the Turini was also characterized by drama of a more

Left: Walter Röhrl in the superb Audi Quattro E2 S1 in the 1986 rally.
Below: Gareth MacHale in a Ford Focus during the 2006 event.

gratifying kind, when the stage was run at night. Known as 'The Night of the Long Knives' by the hardcore fans who braved sub-zero temperatures to witness the spectacle, the name is a wonderfully dramatic description of the sharp slashes of intense white light that would spear into the darkness from the rally cars' blinding array of spotlights.

The rally organizers stopped running the Turini stage at night long ago, one suspects because of commercial television pressures as much as anything else. In fact, the Turini was missed out all together in the 2007 Monte Carlo, much to the dismay of the fans and many of the drivers. The times may be changing, but when you drive it for yourself you'll know that WRC or not, the call of the Col remains as strong as ever.

MINI COOPER S –
MONTE ZOOMER'S REVENGE

The story of the Mini Cooper S and the Monte Carlo is one of the most famous tales in rallying. The inspiring tale of how the plucky little red cars dominated rallying's most prestigious event, suffered at the hands of bitter French subterfuge then fought back with a climactic twist of sweet revenge is the stuff of Hollywood scriptwriters. Yet it all happened on the snowy mountain roads of the Alpes-Maritimes.

The Mini's Monte Carlo ascendancy began in 1963, when the Finnish driver Rauno Aaltonen and his co-driver Tony Ambrose finished in third place. The following year saw Paddy Hopkirk and co-driver Henry Liddon score the Mini's landmark first Monte win, with Timo Mäkinen and Paul Easter scoring the Mini's second consecutive win in 1965.

When Mäkinen and Easter repeated the feat in 1966, and teammates Rauno Aaltonen and Paddy Hopkirk locked out the remaining podium places it should have been the Mini's finest hour. Unfortunately the French organizers (plus a few of the French manufacturer teams) didn't find a Mini Monte hat trick quite such a joyous prospect, and subjected all three Minis to a near-forensic level of scrutiny in the post-rally checks.

After eight hours and the discovery of numerous 'irregularities' that the BMC team confidently rebuffed, the organizers eventually disqualified all three Minis (and a fourth-placed Lotus Cortina) for lights that didn't comply with French headlight-dipping regulations. Hardly a performance-enhancing infringement, but there you go. The result? A Citroen DS in first place, and a scandal that brought the Monte Carlo Rally into disrepute and placed the Minis firmly in the spotlight.

It was a sorry affair, and one that the Citroen's driver, Pauli Toivonen (father of the late Group B hero, Henri) wanted no part in. He reluctantly accepted the trophy but vowed never to drive for Citroen again.

By 1967 the desire to win burned even more strongly within the BMC team. After a heroic drive in appalling conditions, and against rivals in much more powerful machinery, Rauno Aaltonen did just that. Justice was served, the Mini Cooper S entered the pantheon of rally greats, and the tale of how this diminutive British car reigned supreme in Monaco transcended rallying to become a defining moment of the 60s.

RALLY FINLAND

Finland has a population of just 5 million people, yet cast an eye through the long and distinguished history of rallying and you could be forgiven for thinking at least 4.9 million of those are professional rally drivers.

In a way that's not so far from the truth, for when the unique hard-packed gravel roads that cut through the Finnish forests aren't being used as World Rally Championship stages they are regular public highways. Connecting remote villages and isolated farms to each other and the outside world, these epic unmetalled arteries make every Finnish school run and shopping trip a special stage adventure.

The origins of Rally Finland are unusual, in that it was born of the Finnish rally community's desire to compete in the Monte Carlo Rally, rather than wanting to create a rival domestic event. Back then countries were given a certain allocation of entries for events such as the Monte Carlo, and in Finland, where rallying was (and remains) a part of life, demand for those places comfortably exceeded supply. To arrive at a fair means of deciding which rally crews would represent the country, an event known as the Hanko Run was held as a kind of selection competition, with the best finishers earning their Monte entry.

While no one disputed that the principle of the Hanko Run was sound, many competitors complained that because the regulations were very different from those of the Monte Carlo, its demands had little relevance. It was during the after-event dinner of the 1951 Hanko Run that a group of experienced Monte Carlo competitors set about devising a better solution to their selection

issues. The answer they arrived at was to hold an annual competition run as closely as possible to Monte Carlo rules and regulations, and using the centrally located city of Jyväskylä as the start and finish point.

Just two months after laying the ground rules for their new event, 26 competitors started the rally, which, thanks to the large amount of prize money on offer, was called the Jyväskylä Grand Prix. Some 1,000 miles (1,600km) in length, the route took the crews to the Arctic Circle and back, and was mainly comprised of timed road sections, which demanded great concentration and accuracy from driver and co-driver. There were also two special stages: one

held on a 0.8-mile (1.3km) hillclimb, the other an acceleration and braking test close to Jyväskylä.

The Grand Prix was a great success, and Jyväskylä has remained the home of Finnish rallying to this day. By 1954 the event's name was changed to the enduringly evocative and perfectly descriptive 'Rally of the Thousand Lakes', before eventually this too was shortened to the '1000 Lakes Rally' during the 1980s. Sadly, with the dawn of the modern WRC era came the simple but insipid naming formula of 'Rally' followed by the name of the host nation. For a country peppered by some 188,000 lakes, Rally Finland seems painfully bland, but that's progress for you.

Left: The Peugeot 307 WRC of Marcus Grönholm on its way to victory in the 2004 race. **Right:** Kosti Katajamaki in his Ford Focus in 2006.

'It turns out that in his youth, Kankkunen used to regularly drive the road at night when travelling to and from his girlfriend's house...'

Fortunately, while the name became increasingly nondescript, the rally itself has developed into an absolute classic. Just as Spa-Francorchamps is by common consent a favourite of Formula One drivers and fans alike, so WRC drivers, co-drivers and spectators revel in the challenge and spectacle of Rally Finland's unique roller-coaster stages. It's an appropriate parallel, for Finland is the fastest event in the World Rally Championship, and is often referred to in reverential tones as a Grand Prix on gravel.

It's easy to see why when you get out onto the stages. They might be carved through a forest in the middle of nowhere, but unlike the coarse, loose and heavily cambered gravel forest roads so typical of Rally GB, Finnish gravel is finely textured and near-solid. This gives the rally cars a much more even and consistent surface on which to run, enabling them to accelerate, corner and brake more effectively than you would ever believe possible. That they are public roads rather than access roads for forestry workers also makes a big difference, for it means they're wider and more regularly graded to maintain the surface quality. Before the rally cars come through they look smoother than some British B roads!

Above: Marcus Grönholm's final victory for Peugeot came in 2005.
Right: Another year, another victory for Grönholm. This time in a Ford Focus WRC

If you think that makes Rally Finland sound like a piece of cake to drive then think again. The roads might be wide and smooth and the corners gracefully sweeping arcs, but they are also a minefield of blind crests and hidden hazards. As most of the crests are approached flat out in top gear, you can appreciate how absolute faith in your co-driver and your pace notes is essential if you're to remain on the road, let alone on the pace of the aptly named Flying Finns, who have unrivalled local knowledge.

Two-time Rally Finland winner Juha Kankkunen is a prime example, for aside from his famously piercing gaze and super-quick moustache he's noted for two legendary Rally Finland tales. In one, his co-driver makes a rare error and gets lost in his pace notes. Untroubled, Kankkunen is heard to say 'Don't worry, I know this stage', before proceeding to complete it at unabated speed. It turns out that in his youth, Kankkunen used to regularly drive the road at night when travelling to and from his girlfriend's house…

Rallies

The second story proves what you know is often dictated by who you know. It was only when some rally photographers were comparing shots from the same corner that they noticed Kankkunen's car was at a totally different angle and much closer to the inside than all his rivals'. Some years later Kankkunen wryly revealed that he knew the landowner who lived on that particular corner, and had been tipped off that although the owner left his post box in position at the apex of the corner during the rally's recce – prompting all the other co-drivers to mark a 'Caution, don't cut' warning in their pace notes – it was always removed for the rally itself, allowing Kankkunen to take huge liberties and steal some time.

It's a fair bet that if Kankkunen had his own particular secrets then so too do the other Finns. That would certainly explain why only three non-Scandinavian crews have won the rally since 1951, and why of those victorious Nordic nations, the Finns are by far the dominant force on home gravel.

Many have claimed multiple victories: 1960s hero Timo Mäkinen has four wins and Hannu Mikkola has seven, both drivers having scored hat tricks along the way. Markku 'Maximum Attack' Alén has six (including the obligatory hat-trick), while Tommi Mäkinen scored a record five wins on the bounce from 1994 to 1998. But even he bows to the current King of Finland, Marcus Grönholm, who has scored six wins and counting: a pair of hat tricks split by Estonian Markko Märtin's audacious win in 2003. Clearly, when it comes to Rally Finland the names on the trophy may change, but the nationality almost always remains the same.

Sometimes, though, even the local experts get caught out. In the 2005 event the drivers tackled a new stage called Vellipohja. Although they all recced the stage several times before the start of the rally, they'd never driven it at full speed, making the 21 miles (34km) of gravel track a journey into the relative unknown. Just a mile or so from the end of the stage many of the top professional crews were caught out by a particularly deceptive crest, where the road literally fell away on the blind side. None

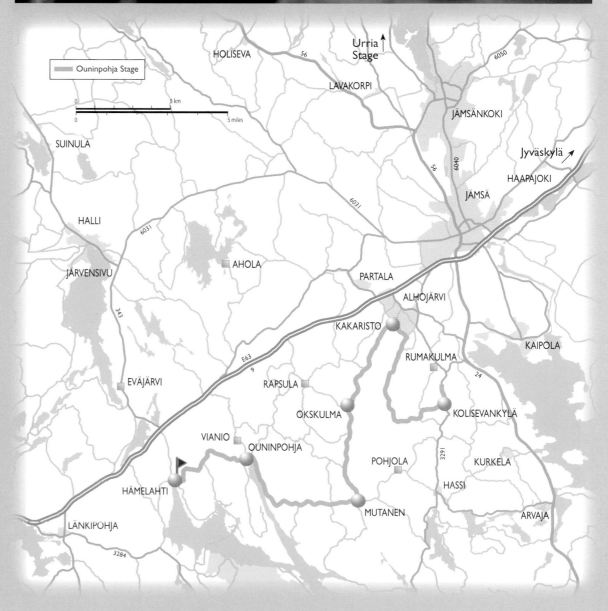

crashed, but the ferocity of the resulting impacts left several co-drivers, including Timo Rautiainen (Grönholm's co-driver) in agony after severely jarring their backs.

During the rally it's easy enough to find the stages – simply follow the buses, camper vans and cars to the well-signed parking areas – but if you make the trip during the rest of the year it gets trickier. As you can imagine, with 10 per cent of the country covered by water and more than 70 per cent smothered in pine and birch trees, the minor gravel-surfaced roads that thread their way through the wilderness are labyrinthine in nature, and easy to miss when you're cruising along the main highways.

While the names of the stages do correspond with the local place names, they don't always start in the village that the stage name suggests. Take the legendary Ouninpohja stage (see box page 120) for example. Although it passes through Ouninpohja, it actually starts in the adjacent village of Hämelahti, which is some 5 miles (8km) or so to the west. This defining stage of Rally Finland has additional complications, since recently it has been split into two stages, the second part of which actually starts 10 miles (16km) or so east of Ouninpohja and only takes the cars further away.

The good news is that while the rally is based in Jyväskylä (three hours' drive north of Helsinki), many of the stages are centred around Jämsä (including Ouninpohja), which is almost an hour further south, meaning you can get a vivid taste of Rally Finland without having to do the whole route. In truth, whether you find yourself driving the Ouninpohja, Ruuhimäki, Urria or any of the other special stages, or simply decide to explore many of the other country roads that share their character, you're sure to find an authentic Rally Finland driving experience.

What's certain is you'll never get used to way the forests seem to go on forever, nor how the crests interrupt your vision. In fact almost from the moment you turn off the main highways you'll be constantly straining against your seatbelt for a better

OUNINPOHJA – HOME OF THE YUMP

If there's one stage that defines what Rally Finland is all about, it's Ouninpohja. The fastest, fiercest stage in the entire World Rally Championship, this majestic, malevolent stretch of Finnish gravel is the ultimate test of skill and nerve that a driver and co-driver can face.

Nowhere do rally cars spend more time with their throttles pinned wide-open, or their wheels off the ground. In 2003, Estonian driver Marrko Märtin and his co-driver, the late Michael 'Beef' Park, set an all-time yumping record on their way to an historic Rally Finland victory. No doubt egged on by the presence of a radar speed trap just before Ouninpohja's legendary 'yellow house' yump, Märtin took the crest at 107mph (172kph) and the pair proceeded to fly at an altitude of 10ft (3m) or so for an incredible 62 yards (57m). Images of their Ford Focus WRC caught in mid-flight are now among the most iconic in rallying.

The following year, Subaru World Rally team driver Petter Solberg and his co-driver Phil Mills set a stage record for Ouninpohja, covering the stage in 15:18.5, shattering Colin McRae's previous record of 15:25, and exceeding the FIA's 81mph (130kph) average speed threshold in the process. As a result Ouninpohja was split into two stages in an attempt to reduce the average speed without neutering the challenge that is its essential character. Solberg and Mills' reward for such a heroic effort was the prospect of their record time never being beaten, but if rumours that the full Ouninpohja is set to return prove true, we have the prospect of further record-breaking performances to look forward to.

For now, though, the legacy of Solberg's incredible time is Ouninpohja Länsi and Ouninpohja Itä: the two halves of the old monster. Fortunately the 8.69 mile (13.98km) and 10.29 mile (16.55km) stages are just as daunting and exhilarating, and the drivers still love them. Proof, if any were needed, came in last year's rally, when data from Marcus Grönholm's Ford Focus WRC revealed he had spent 46 seconds flat out in top gear during his passage through one of the revised Ouninpohja stages, during which time he averaged 106mph (171kph).

Additional information revealed by the Subaru World Rally Team provides us with further enlightenment about the stage's unique demands. The highest recorded peak speed for a Subaru Impreza on Ouninpohja was 123mph (198kph), while the team's engineers have calculated that there are approximately 50 jumps in the two Ouninpohja stages. They also reckon that the average distance travelled at each of those yumps is 32ft (10m), which means that by the end of the stages the car has travelled some 0.3 miles (500m) in the air. That's more than 15 seconds airborne. No wonder the drivers say there's nothing like it.

To see footage of Petter Solberg's record-setting run through the old Ouninpohja stage, log-on to http://www.carspace.com/videos/play!id=.5a06afee

view of the road ahead. It's a largely futile reaction, but in the absence of a skilled co-driver it's the best you can do. The deep, car-swallowing ditches and proximity to the trees are also pretty daunting, particularly when you contemplate what it must be like to whistle along these roads – and through the air - at anything up to 120mph (193kph). The legendary rally photographer, Reinhard Klein, sums it up best when he describes Finland as 'a three-dimensional rally.'

Despite the absence of tarmac, it doesn't take long to feel confident on the gravel surface. There's some dust if the weather is dry, but you don't feel the car slipping around beneath you, and for the most part you can drive just as you would at home. The benefit of travelling at sane speeds is the time you have spare to look around you. Shimmering expanses of water are never far away, and the stages sometimes pass along the fringes of the lakes, affording breathtaking vistas across this pure, unspoiled natural wilderness. During the rally the woods are inhabited by fanatical and spectacularly inebriated Finnish and Estonian fans, but for the rest of the year your concern should be focussed on the mosquitoes, which sound like Spitfires and have a voracious appetite.

Another Finnish hazard are the police, who enthusiastically enforce speed limits that are among the strictest in the world. Predictably they're especially vigilant around late July and early August, when the rally is held, but they never really drop their guard. It's always best to drive responsibly, though, if for no other reason than it's going to be hard to explain how you managed to park your Ford Focus rental car halfway up a pine tree, let alone what you were doing on the road to Ouninpohja…

Below: Headlights streaming through the forest in 1990, when the event was still known as the 1,000 Lakes Rally.

TOUR DE CORSE

DISTANCE: VARIES FIRST RACE: 1956 LOCATION: CORSICA, FRANCE

The Tour de Corse, or 'The Rally of 10,000 Corners' was first held in 1956. As it's unofficial name suggested, it was a punishing circuit of the island, taking the best part of a week to complete and requiring the rally crews to tackle most of Corsica's wild and unruly mountain roads, often at night. It wasn't a challenge for the faint-hearted.

A field of 43 competitors began that first Tour of 1956, but only 24 made the finish. The following year two events were run in parallel: one was a round of the French GT championship run in the spirit of the Tour de France and the great Italian road races, the other an event called the L'Ile de Beauté rally.

In 1973 the introduction of the World Manufacturers' Championship for rallying gave the directors of France's National Motorsport a tough job deciding between the Tour de Corse and Tour de France as the event to put forward as the French round of the new World Championship. In the end they chose the Tour de Corse, and it has remained as a round of the World Rally Championship ever since.

In 1979 the sport's governing body, the Fédération Internationale du Sport Automobile (FISA) supplemented the Manufacturers Championship with a World Drivers' Championship. This cast the spotlight on the achievements of the individual as well as those of the works teams. As the ultimate tarmac rally, Corsica soon became one of the events a driver longed to win, as it demonstrated their mastery of one of rallying's three main surfaces.

Right: Didier Auriol en route to victory in his Lancia Delta Integrale in the 1992 Tour de Corse. **Opposite:** The red rocks of the Calanches de Piana on Corsica's northwest coast.

As the World Championship matured, teams grew wise to the specialized demands of a tarmac event like Corsica, which gave rise to tarmac experts being drafted in to score maximum points for the team. In the modern era, drivers like Gilles Panizzi (co-driven by his brother) dominated the event (and other tarmac rallies) for Peugeot, setting extraordinarily fast stage times to score memorable wins in 2000 and 2002. Corsica has also been a happy hunting ground for privateers with a penchant for tarmac. Indeed, Bernard Darniche is the most successful driver of all on Corsica, winning no fewer than six times between 1970 and 1981, an honour he shares with fellow Frenchman Didier Auriol, who scored six wins in eight years.

More recently, the advent of 'complete' rally drivers, such as Petter Solberg, Sébastien Loeb and Marcus Grönholm – three men who have won on every surface – has made it harder for the tarmac specialists to get a look in. Of the trio, Loeb is the master, having won his first Rally France (the new name for the Corsican WRC round) in 2005 in unprecedented fashion by claiming fastest time on every special stage. After such a virtuoso performance few were surprised when he conquered the Corsican mountains again in 2006.

With more than 600 miles (966km) of coastline, 21 mountains with summits of more than 6,500ft (2,008m), the highest of which, Monte Cinto, reaches 8,878ft (2,706m), and a snaking network of

'Fighting to control their over-powered and ill-tempered cars took huge reserves of mental and physical endurance'

Above: Philippe Bugalski in a Citroen Xsara WRC in 2003. **Right:** Stephane Sarrazin spins his Subaru Legacy during the 2005 event.

near-deserted roads, Corsica could have been designed with tarmac rallying in mind. When the Tour de Corse still involved a full exploration of the island's roads, the crews would face a huge number of stages, including 'Les Calanches', where the route followed the winding coast road before climbing into the mountains near Porto on the northwestern side of the island. At one point the road actually passes between a narrow gap in the spectacular rock formations that give the stage its name. On other sections of the road all that stands between you and a dizzying 1,300ft (400m) drop into the sea is a shin-high stone wall. Driving with full commitment though here must have been hair-raising, and confirms that co-drivers, in particular, are insane.

The current, greatly reduced, dash through Corsica rarely ventures north of its HQ in the port of Ajaccio (birthplace of Napoleon Bonaparte) on the southwest coast. In fact, last year the only stage

to do so was the 21.3-mile (34.3km) sprint from Vico to Plage du Liamone. The longest stage of the rally, it's one of the few stages to resemble the great tests of the Tour de Corse, clinging as it does to the precipitous and distinctively red cliffs.

It's a stage made doubly challenging by the fact that the road runs largely downhill. Narrow and twisty for the first 15 miles (24km) or so it passes through a couple of small mountain villages before joining a wider and more flowing road for the last 6 miles (10km), where it finishes at the beach. Tyres and brakes take a real pounding on this stage, with many of the top drivers complaining of shot rubber and no stopping power by the end.

Other modern classics include the 16-mile (26km) Ucciani–Bastelica stage, which can be found

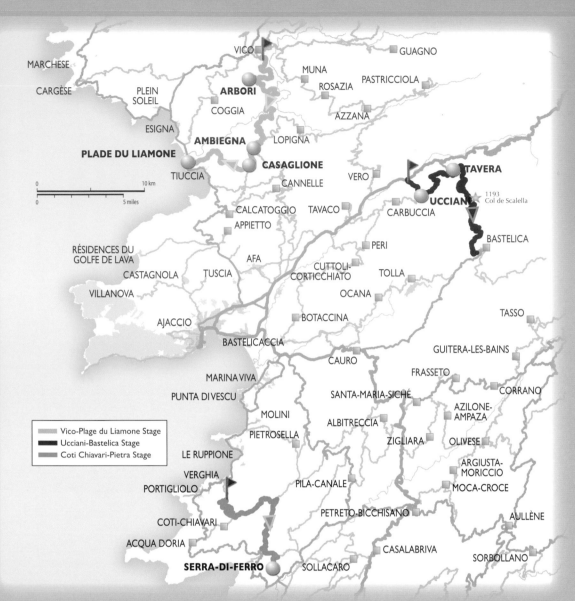

Above: Bullet-ridden Corsican road signs. **Right:** The Lancia S4 of Henri Toivonen during the tragic 1986 race.

climbing the 3,913ft (1,193m) Col de Scalella directly to the east of Ajaccio, and the 15-mile (24km) Penitencier de Coti–Pietra Rossa stage, which is the fastest in the rally.

The former starts on a very fast main road, which passes through a village before turning onto a much twistier road – the D27 – which is often dusty and dirty. If it rains, as it often does in the Corsican mountains, the road surface can be lethally slippery. As the road crests the Col the surface becomes rougher and more broken, before levelling off for the last mile or two to the finish. The latter has tree cover for the bulk of the climb, which is unusual for the island, before turning onto a much wider road that the crews take flat out, apart from the series of hairpins that punctuate the 7-mile (11km) run to the end of the stage.

Compared to the Tour de Corse at the height of the Group B era these fierce modern WRC stages are a walk in the park. In 1986 some stages could take crews an hour to complete, despite

driving flat out in monstrous 500bhp machines. These were the days before teams could only work on their cars in the centralized service area at rally HQ, and some of the teams – most notably Lancia – took full advantage, conducting mid-stage Formula One-style pit stops where they would change tyres and even replace brake pads in an effort to keep their highly stressed cars in perfect order.

Unfortunately nothing could be done to refresh the drivers and co-drivers, who had no choice but to battle on regardless. Fighting to control their over-powered and ill-tempered cars took huge reserves of mental and physical endurance, and for some drivers the effort of sustaining sufficient concentration to control these unforgiving cars at such high speeds for such extended periods led them to develop tunnel vision from always trying to focus on the rushing road ahead.

It was a fabulous era to be a spectator, but a difficult and dangerous time to be a driver, for in

truth few had the courage and natural ability to truly master the demands of a Group B car rally car, particularly on a high-grip tarmac surface like Corsica. One of the few drivers to inhabit that elite group was the young Finnish hero Henri Toivonen.

Fast and fearless, Toivonen had a reputation for conjuring eye-watering speed from his cars. It's true that he also teetered between triumph and disaster, and his early rally career was punctuated by some enormous accidents, but when you have the ability to take whole minutes out of your rivals' times on just one stage, teams tend to forgive you the odd written-off car.

Toivonen was also an accomplished circuit racer, having made a one-off appearance for Eddie Jordan in Formula Three, and at Le Mans driving a Porsche 956. As a consequence his confidence on tarmac – normally an alien surface to a rally driver – meant he had the skill and sensitivity to push his car to extraordinary lengths on Corsica's treacherously twisty roads. Ironically it was this ability and desire to extract the maximum from his savagely powerful Lancia Delta S4, which was both turbocharged and supercharged, that ultimately put him at greater risk on this least-forgiving rally in the World Rally Championship.

The Tour de Corse had bared its teeth the previous year, when Italian Attilio Bettega lost his life during the 1985 Tour de Corse, while driving a rear-wheel drive Lancia 037. For 1986 the Lancia squad came with their all-wheel drive S4, a car that was both more powerful and harder to tame than the underpowered but sweet-handling 037. It was in this ballistic that the mercurial Toivonen was expected to shine.

True to form, and despite the debilitating effects of flu, he and his American co-driver, Sergio Cresto, more than lived up to the expectations, setting successive fastest stage times and pulling into a commanding lead. Despite his apparent mastery of

the car and the Corsican roads, Toivonen knew how hard he was pushing and admitted that he was struggling to keep up with the speed of his car. Speaking to reporters during the rally he said of the Tour de Corse 'This rally is insane, even though everything is going well at the moment. If there's trouble, I'm as good as dead.'

His words were to prove chillingly prophetic, for just 4.5 miles (7.25km) into Stage 18 of the rally on the fast twists and turns that runs between Corte and Taverna in the mountainous centre of the island, he lost control of his Lancia. The left-hand curve was typical of the stage, with the craggy mountain on one side and fresh air on the other, and the Lancia skidded off the unprotected edge of

the road and down into a rocky ravine. The S4's fuel tank ruptured as it clattered into a small clump of trees and came to rest on its roof. The car caught fire with the hapless Toivonen and Cresto trapped inside. The resulting inferno was so intense that nothing could be gleaned from the wreckage, leaving the cause of the tragic crash a mystery to this day.

A simple marble memorial stands at the place where the accident happened, and local people still place fresh flowers there every day. There's also an unopened bottle of Martini there, as a reference to the distinctive sponsorship livery of their Lancia, and rally fans from all over the world drive along the stage to pay their respects to an enduring hero.

In the immediate aftermath, motorsport's governing body banned Group B (and the mooted Group S) for the following season, prompting an initiative for safer cars and shorter rallies, a move that has undoubtedly saved the lives of many rally crews since.

Each year when the World Rally Championship visits Corsica, thoughts are spared for Bettega, Toivonen and Cresto. The rally and the cars are safer now – largely thanks to their sacrifice – but the enthralling roads of this French island outpost remain as demanding and thrilling as ever, and a fitting venue for the finest drivers in the world to continue to display their talent.

24 Grand Prix Circuits

Jarno Trulli in action during practice for the 2007 Monaco Grand Prix at the wheel of his Toyota TF107.

SPA-FRANCORCHAMPS

DISTANCE: 9.3 MILES (15KM) FIRST RACE: 1921 LOCATION: BELGIUM

Ironically, it's a dull drive to get to Spa-Francorchamps. Firm favourite of past and present Grand Prix drivers and one of the last truly spectacular 'natural' circuits on the Formula One calendar, Spa sits at the end of a tedious three-hour motorway haul along the industrial coast of France, the flat fields of Belgium and the concrete sprawl of Brussels.

The motorway monotony is eventually broken by a series of large brown-and-white signs bearing the

Below: The Porsche 996 GT3 RS of Emmanuel Collard, Luca Riccetelli and Romain Dumas during the 2006 FIA GT Championship race at Spa. **Opposite:** The famous plunge down the hill to Eau Rouge at the start of the 1958 race.

legend 'Spa-Francorchamps' against a background illustration of a racing car, crash helmet and chequered flag. As road signage goes they're pretty inspiring, for they mean you're just a few miles from what many consider to be the greatest motor racing circuit of them all.

Like the Nürburgring, Spa-Francorchamps is set in dense pine forests, in this instance cloaking the Ardennes Mountains. It's a region of Belgium that 'enjoys' similarly changeable weather to the legendary German circuit's Eifel Mountain home, but then as the two are separated by barely an hour's drive that's hardly surprising.

As you'll discover if you visit the region, water is a recurring theme at Spa. There's a hint in the name,

thanks to the Romans' discovery of iron-rich mineral water here, which led to the development of a town where people would come to take the waters for medicinal purposes. The famous Eau Rouge corner is named after the red-tinged stream (caused by the iron deposits) that runs through the bottom of the valley, while at one stage in the circuit's history it had rained for 20 consecutive Belgian Grand Prix meetings.

Racing first came to the region as early as 1902, on the Circuit des Ardennes. This was a new development in motorsport, for the vogue then was for city-to-city races rather than events held on a defined circuit. In its original configuration the circuit covered a lap of some 53.5 miles (86km), but this was extended to a faintly ridiculous 73.4 miles (118km) in 1904 before the course faded quietly into obscurity soon after.

With the appeal of Spa's medicinal waters on the wane, a casino was built to attract wealthy visitors to the area, and it was with their continued amusement in mind that local man Jules de Thier hatched a plan to bring motor racing back to the region. Using the country roads near the village of Francorchamps as his template, de Thier devised a 9.3-mile (15km) circuit that plunged down into the valley and over the l'Eau Rouge stream before climbing once more towards Les Combes. From this high ground the circuit then descended once more through fast, sweeping curves into the village of Burneville, where it changed course at the Malmedy road junction, spearing along the valley floor in the direction of Stavelot through the sleepy hamlet of Masta. One final direction change saw the course veer away from Stavelot, avoiding the town in favour of making the climb back towards Francorchamps via another small settlement called Blanchimont.

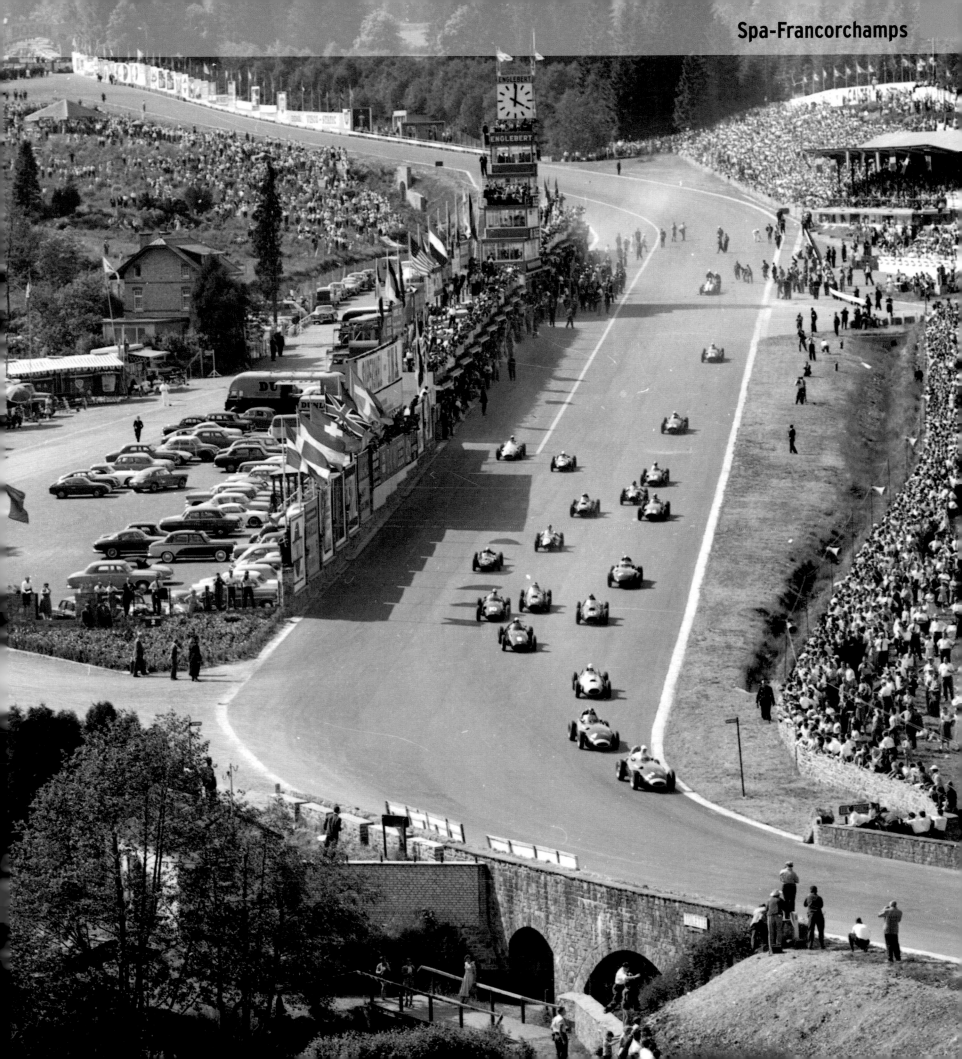

'Terrible conditions frequently added to the perils of this pure road circuit, mist and spray hanging in the dank forest air'

If you think many of those names sound familiar, they should, for they form the majority of the corner names on today's Spa-Francorchamps circuit, despite the fact that this relatively new circuit is just half the length of the formidable original and has now been made into a permanent facility rather than one that relies on public road closures as it did in the past.

First used in 1921, de Thier's vision remained it its original configuration until 1930, when it was fractionally shortened, then tweaked again in 1934. In 1939 the circuit underwent a more significant alteration for that year's Belgian Grand Prix with the creation of the towering Eau Rouge corner, an addition which has since come to define the circuit. Apart from a later mild change in 1956 this was to remain the circuit's layout until safety concerns forced F1's withdrawal from Spa in 1970 and the circuit's closure and subsequent redevelopment in 1978.

Despite more than three decades having passed since the old Spa-Francorchamps' demise, it's still

Below: Richie Ginther rounds the hairpin at La Source in his Honda RA272 in the 1965 Belgian Grand Prix. **Right:** Rubens Barrichello in practice for the 2004 race at the wheel of his Ferrari F2004.

possible to retrace the route of this magnificent circuit. It's a process that takes a little while, for the recent redevelopment of the circuit to bring it in line with modern F1 standards has seen a warren of link roads cut into the woods.

After making your way out of Francorchamps by heading down towards the modern circuit's La Source hairpin, you need to take a right at a roundabout just after the fuel station, at which point you head into the trees. Having meandered your way to another new roundabout (where you continue straight on past the new circuit entrance) you begin the climb towards the elevated area known as Les Combes. This is the highest point for miles around. It's also where the new circuit turns hard right then left at the end of the Kemmel straight and where the old circuit would have continued headlong towards Burneville. All of which means the road's endless and frankly innocuous-looking left and right sweepers that head down to Burneville are the self-same corners that tested the mettle of every Grand Prix hero from Tazio Nuvolari to Jim Clark.

Old strips of Armco line parts of this stretch of the N62C. Given Spa's formidable reputation you'll doubtless find the barrier's flaking black and white

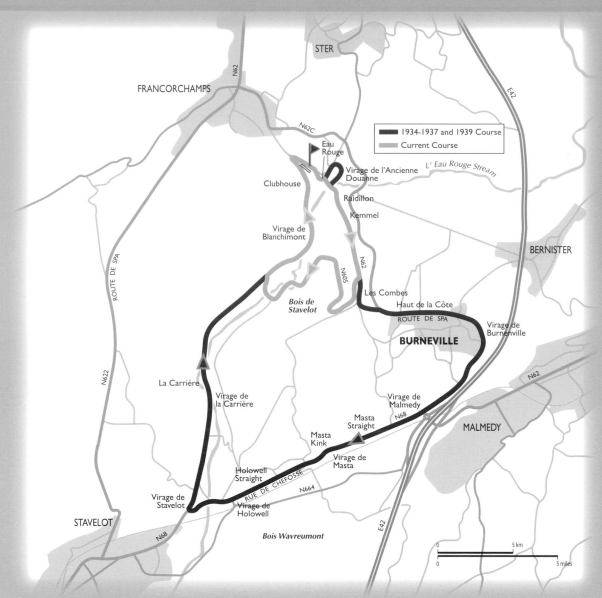

Map legend:
1934-1937 and 1939 Course
Current Course

Above: The 2004 24-hour race, part of the FIA GT Championship.
Right: The 2005 European Le Mans Endurance Series race at Spa.

paint sufficiently redolent of this super-fast road's racing past to send a slight chill down your spine. At legal speeds this section is nothing, while the smattering of housing adds to the impression of suburban calm, but at racing speeds this was one of Spa's sternest tests.

Even before the outbreak of the World War II, concerns were mounting about the dangers of racing modern Grand Prix cars around Spa's relentlessly rapid and largely unprotected curves. Terrible conditions frequently added to the perils of this pure road circuit, mist and spray hanging in the dank forest air. When the Englishman Dick Seaman died from his injuries after crashing his Mercedes-Benz into the trees (which subsequently caught fire) in 1939 the dangers were illustrated in tragic fashion. Were it not for the war and its aftermath which brought racing to an end until 1947, steps may have been taken then to tame the circuit, but the post-war world was a different place with a new perspective on life and death, and when the World

Driver's Championship was inaugurated in 1950 Spa-Francorchamps became a permanent fixture in the F1 calendar.

By the 1960s speeds were getting out of hand. With just one corner – La Source – requiring the drivers to slow significantly, and cars designed simply to be as fast as possible, rather than as fast and as safe as possible, as they are now, Spa exacted a heavy toll on a lost generation of racing drivers.

In the 1960 Belgian Grand Prix two young British drivers were killed during the race – Chris Bristow and Alan Stacey – while Stirling Moss also suffered a serious accident. The 1966 GP was also marked by several major accidents, including one involving Jackie Stewart, who would later claim that his pioneering quest for greater safety stemmed from this traumatic incident.

By 1969 Stewart and the other drivers – now united by the recently formed Grand Prix Drivers' Association – refused to race at Spa on safety grounds and the GP wasn't held. They returned for

1970 thanks to the introduction of a new chicane, but average speeds remained alarming, as Pedro Rodriguez's winning average speed of 149.94mph (241.25kph) proved.

Unsurprisingly the Grand Prix drivers never returned to the old Spa, but in a display of callous indifference that typifies the attitude of the sport in those not-so-distant days, other racing continued throughout the 1970s, even in the bloody aftermath of the 1973 Spa 1000km race, in which three drivers lost their lives. In the face of mounting pressure, the chequered flag finally fell on the old circuit's configuration in 1978.

During the next 12 months the monstrously fast loop from Les Combes to Burneville, Malmedy, Masta and Stavelot was replaced by a purpose-built section, which packed ten corners into just a few miles, rejoining the old road circuit at the approach to Blanchimont. Racing returned in 1979, but it wasn't until 1983 that the Belgian Grand Prix returned to a much safer and more sanitized but still spectacular spiritual home.

While F1 drivers profess a universal love of today's Spa-Francorchamps, it's doubtful many would even consider facing the risks their predecessors confronted, carbon-fibre survival cells or not. As you leave Malmedy behind you and tackle the long straight run towards the Masta Kink, you really couldn't blame them, for this slightest of left-right shimmies must have been like threading the eye of a needle, with the consequences of a misjudgment or mechanical failure too grim to contemplate. A classic test of raw courage, Masta was the kind of curve where a driver's brain would tell his right foot to stay flat, only for some primeval preservation instinct to endow said foot with a mind of its own. Only the bravest, or most foolish, could claim to take Masta flat.

Above: The Formula 3 race at Spa during the 2006 British Formula 3 Championship.

It's a sharper turn than it once was – there's no way even a current F1 car could tackle it without lifting – but the clues to its former trajectory are there in the form of an incongruous section of kerbing set some way back from the current curve and forming the edge of a large lay-by. Stand here and the kink's radius is eased considerably, but still the prospect of manoeuvring a 1960s GP car through here in the pouring rain makes you appreciate what separates mere mortals from the racers of that deadly era.

After the hilly confines of Les Combes, the charge from Masta to Stavelot is through open scenery in the valley floor. Framed by foreboding forests and a mournful grey sky, the road is your focus, spooling before you with just the gentlest direction changes. For every piece of Armco along here, there must be at least a dozen unprotected telegraph poles or stout trees, yet this is almost exactly as the circuit would have been raced.

On the entry to Stavelot village, you'll see a long, inviting upward sweep of road that climbs to the right. Gently banked and clearly exceptionally fast, it's one of the original segments of the old circuit. Much of the tarmac has the integrity of an old digestive biscuit, while the original barriers still bear the scuffs and scars of battle, but this decrepitude makes the history feel so much more real.

As the road cuts through the woods towards Blanchimont, a huge set of security gates prevent you from merging with the modern circuit. At first it feels frustrating, but then you see just enough of the neatly mown grass run-off, billiard-smooth surface and multiple layers of fresh barriers to appreciate that this is the place where the heroism of the 20th century and the commercialism of the 21st meet. Like oil and water, they don't mix.

REIMS

DISTANCE: 4.9 MILES (7.8KM) **FIRST RACE:** 1925 **LOCATION:** FRANCE

If there are ghosts of motor racing's past it's hard to imagine a more appropriately haunting place for them to reside than the skeletal remains of the once-great Reims circuit.

Abandoned after racing ceased in 1970, Reims' grandstands, pit boxes and administrative buildings

Below: Mike Hawthorn at Reims in the 1958 French Grand Prix, at the wheel of a Ferrari Dino 246. **Opposite:** Phil Hill, Wolfgang von Trips, and Richie Ginther lead the way at the start of the 1961 French Grand Prix.

have stood disused for nearly 40 years, left to fade and flake under the warm French sun. Now, thanks to the efforts of Les Amis du Circuit de Gueux (ACG), the site is being refreshed in a well-meaning but controversial effort to preserve it.

It seems we've grown so used to the uniquely careworn patina that the shock of fresh paint and a bit of care and attention seems like an act of organized vandalism. In truth, if the ACG hadn't stepped in, the remains of the circuit's infrastructure would have crumbled to dust, or succumbed to

the threat of the bulldozer and wrecking ball. Either way, it's surely better to preserve what's there now than rue the loss of this magnificent monument to an age when Grand Prix racing took place on public highways.

And what highways they were. Few road circuits can claim to have been so completely dedicated to speed as Reims. Essentially three long straights linked by a trio of simple hairpins, it's hard not to suspect the 4.865-mile (7.833km) circuit was designed with nothing more than a pencil and ruler.

Of course, when you drive what remains of the circuit, you appreciate that there was a little more to Reims than a series of drag races and heroics under braking, but the fundamental purity of the layout still exudes the impression that here, perhaps more than on any other road-based race circuit in the world, if you boiled this place down you'd find that speed really was its essence.

Using roads cut through the rolling cornfields of northeastern France, this startlingly simple circuit lies just 4.5 miles (7.25km) to the west of the cathedral city of Reims, in the heart of France's famous Champagne region: a handy location, given the time-honoured bubbly-spraying enjoyed by generations of racing drivers.

Also known as the Circuit de Gueux, thanks to the nearby village that the original circuit passed through, the roads were first closed for racing in 1925 when they played host to the Grand Prix de la Marne, named after the regional department in which the circuit is situated. In 1932, Reims' status was elevated when it was bestowed the honour of hosting the French Grand Prix, which was won by Tazio Nuvolari in an Alfa Romeo. From this point on Reims was a regular stage for the very highest level of racing.

'...with every race becoming a perilous slipstreaming battle as drivers tucked into each other's wake to try and gain a speed advantage'

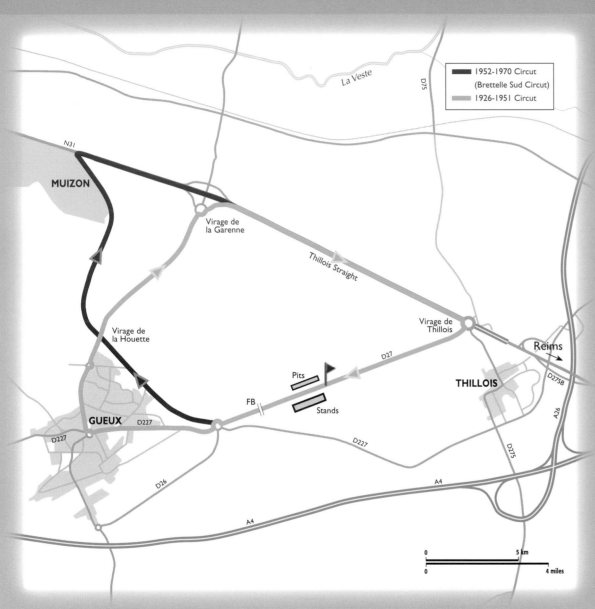

Map legend:
- 1952-1970 Circuit (Brettelle Sud Circut)
- 1926-1951 Circuit

La Veste · D75 · N31 · MUIZON · Virage de la Garenne · Thillois Straight · Virage de la Houette · Virage de Thillois · Reims · D27 · THILLOIS · D275B · Pits · Stands · FB · GUEUX · D227 · D227 · D26 · A26 · D227 · D275 · A4 · A4

0 ———— 5 km
0 ———— 4 miles

Above: The flaking remains of this once great circuit. **Right:** Signs of the efforts of the ACG to preserve what remains of the circuit grandstands and pit boxes.

There was a five-year hiatus before the blue riband race returned in 1938. This was the era of the Silver Arrows, when the German marques of Mercedes-Benz and Auto Union built extraordinary Grand Prix machines, the like of which had never been seen before. Given their unrivalled power and sophistication, it came as no surprise when the 1938 race was won by Mercedes' Manfred von Brauchitsch, nor when H P Müller took the spoils for Auto Union in 1939, shortly before the outbreak of World War II.

This successful pre-war phase saw Reims become firmly established amongst the finest circuits of the day, a fact that was reflected in the permanent pit and grandstand structures that were erected along the start/finish straight. Not only were they impressive facilities for the day, but they also underlined the dual usage of these otherwise typical French roads, something they continue to do to this day.

Two sides of the Reims triangle remained unchanged from the circuit's inception to its demise, but the third, from Gueux to Muizon, was altered several times. In its original guise the circuit's start/finish straight (the D27, to give it its public road designation) began to curve gently shortly after passing the pits, entering the village of Gueux. Passing between a grocer's shop and a duck pond, the circuit then took the D26 heading north out of

the village on a gentle zigzag to the tight Virage de Garenne, a 90-degree right-hander that joined the Route Nationale 31 heading in the direction of Reims for more than a mile before an even tighter right-hander at Thillois rejoined the D27 for the long charge towards the grandstands and the start of another lap.

After the war the circuit was revised, and many trees and buildings were cut down and demolished to make way for the changes. However, unlike the kind of circuit changes we're used to in the modern era, designed to slow things down and make the track safer, the alterations were actually designed to make Reims faster.

Instead of running through Gueux, the new purpose-built section of the circuit bypassed the village, with a more defined right-hand curve after the pits flowing into a short straight, which crossed the northbound path of the D26, before another fast right – the Virage de la Houette – turned the cars directly north to join the RN31 with a tricky left that immediately fed into a hairpin right. This was the first section of the Reims circuit

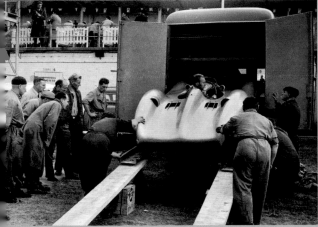

Above: The Mercedez-Benz team unload the W196 cars from the team transporter in the paddock at the 1954 French Grand Prix. The cars would be driven by Juan Manuel Fangio, Hans Herrmann and Karl Kling.

permanently dedicated to racing, but in an ironic twist it became public road – the D27e – when the circuit fell into disuse.

The result was an even longer run down the Thillois Straight, with speeds touching 180mph (290kph) or more. This heightened the intense nature of the racing that took place, with every race becoming a perilous slipstreaming battle as drivers tucked into each other's wake to try to gain a speed advantage.

Back in the 1950s and 60s, Grand Prix cars were shaped to minimize drag rather than maximize downforce. Some teams – most notably Mercedes-Benz – went to extraordinary lengths to make their cars cleave the air with absolute efficiency, and fielded a special streamlined W196 for the ultra high-speed GPs. Clothed in magnificently smooth and elongated aluminium curves, it remains one of the most spectacular racing cars of all time, and made its debut at Reims.

Perhaps as a consequence of its uniquely demanding nature, Reims always enabled the best drivers to shine, but it also made for some surprise results. The supremely talented Fangio won the 1950 French GP, then followed it with another win in 1951, although he had to take over his teammate's car to do so as his own car broke down during the race. English ace Mike Hawthorn (another World Champion) won in 1953, but Fangio fought back in 1954 with the help of his streamlined Mercedes.

It was at Reims in the 1958 French GP that Fangio took part in his final race. Having witnessed the scene of Luigi Musso's fatal accident at the difficult Muizon corner, and knowing that he had achieved more than any other man in the sport, he simply realized his motivation had deserted him. On finishing fourth, the 47-year-old maestro decided to call time on his career with immediate effect.

Other notable moments in the 45-year history of the Reims circuit are Giancarlo Baghetti's win for Ferrari on his Grand Prix debut in 1961 (a feat that remains unmatched to this day) and Jack Brabham's 1966 victory in which he became the first man to win a Grand Prix driving a car bearing his own name. This was also the fastest race in the circuit's history, with Ferrari's Lorenzo Bandini setting a lap record of 2m 11.3sec at average speed of 142.09mph (228.62kph).

Today, although the Thillois Straight has long since been buried under a four-lane autoroute and the landmark row of trees that lined the exit of the Virage de Muizon has yielded to the rasp of the chainsaw, there's still a very real sense that great and terrible things once happened here.

Thanks to the traffic-reducing effects of the modern road network, you can power up the D27 in blissful isolation, blasting towards the angular outline of the semi-ruined grandstands. The surrounding countryside is wide open but the road itself is confined, with sufficient room for two dicing Grand Prix cars to pull side by side, but no more than that.

The temptation to power through the concrete canyon that runs between the pit boxes and grandstands is powerful, but curiosity always wins the day, forcing you to pull over (in the pits, naturally) get out of your car and explore. Fresh paint or not, there can be few more evocative locations to stand and absorb the atmosphere. On a hot summer's day the peace is so absolute that your ears begin to play tricks and your mind works overtime, to the point when you'd swear you can hear the bark of a highly tuned racing engine ricocheting off the scalloped roof of the concrete grandstands, when in reality all you can hear is a solitary skylark and the chirrup of crickets in the long, golden grass.

Those without a head for heights might blanch at the prospect, but a moderate burst of athleticism is sufficient to scale the steps that rise above the pit boxes and gain you access to the Control Tower. Taking care all the while – and respecting the crumbling nature of the structure – it's worth making the ascent, for you're rewarded with a new

and fabulous perspective on the circuit and the arrow-straight D27 in particular.

Old and essentially dilapidated it may be, but the view from up here does more to bring the circuit alive than any words or photos can manage. Consequently it's with a new sense of purpose and perspective that you power away from the pits and take a right turn at the roundabout onto what was the permanent section of circuit built to bypass Gueux. Even if the road is blocked – as it can be – by hefty red-and-white barriers, make the effort to see the gracefully swooping curves that flow through the fields towards Muizon, for they encapsulate the need for speed and commitment that made Reims such a special place to hold a motor race.

Such is the lasting allure of this glorious throwback of a circuit that you're unlikely to be alone. In fact, the chances are there will be someone bold enough to have nipped around the barriers to complete a slow pass along this redundant road. If you don't want to drive, take the time to walk at least a portion of it, for the farther you get from the still active D27, the easier it will be to conjure images of Fangio flashing through here in his teardrop-shaped W196 Streamliner, drifting from curve to curve on his way to victory in the wind-cheating Silver Arrow's debut race.

Anywhere else such moments seem locked in grainy black-and-white photographs, action-packed images from a bygone era, but at Reims, in the midst of this ageing monument to speed, that history is alive in vivid colour, and so close you can literally reach out and touch it.

Left: Philippe Etancelin in the Lago-Talbot T26C-DA flashes past a pit board during the 1950 French Grand Prix at Reims. **Above:** Haunting monuments like this disused timing board hint at the circuit's past.

NÜRBURGRING NORDSCHLEIFE

DISTANCE: 13 MILES (21KM) **FIRST RACE:** 1927 **LOCATION:** GERMANY

A dark and ancient tower silhouetted against the skyline is the first clue you're drawing near. All around, seemingly impenetrable pine forests swathe the hillsides. Then you see it. The briefest glimpse at first, then slowly, tantalizingly, a majestic swoop of tarmac and the dull glint of galvanized steel become visible. Your pulse races: you have arrived.

So many elements combine to endow the Nürburgring with irresistible magnetism. Steeped in history – both triumphant and tragic – notoriously unforgiving and hugely intimidating yet completely addictive and totally absorbing, the Nürburgring is one of the last remaining links between us and the heroes of motor racing's past. Incredibly this sensational circuit is also open for us to drive, with public sessions held most weekday evenings and selected weekends throughout the year. Drawing countless thousands of enthusiasts from all over the world, it is the ultimate everyman experience.

Such global appeal isn't so far from the original concept that Eifel District Councillor Dr Otto Creuz presented to the German government back in 1925. Creuz's vision was for a dedicated development facility for the German automobile industry and a racetrack to surpass anything yet built. He also believed that this circuit would provide the economically depressed Eifel region with years of employment while the circuit was being built and a future source of income once it was completed. Now, more than 80 years after Creuz first submitted his bold scheme, the circuit defines the entire region.

Convinced by Creuz's plan, the government pledged a grant of 14.1 million Reichsmarks, and the first foundation stone was laid on 27 September 1925. It started a gargantuan engineering project, involving the toil of more than 2,500 labourers for

nearly two years. Encompassing four villages, the imposing hilltop castle, streams, forests and farmland, the circuit builders faithfully and sympathetically followed the Eifel region's magnificently undulating terrain to create a circuit of unrivalled character and complexity.

Nowadays we most commonly refer to the original Nürburgring as the Nordschleife, or North Loop, but when it was first built the Nürburgring comprised two circuits – the Nord and Südschleife – which could be used separately, or joined together to make one vast 17.6-mile (28.3km) circuit. The Südschleife or South Loop was 4.8 miles (7.7km) in length and primarily intended for vehicle testing and club racing, while the Nordschleife existed as the ultimate statement of Germany's engineering might. It also stood as the greatest test a racing driver could face.

Today only the Nordschleife remains, for much of the Südschleife was sacrificed in the making of the modern Nürburgring GP circuit, which opened in the 1980s. Sections of the old South Loop that survived have either been incorporated into the road network that surrounds the new GP circuit complex or lie overgrown and unloved by all except the hikers and mountain bikers who also flock to the Eifel region.

Fortunately the surviving Nordschleife provides ample and epic compensation for the loss of its little brother. At a fraction under 13 miles (21km) in length, it is four or five times longer than most modern racetracks, yet even this fact fails to emphasize the extraordinary magnitude of this unique circuit. With a 1,000ft (300m) elevation change, 73 corners and often little more than a car's width of grass between you and the Armco the years have done little to diminish its intimidating nature.

Of course, all things are relative. As recently as the 1960s, the Nordschleife was a much wilder place than it is today. Lined by earth banks, ditches, hedges and other more substantial vegetation – which often came right to the edge of the tarmac – crash barriers were almost non-existent. Yet when the circuit underwent major remodelling and Armco was installed for the 1971 German GP – essentially creating the circuit as it is today – some experienced drivers, including former F1 World Champion Phil Hill, said the place had been emasculated!

Taken in the context of Hill's racing experience, his sentiments are doubtless true, but there was no denying that Armco or not the Nordschleife remained a perilous place to race. Throughout its history, the circuit has divided opinion among the greatest drivers of the day. Some, like Fangio and Moss, loved it. Others – most notably Jackie Stewart – detested the place for its fickle weather and lethal reputation. And yet, despite such open loathing for the circuit, Stewart displayed total commitment around the circuit he so famously christened 'The Green Hell'. In 1968, before the safety changes and racing in the worst weather conditions imaginable, Stewart drove through the rain and fog to win the German Grand Prix, beating his nearest rival by an astonishing four minutes. He won on the revised circuit in 1971, and again in 1973, confirming his mastery of this monstrously challenging circuit. Despite his success he never changed his opinion of the place.

Though the alterations for 1971 did make improvements to safety levels, the revisions couldn't keep pace with the cars, and the Nürburgring was

Opposite: The BRM P57 of Richie Ginther leads the Cooper T66-Climax of Bruce McLaren and Graham Hill's BRM P57 during the 1963 German Grand Prix.

'you always want to strain at your seat belt in an effort to get a better view of the road, for seemingly every corner is hidden on the blindside of a brow or crest'

Above: Jackie Stewart on his way to victory in the 1968 German Grand Prix at the wheel of his Matra MS10 Ford. **Right:** A BMW M3 tackles one of the many hairpin bends on the circuit.

becoming increasingly unsuited to Formula One. The new 3.0-litre-engine cars were tremendously fast – as witnessed by Niki Lauda's first sub-7-minute lap in 1975 – but the circuit left no room for error or mechanical failure, while its vast scale and relative inaccessibility made it extremely difficult to marshal effectively. Surprisingly, the Nürburgring's safety record was no worse than any of the other major international circuits of the day, but Lauda's grisly and near-fatal accident in 1976 proved the final straw, and Formula One was never to return.

Top-level sports car racing continued well into the 1980s, while the German Touring Car Championship (DTM) still raced around the Nordschleife in the 1990s. Now, only the VLN Endurance series for production-based cars uses the circuit, together with the Nürburgring 24 Hours, which takes place every June. With an entry list of some 220 cars, varying from the fastest professional drivers in highly developed Porsche 911s to rank amateurs in ageing hot hatchbacks, it is the biggest 24-hour race in the world and one of the greatest spectacles in motorsport.

While Creuz's vision for a professional industry-standard test facility and world-leading venue for the highest level of motorsport has come to fruition, even the far-sighted Herr Docktor couldn't have foreseen the Nordschleife's unparalleled popularity as a destination for car enthusiasts from around the world. In the last 20 years or so a whole tourist industry has sprung up around the circuit to service the endless flow of bikers and drivers who are drawn there like moths to a flame.

In Nürburg and the surrounding villages many guesthouses now have large and well-equipped workshops, which guests can use to fettle their cars. Bars and restaurants are thick on the ground, and from early spring through until late autumn the region buzzes with enthusiasm for the grand old circuit.

No matter how many times you visit, the sense of anticipation never wanes, nor does the sense of amazement at how simple it is to get onto the track. Just head out of the old village of Nürburg with the castle on your left and within moments you'll arrive at the purpose-built car park, restaurant and ticket booth. Once here you have a choice of single or multiple lap tickets, while the most hardened veterans buy season passes at €750 a pop. However, as opening times vary, it's best to check at

Above: En route to the famous track. **Left:** Niki Lauda on his way to setting the first sub-7-minute lap time in 1975 in his Ferrari 312T.

www.nuerburgring.de for the latest schedule before planning your trip. One thing is certain: the moment you slide your ticket into the automated barrier, your life is unlikely to be the same again.

Whether you're completely new to the place or have 'driven' thousands of virtual laps on your Playstation3, nothing truly prepares you for your first actual lap. Accelerating down the straight you almost immediately pass beneath the bridge, followed by a gradual kink. Unfortunately you never get to approach this section at full speed on a public day for flying laps aren't permitted. Suffice to say it's a great deal more than a gradual kink at 180mph (290kph).

You don't so much learn the Nordschleife corner by corner as you do on a conventional circuit, rather you gradually become familiar with certain sections, piecing the elements of each section together until you begin to feel more familiar with it and mentally move on to the next.

The first of these sections is Hatzenbach, which runs steeply downhill just after the old pit area. Building speed all the time, you plunge through a pair of fast left-handers, noting how bumpy the surface feels even in a normal road car, before braking hard and peeling into a tight right-left. It's easy to trip up here, as the cambers are shifting all the time and you're forced into braking while turning.

It's an early wake-up call, which is just as well, for the next few miles are among the fastest of the lap. Having exited the corkscrew Hocheichen, you dive between the concrete walls of a flyover before accelerating up what appears to be a sheer face of tarmac. Hold your nerve, keep to the left and you'll pop up and over the famous Flugplatz, or Flying Place, with just enough time to catch your breath as you turn into a long, long right-hander. Already you'll feel the speed, and how it seems to build, regardless of crests, dips or corners as you make

the roller-coaster run towards the perilous Schwedenkreuz left-hander and looping downhill hairpin at Aremburg.

A flash of red-and-white kerb followed by a blur of concrete as you pass beneath another bridge heralds the terrifying plunge down the Fuchsröhre, or Foxhole. Nowhere on the lap does the speed feel so intense as here, as you charge between the trees, funnelling down to a wicked compression before climbing once more to the Adenauer Forst chicane. Plenty of people tend to gather in the spectator areas here, but don't be tempted to play to the crowd unless you're confident you can steer cleanly between the tall, sump-splitting kerbs.

From Adenauer Forst you begin the descent towards the bridge over Adenauer, called Breidscheid. It starts gently at first, the straight run to Metzgesfeld being almost level, but from the moment you head towards Kallenhard the track begins to plunge in earnest.

In addition to the relentless speed you'll also notice that you always want to strain at your seat belt in an effort to get a better view of the road, for seemingly every corner is hidden on the blindside of a brow or crest. The ability and awareness to decode the landmarks and read the road ahead are vital Nordschleife skills, and make driving here more like driving along an unfamiliar B road than a typical racetrack.

It pays to take things easy as you approach Wehrseifen and Breidscheid, for you've been relying on the brakes for corner after corner without much respite. As you'll see from the scrapes and smears that run along the concrete barriers many a driver has come steaming down here only to discover that his brakes have overheated.

Safely over the bridge you begin the long, long climb towards the famous banked saucer of concrete called the Karussell, passing the scene of Lauda's crash at Bergwerk along the way. It's bumpy

TESTING, TESTING... – THE INDUSTRY POOL

It's often claimed that a high-speed mile at the Nürburgring is worth ten road miles, which tells you all you need to know about the demanding nature of the circuit. It also explains why an elite group of motor manufacturers, known as the Industry Pool, spend most of the year pounding around the Nordschleife's punishing twists and turns in an effort to finely hone the performance of their forthcoming products.

Chassis engineers love the Nordschleife because it requires them to think about every aspect of the car's feel and behaviour. If a car feels edgy and unpredictable here then the chances are it won't inspire confidence on the road. Likewise, if a car copes well with the intense demands of the circuit's many cresting corners, tricky surface changes, awkward braking areas and savage compressions then it will be well-prepared for what the real world has in store for it.

Such is the kudos of using the Nordschleife as part of the development process that many manufacturers mention the circuit specifically in publicity material.

Many – including Porsche, BMW, Opel, Aston Martin, Jaguar, Alfa Romeo, even Japanese companies Nissan, Honda and Toyota – have dedicated facilities within sight of the circuit, from which their test and development engineers can operate more effectively.

Inevitably some of these manufacturers also started to claim 'unofficial' lap times, which kick-started a battle of honour to see who could achieve the most impressive laps. Although now rendered largely irrelevant by superfast times set by tuning companies in one-off specials and low-volume sports car builders in racing cars with number plates, Nordschleife lap times remain a constant source of intrigue and in-fighting, particularly among proud German manufacturers.

The current production car 'record' stands at a little over 7min 30sec, but as anyone who has driven there will tell you, any car (or indeed any driver) capable of clocking close to 8mins is doing very well indeed. To put this in perspective, the outright lap record is a mind-blowing 6min 11sec, set by the late Stefan Bellof in a Porsche 956.

as hell around the Karussel, but worth the odd scuff on your chin spoiler for there can be few more noble battle scars than those gained here.

As you're spat out of the Karussel, the road climbs away even more steeply on the slog towards Hohe Acht (High Eight), which is the highest point on the circuit. The character of the circuit changes here, the long and gently meandering climbs swapped for a more intense and sinuous descent through the

Wipperman section. Small, nimble cars excel through here as they can carry plenty of speed between the kerbs, but there's zero run-off and plenty of mistakes to be made.

Brünnchen is another spectator favourite, thanks to the high banks and long arc of track visible from the viewing areas, but you soon escape their gaze, powering up and over the Eiskurve towards Pflanzgarten, where a nasty crest and dip sit right in your braking zone. It's common to get some air under your tyres here, but hopefully not as much as Manfred Winkelhock, who flipped his Formula Two car here in spectacular fashion in 1980.

The second part of Pflanzgarten is another jump, this time in the middle of a 100mph (160kph) corner, but having held your heart in your mouth for most of the lap you'll be relieved to know that there are just a handful of corners – including the less severe Kleines Karussel – to negotiate before you emerge back onto the Döttinger straight, at which point you'll feel your whole body tingle with the adrenaline rush. It's a feeling you'll never forget and an experience you'll want to repeat. Welcome to your Nordschleife addiction.

Below: Jaguar is one of the many brands to have a test centre at the Nürburgring circuit. Here, an XKR prototype is put through its paces.

PESCARA

Nestled at the foot of the Abruzzi Mountains on the sun-baked Adriatic coast of Italy, Pescara is an unlikely setting for the longest and most feared circuit in the history of Grand Prix racing's post-war era.

Like the many other seaside towns between Rimini and Bari, Pescara's façade is one of busy bars and hotels that line a 10-mile (16km) stretch of inviting beaches. Up in the hills sweet-scented orchards flourish in the cooler air. But it's a picture-postcard scene that belies a racing past every bit as brutal and dramatic as any of its great road course contemporaries.

Even in 1957, when Pescara hosted its first and only World Championship Grand Prix, it was regarded as something of a dinosaur, and a T-Rex at that. Dating back to 1924, the circuit had become famous for holding the Coppa Acerbo throughout the 20s and 30s, with a certain Enzo Ferrari winning the inaugural event back in the days when he raced cars rather than bestowed his name upon them.

A road race venue in its most rudimentary sense, Pescara's concession to safety had always been little more than closing the roads to non-race traffic. No crash barriers or room for error, just point-blank speed and peril at every turn. It was this throwback of a circuit – unchanged in 33 years – that greeted the teams and drivers entered in the 1957 Pescara Grand Prix.

What separated Pescara from the other Grand Prix road circuits such as Reims and Spa-Francorchamps was its length and its proximity to the town and its people. Far from relying on the isolated country roads preferred by the French and Belgian circuits, Pescara's spirit is shared with those all-encompassing Italian road races, the Mille Miglia and Targa Florio.

At 15.99 miles (25.73km) in length, the Pescara road circuit wasn't as sprawling as the Targa course, but with two monstrous 5-mile (8km) straights linked by a tortuous climb through a series of villages and hamlets, it combined the challenges and hazards of the great Sicilian road race with a few tricks of its own. Among them was a sharp right turn between a church and some houses, a railway crossing and a special timed section on the descent from the mountains towards Pescara known as 'The Flying Kilometre', where race organizers would award a prize of 200,000 lire (£115 or thereabouts) to the driver of the fastest car.

As if this wasn't sufficiently challenging, where the Targa and Mille Miglia started competitors singly at regular intervals, the 1957 Grand Prix would see 16 open-wheel racers take a massed start, with drivers jockeying for position into

The 1938 Coppa Acerbo at Pescara. **Left:** Hermann Lang in the Mercedes-Benz W154. **Right:** An exhausted Tazio Nuvolari (Auto Union) retires from the race due to lack of fuel pressure.

'From sublimely contorted lanes rising into the Abruzzi foothills to the ridiculous headlong descent back towards the sea, Pescara was a circuit for the purist'

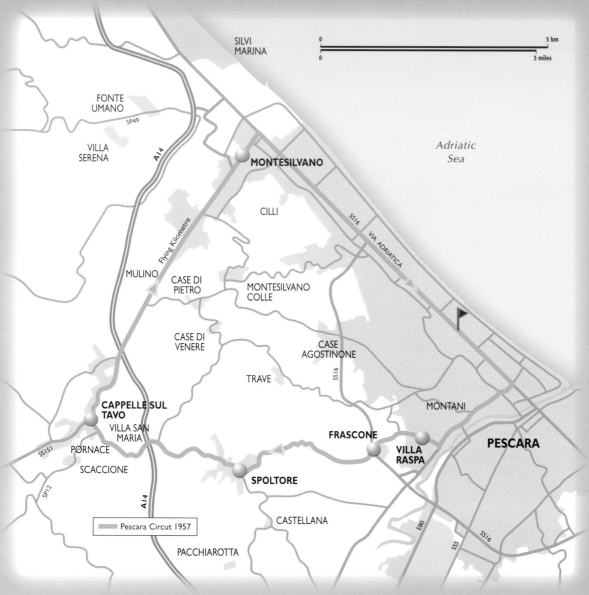

the first corner and continuing to tussle fiercely as the grid charged into the narrow and knotted 6-mile (10km) mountain section. Scheduled for 18 laps or 287 miles (462km) it would be a Grand Prix like no other.

Such remorseless wheel-to-wheel racing was a recipe that had served Pescara well over the decades, elevating the Coppa Acerbo to the very highest level in the years before World War II, and afterwards as a regular non-championship race contested by the teams and drivers competing in the new FIA World Championship.

Before the war all the great works teams regularly made the trip to the Adriatic coast, including Mercedes-Benz and Auto Union, who challenged the supremacy of the home-grown Alfa Romeo and Maserati teams. The German teams boasted a stellar line-up of drivers, including Rudolph Caracciola, Achille Varzi and Bernd Rosemeyer, and proceeded to dominate the race until the outbreak of war.

Right: The Maserati 250F of Masten Gregory in the 1957 Italian Grand Prix at Pescara.

With the arrival of the German superteams in 1934 the speed of the cars seemed to be growing exponentially, to the point where the organizers felt compelled to slow the cars' progress by introducing a chicane into the start/finish straight. It worked to a degree, but the race was still fraught with danger. The great Caracciola left the road at high-speed and rolled into a field, only to emerge from the wreckage unscathed, while Guy Moll, driving an Alfa Romeo for the recently formed Scuderia Ferrari, was less fortunate, crashing to his death when a gust of wind blew him off the road as he tore through the flying kilometre at more than 160mph (258kph).

By 1937 both the Mercedes and Auto Union machines were living up to their collective nickname – The Silver Arrows – by topping 200mph (322kph) on both Pescara's straights, despite the sizeable chicane. Nothing could keep up with these ballistic cars. Having won the previous year, Auto Union's hero Bernd Rosemeyer took the Coppa Acerbo again in 1937. Mercedes' ace Caracciola won in '38, but with war looming in 1939 the German teams withdrew from racing, leaving the Coppa Acerbo to the Italians once more.

Racing returned to Pescara in 1947, but the Coppa Acerbo name had gone. Originally dedicated to Tito Acerbo – a local war hero who was killed in battle in 1918 – the Acerbo family name fell out of favour after the war because Tito's older brother, Giacomo, had been a prominent member of Mussolini's fascist government. And so the Coppa Acerbo became known the Circuito di Pescara, or the Gran Premio di Pescara.

Above: Another Maserti 250F in 1957. This is Giorgio Scarlatti's car.
Right: The Vanwall VW11 of Stuart Lewis-Evans at the same race.

The name may have changed but the circuit's malevolent nature remained. There's every likelihood that had it not been for the knock-on effects of the Suez Crisis the previous year, Pescara would never have been elevated to full FIA Championship status in 1957. But with the prospect of a greatly reduced calendar, and a local automobile club keen to restore its circuit to the top level, Pescara got the nod even though it remained untouched by advances in safety and was still uncensored, despite the horrific accident that had marred the Mille Miglia just a few months earlier.

Though new to the World Championship, the circuit wasn't new to many of the drivers, as most

had taken part in at least one of Pescara's non-championship races during the first half of the 1950s. For some this made the Gran Premio di Pescara a race to relish, while for others it was an event to dread.

On closer investigation it's easy to see why both factions should feel so strongly. Here was a circuit comprised entirely of public roads, the straightest of which had been laid originally by the Romans. There were no purpose-built sections, no permanent pit or grandstand structures, no special race-friendly resurfacing. From sublimely contorted lanes rising into the Abruzzi foothills to the ridiculous headlong descent back towards the sea, Pescara was a circuit for the purist.

For Stirling Moss such a raw and unreconstructed challenge was manna from heaven. After conquering both the Mille Miglia and Targa Florio in 1955 and with a burgeoning GP career, Moss was commonly regarded as the world's finest exponent of open-road racing. Poised to usurp his hero Fangio – who was also racing at Pescara – and equipped with a fast and sophisticated car built by the British Vanwall team, Moss was in his element.

Reflecting on his racing exploits at Pescara, Sir Stirling's passion for road racing remains undiminished, even in an age when such risk-laden racing environments have long been eradicated. 'I thought it [Pescara] was fantastic', says Moss. 'It was just like being a kid, out for a burn-up. A wonderful feeling. What racing's all about. As a driver you got a tremendous amount of fulfilment from it. The races we had at Silverstone and Goodwood and so on were never the same sort of thing.'

It's a view shared then and now by Moss's Vanwall teammate Tony Brooks. Another die-hard road racing purist, he was also an advocate of Pescara's unique character. 'To me road racing is the only form of racing', he said in an interview with Richard Williams. 'Motor racing started with races from city to city, and the further you get away from that, the further you get away from the spirit of Grand Prix racing.' In complete contrast, Sir Jack Brabham's typically blunt reminiscences are rather less fond. He told Williams 'Those road courses were bloody dangerous and nasty, all of them. And Pescara was the worst.'

Starting close to Pescara's town centre, towards the end of the 5-mile (8km) straight along the Via Adriatica, the circuit turns hard right near the station building, then left-right again before heading out of town. Approaching Montani and Villa Raspa the road starts to climb, eventually charging into Spoltore and the narrow church turn. That the drivers found the room to race along here is a testament to their determination and skill. That they did so with no quarter asked or given, between trees, telegraph poles and lethal kilometre markers standing like tombstones at the road's fringe, while surrounded by twenty gallons (91 litres) or more of highly volatile racing fuel is a mark of their courage and unshakable self-belief.

After a long climb the road tumbles briefly downhill to a plateau before climbing once more to Pornace and Villa San Maria. After 6 miles (10km) or so of relentless twists and turns the road makes an extremely tight right-hand switchback at the village of Capelle, throwing in a few more snaking turns before unfurling into the seemingly endless rush down through a high-speed kink at tiny hamlet of Mulino before heading on through the organizers' 'Flying Kilometre' and the 90-degree right at Montesilvano. Ahead of them lay the shimmering Adriatic.

The sight of those sun-dappled waters must have been mighty tempting to the 16 drivers engaged in the 18-lap, 288-mile (464km) battle as they fought each other for three unrelenting hours in the scorching 109°F (43°C) heat. Had an administrative error not led most of the teams to arrive at Pescara with unsuitably short gearing for the circuit's endless straights they would have completed the race slightly sooner, but as the promised trio of chicanes had been reduced to one, just before the start/finish line, the cars soon ran out of revs in top gear on both straights.

Despite being hobbled, all but the diminutive rear-engined Coopers (driven by Jack Brabham and Roy Salvadori) would still touch 170mph (274kph) at numerous points around the lap. Indeed, along the 5-mile (8km) start/finish straight they would keep their throttles pinned to the stop for more than two minutes as they flashed between the packed stands and hotels to complete each lap.

As the race unfolded Moss ran away and hid from the field with a series of blistering laps in which he repeatedly beat his qualifying time. It was a master class that culminated with a lap that matched the pole position time of his great friend and rival, Fangio. Once Ferrari's Luigi Musso retired from second place Moss eased back, safe in the knowledge that Fangio was trailing. As the chequered flag fell Moss finished a mighty 3 minutes ahead of the legendary Argentinean's Maserati.

Pescara would never host another top-level Grand Prix. In fact it would only hold two more races – a lowly Formula Junior race in 1960 and a four-hour sports car race in 1961, which was fittingly won by a Ferrari some 37 years after Enzo Ferrari won the inaugural Coppa Acerbo.

The racing cars have long left Pescara, but the roads are still there, fast and pure, just as they always were. Unchanged for the best part of a century, they enable us to experience exactly the same twists and turns as Ferrari, Rosemeyer, Fangio and Moss. It truly is the track that time forgot.

MONACO

DISTANCE: 2 MILES (3KM) **FIRST RACE:** 1929 **LOCATION:** MONACO

Given that seemingly half the world's professional racing drivers live in Monaco you'd think the traffic would move a bit faster. Sadly, while the Nomex-wearing residents all enjoy the kudos and fiscal benefits of an address in the principality, when it comes to negotiating Monte Carlo's chronic congestion a moped is far more useful than an FIA Superlicence.

So the traffic is a pain. Who cares? When you're in Monaco you don't have to drive fast to feel the magic. In fact, whether you're a first-time visitor or a seasoned veteran, there's so much to take in it's doubtful you'd want to drive fast even if the opportunity presented itself.

With far-flung countries queuing up to win a place on the F1 calendar, Grand Prix racing is a sport used to being the centre of attention. Where it goes glamour follows, except in Monaco, when the roles are reversed. No matter how monumental in scale and expenditure, there isn't a clean sheet racetrack on earth that can compete with Monaco's wholly unsuitable streets for intensity, spectacle or sense of history. Yet taking all this into account it's a struggle to see how a circuit so patently incompatible with the cut and thrust of state-of-the-art Grand Prix racing continues to keep its end-of-May appointment with F1. According to Bernie Ecclestone the reason is simple: 'This place gives us more than we give it.'

As you wind your way down from the autoroute that carries traffic along the Côte d'Azur from Nice you can immediately see what Ecclestone means. Sandwiched between the Alpes-Martimes and the

sparkling Mediterranean, with a palace perched on a caramel-coloured rock overlooking the sea, surrounded by lavish hotels, a grand casino and countless apartments that spill down to a yacht-packed harbour, Monte Carlo has a unique, breathtaking setting.

Cars have raced around the streets since 1929, thanks to the inspired suggestion of Anthony Noghes, son of the fabulously wealthy and influential Alexandre Noghes, who was responsible for co-founding the Monte Carlo Rally some 18 years earlier. Close friends and confidantes of the ruling Grimaldi family – who have presided over

the world's smallest sovereign state for more than 700 years – the Noghes had a pivotal role in the creation of the Grand Prix and are honoured by the name of the circuit's last corner: Virage Anthony Noghes.

Incredibly, despite the pace of development and expansion that leaves Monaco itself in an almost constant state of flux, very little of that original 1929 circuit has changed. A significant number of the corners have been reprofiled at some point, either to

Right: Stirling Moss drifts his Maserati 250F around Mirabeau on his way to victory in the 1956 Monaco Grand Prix.

Right: The 2006 Monaco Grand Prix. Eventual winner Fernando Alonso (Renault R26) leads Kimi Räikkönen (McLaren MP4/21-Mercedes-Benz) and David Coulthard (Red Bull RB2-Ferrari).

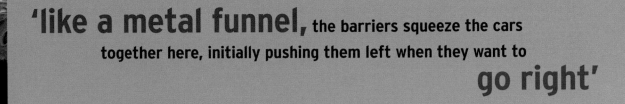

'**like a metal funnel,** the barriers squeeze the cars together here, initially pushing them left when they want to **go right'**

ease their radii or to make them more severe, while the tunnel and swimming pool sections have also been redeveloped over the years, but the course and location of the circuit are remarkably true to the original. Look at any black-and-white photograph of the race taken in the last 80 years or so and the section of track will be easily recognizable.

It's this continuity, this tangible 2-mile (3km) thread of tarmac which can be traced back to motor racing's infancy that makes the Monaco Grand Prix so special, and explains why even a snail's-pace drive around the hallowed circuit is a memory to cherish.

There's never a good time to drive into the centre of the principality, so you may as well resign yourself to that fact straight away and embrace the chaos. One-way streets, four lanes funnelling into one, double-parking, suicidal superbike riders and 7ft-wide (2m) supercars are all part of the experience, and that's before you've got anywhere near the street circuit itself.

It's not difficult to find your way to a recognizable section of the lap, but it's almost impossible to arrive in such as way as to emerge conveniently

Left: Polesitter Fernando Alonso leads the field round on the formation lap at the start of the 2006 race. **Above:** Giancarlo Fisichella (Renault R26) enters the famous tunnel section during the previous day's practice.

onto the start/finish straight. Better to follow your nose, and the gradient, downhill, skirting the leafy gardens on the far side of Casino Square until you pick up signs for the Grimaldi Forum, a modern exhibition centre right on the seafront. It's not that you want or need to go there, but as you creep your way through the ever-narrowing streets you'll discover that by following the signs you actually merge with the circuit at Portier, which, if you can ignore the confusingly configured roundabout, is the tight right-hander before the famous tunnel.

Fans of Ayrton Senna will remember Portier as the corner where the Brazilian genius stuffed his McLaren into the Armco in 1988 after a momentary lapse in concentration. Distraught at his unforced error, Senna abandoned his crippled car and trudged mournfully back to his apartment, where he remained for several days.

From here it's a short distance to the mouth of the tunnel, which curves with increasing severity almost from the moment you enter its strip-lit maw. Disconcertingly, the tunnel's exit is blind, yet it's the fastest section of the circuit with cars touching more than 170mph (274kph) as they explode into the sunlight. While it's a straightforward part of the lap if nothing goes wrong, plenty of drivers – including Michael Schumacher – have had their hopes dashed in here, emerging in a shower of splintered carbon fibre.

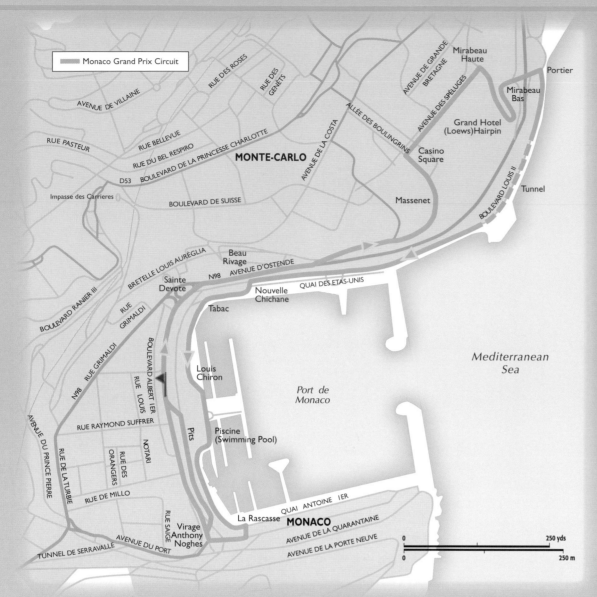

Monaco Grand Prix Circuit

MONTE-CARLO

Mediterranean Sea

Port de Monaco

MONACO

Exiting the tunnel, you get the first opportunity to appreciate how close the circuit runs to the sea, and also that the road is still running downhill. As it levels off you arrive at the Nouvelle Chicane, which is actually a tricky staggered junction in regular usage. You can take a more direct line through here than the modern F1 cars do, following the truer diagonal path used up until the mid-1980s.

It's the closest you get to the water for the whole lap, and a place where, before the circuit revisions were made, drivers would simply dab the brakes and jink left-right in the blink of an eye, carrying as much speed as possible. Three drivers have carried a bit too much and landed themselves in the harbour: Alberto Ascari in 1955, Paul Hawkins in 1965 and the actor James Garner, whose character, Pete Aron, crashed his Jordan-BRM into the Med in the John Frankenheimer 1966 epic *Grand Prix*.

After the chicane you head towards the tricky Tabac corner. Demanding absolute precision, this unsighted left-hander is hellishly quick in an F1 car,

and the Armco stacked high on both sides creates the illusion of careering into a wall of steel. The very quickest drivers will just brush the barriers on the exit, while the slightest misjudgment on turn-in will see them clout the inside barrier with their left front wheel before connecting with the outside barrier a split second later.

After rounding Tabac, you're treated to a broad view of the Swimming Pool complex and the left-right chicane that marks its entry. This used to be as confined and daunting as Tabac, but recent changes – made possible thanks to an enormous engineering programme that saw 54 acres (22ha) of land reclaimed from the sea – have given the drivers the rare luxury of some room for error. Nevertheless it's a section that demands total commitment and complete faith in the adhesive qualities of racing tyres and aerodynamic downforce.

Right: The Williams FW28-Cosworth of Mark Webber flashes past the steps of the Hotel de Paris during the 2006 race.

Next up is the awkward La Rascasse hairpin, which passes so close to the restaurant that shares its name that the drivers all but power between the downstairs tables. It's best to pick your line carefully here, for, as Michael Schumacher proved in 2006, even the best can make an innocent mistake and run out of road…

Squeezing between La Rascasse restaurant on your right and the taller buildings on your left, the road makes an awkward kink to the right at Anthony Noghes before feeding you onto the unmistakable start/finish line. A straight by name but most definitely not by nature, the road sweeps gently but insistently to the right, spearing between the new permanent pit buildings and prime apartment buildings. If you fancy renting one with a balcony from which to have a bird's-eye view of the race, all you need is £15,000 or so.

Approaching St Devote – Monaco's infamous first turn – you can see why it causes the world's best drivers so much trouble. Like a metal funnel, the barriers squeeze the cars together here, initially pushing them left when they want to go right, then taking a wicked 90-degree turn to the right before the steep climb up Beau Rivage. On race day the F1 cars stampede up this smooth and sinuous ascent at 160mph (258kph) , but you'll be lucky to hit a tenth of their velocity as you pick your way through the blockade of AMG Mercedes and Bentley Continental GTs that have been semi-abandoned by their owners outside the numerous designer boutiques.

It's here you notice the road is smothered in painted road markings. Innocent enough on a sunny day at walking pace, when you're accelerating an F1 car up here in the pouring rain these highway hieroglyphics are like patches of ice. Just ask Nigel Mansell, who spun his Lotus into the barriers while pushing his luck too far in the quest for his maiden GP win.

As you crest the brow and begin to turn left, the level of surrealism ratchets up a few notches as you enter Casino Square. Stripped of the barriers that define the circuit's testing off-camber left and right, you'll doubtless be distracted by the casino, complete with lush gardens, gushing fountains and mouth-watering array of prestige cars precisely valet parked for all to see.

If you can tear yourself away and continue downhill past the Mirabeau Hotel, you'll find yourself in one of the few potential overtaking zones in the whole lap. Those incongruous red-and-white kerbs that jump out at you from your television screen are all here, tall and intimidating as you corkscrew right then immediately left into that other great Monaco landmark, the Loews Hairpin. How an F1 car gets around here is anyone's guess, for it takes some concerted arm twirling to negotiate cleanly in a normal road car.

All that remains before you arrive back at the Portier turn is a tightish right-hander, lined on your left by a tall embankment wall and on your right by a conveniently chamfered kerb, which the F1 boys cut greedily to shave a few hundredths of a second from their lap time. Tempting though it is to emulate their line, it's best not to for fear of collecting one of the diamond-collared poodles or chihuahuas that are indigenous to this billionaires' playground.

Despite the certainty that you'll fail to exceed 20mph (32kph) at any point in the entire 2-mile (3km) lap, driving around Monaco's celebrated street circuit gives you an unforgettable taste of Formula One's most enduring challenge and most coveted prize.

Below: The jewel in the F1 crown. The sun-drenched Mediterranean harbour with its palatial array of yachts provides a unique setting for the world's most glamorous motor race.

5 Hillclimbs

Swedish driver Per Ekland's Saab roars through the gravel section of the Pikes Peak course in 2000.

GROSSGLOCKNER

DISTANCE: 15.7 MILES (25.3KM) **FIRST RACE:** 1935 **LOCATION:** AUSTRIA

It's 30 August 1930 and the Austrian Alps are reverberating to the sound of a dynamite explosion. Work has just begun on the epic Grossglockner Hochalpenstrasse (High Alpine Road) to create a convenient north–south passage between Austria and Italy.

Fast-forward to a whisker under five years later and the hills are shaking to a different kind of thunder, as some of Europe's quickest drivers tackle a 12-mile (19km) section of the newly completed 20.8-mile (33.5km) mountain pass, just one day after the President of Austria has declared the road officially open.

Climbing to an altitude of 8,226ft (2,500m), the Grossglockner is the highest road in Austria and one of the most spectacular and vertiginous motorsport venues in the world. Since it opened, more than 50 million tourists have enjoyed the panoramic views it affords, but throughout the 1930s this majestic High Alpine Road presented a towering challenge both to those who built it, and those who competed on it.

After years of preparatory survey work, it took a team of 3,200 engineers and labourers 26 months of solid work to excavate the 1.5 million tons of earth and rock it required to carve a path and build embankments for this epic road. They also built 67 bridges and laid a telephone line along the entire length of the road to give travellers a means of communication if they ran into difficulties. Upon completion, it was calculated that this mammoth achievement had cost the equivalent of £40 million in today's money. The projected costs in 1929 said it would cost just £4.5 million. Clearly when it comes to monumental engineering projects some things never change…

In its original form the Grossglockner Pass had a surface of compacted sand and gravel, which was the approved method of the day for building a road in such an isolated and hostile environment. It was hoped that the inaugural mountainclimb would see the appearance of the Mercedes-Benz and Auto Union teams, but both claimed the surface was too dangerous for such potent machines and so gave the Grossglockner a miss.

Below: Ernst Lammel in his Triumph TR3A tackles the Grossglockner – the highest road in Austria. **Right:** The 1935 Alvis of Erwin Hantke winds its way through the stunning mountain scenery.

The event went ahead regardless, and although history records it as being a poorly organized affair, the mountainclimb was notable for two outstanding performances: one from the tremendously gifted Italian driver, Mario Tadini, who set the fastest time of the day in a Scuderia Ferrari Alfa, the other from the up-and-coming Englishman Dick Seaman, who finished second in his ERA.

By the time the racing cars returned to the Grossglockner in 1938, not only were the previously absent Mercedes and Auto Union machines among the entries, but the event had become the most important climb of the year: the Deutsche Bergmeisterschaft or German Mountain Championship. This, don't forget, was at a time when hill- and mountainclimbing were considered second only to Grand Prix racing in terms of prestige and importance. It was also a time of political tumult, and with both Mercedes and Auto Union enjoying significant funding from Adolf Hiter's ruling Nazi party for their respective racing efforts, it was inevitable that political capital would be made from motorsport whenever possible. It was surely no coincidence that just months after taking control of Austria without authority the Germans decided to make the Grossglockner the chosen venue for the German Mountain Championship.

Despite the imperious Nazi presence, the Grossglockner would not be overshadowed, and the mighty 12,457ft (3,787m) peak provided a larger-than-life backdrop for what would be a fiercely contested prize. Favourite amongst the contenders was Auto Union's Hans Stuck. The undisputed King of the Mountains, Stuck was the Michael Schumacher of mountainclimbing, invariably coping with the solitary, high-pressure demands of this specialized discipline with metronomic consistency. Ranged against him were the Mercedes duo of

Hermann Lang and Manfred von Brauchitsch, both Grand Prix aces in their own right.

The original plan was to run the event along the entire 20.8-mile (33.5km) Grossglockner High Alpine Pass, starting the ascent at Ferleiten (where the northern toll booth is today) and heading south to the finish at Franz Josefs Höhe, which is up a dead-end spur off the main road and some 7,747ft (2,355m) above sea level. It was a flawed plan; as in 1935, the organizers had misjudged the potency of the Silver Arrows and how they would perform on the Pass, as there's a mid-section that actually descends quite steeply and includes some lengthy tunnels.

When it became clear that the section from the Mittertörl Tunnel to Guttal posed too big a risk in the 500bhp V12 and V16-engined racers, the decision was made to split the run into two parts, the first starting at Ferleiten and finishing 7.8 miles

(12.5km) later at the Fuscher Törl, at which point it's possible to see as many as 37 separate mountain peaks. Having successfully completed the first run, the cars were then to be driven 8 miles (13km) or so to the second start point, at Guttal, where the next timed run would complete the remaining 7.9 miles (12.7km) to Franz-Josefs-Höhe.

Despite being the middle of summer, the weather was terrible, with rain and dense cloud shrouding the second leg of the climb. The organizers wanted to continue with the two-stage competition, but with visibility terribly compromised the drivers rebelled, staging a strike until the organizers relented and agreed to hold two runs on the first section. Even so, conditions remained bad, with torrential rain adding to the challenge. As expected, Stuck rose to the occasion and set the fastest time, but Lang was breathing down his neck, with von Brauchitsch trailing in third place.

While much of the surface remained hard-packed gravel, just as it was in 1935, the Grossglockner now featured an elaborate cobbled surface on many of the switchbacks. These hard granite sets must have been lethally slippery in the cold and wet conditions, especially in such hugely powerful cars, yet Stuck and Lang had their cars dancing to the tune of their throttles, tyres spinning, tails sliding and engines wailing as they skittered around the switchbacks.

Fortunately for us, there's now a smooth coating of tarmac covering the High Alpine Road, but where you'd expect there to be modern crash barriers lining the fresh-air side of the road, instead stand regularly spaced stone corner markers that march on into the distance like an advancing column of small grey soldiers. While great at preserving the unspoiled views across the valley, they don't appear to offer much in the way of protection from the

'These hard granite sets must have been lethally slippery in the cold and wet conditions, especially in such hugely powerful cars'

sizeable drops. However, they do give you a clear impression of the view Stuck, Lang and the others had from their open cockpits as they powered their way up the mountain.

Although there are some steep and tangled stretches, on the whole the Grossglockner makes a very gradual ascent and descent of the mountain. If it wasn't for your ears blocking and popping with the fluctuating air pressure – and the dizzying views across to distant snow-capped summits – you wouldn't believe you were driving along one of the highest mountain roads in Europe. If you're a big fan of Stelvio-style zigzags then you might find it a bit lacking in intensity, but what the High Alpine Road lacks in frenzied hairpins it makes up for in beautifully smooth and sinuous progress.

With tremendous views across three, four and sometimes even five sets of corners as they wrap themselves around the contours of the mountain, you can take a clean line, kissing the inner and outer edges of the road with confidence as you power through mile after mile of clearly sighted road. It's possible to find a hugely satisfying rhythm, especially on the faster and more swooping

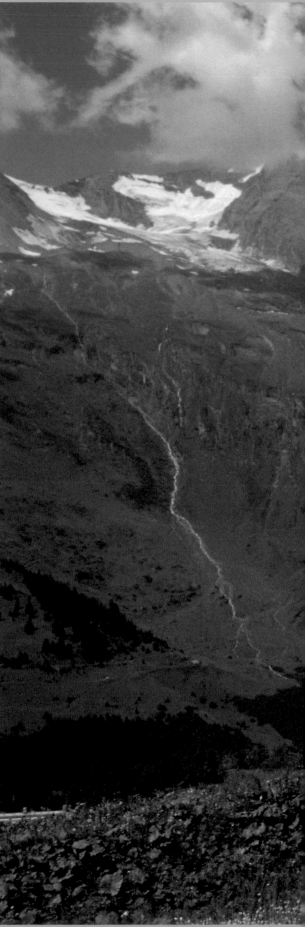

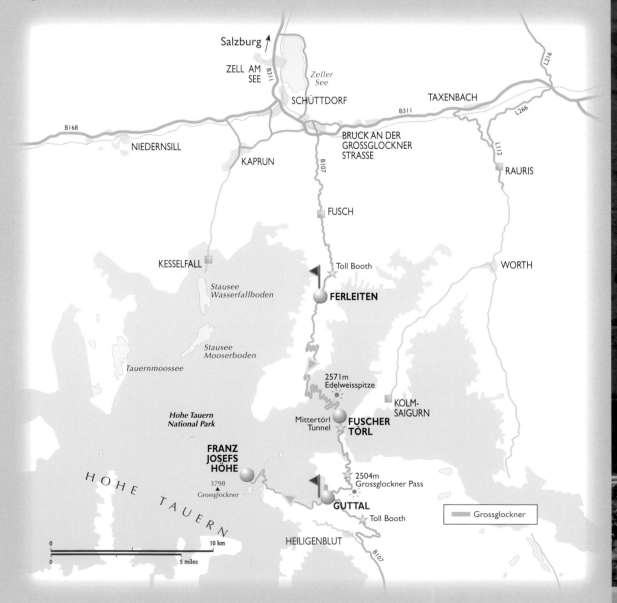

Salzburg ↑

ZELL AM SEE

Zeller See

B311

SCHÜTTDORF

TAXENBACH

L216

B168

B311

L266

NIEDERNSILL

BRUCK AN DER GROSSGLOCKNER STRASSE

L112

KAPRUN

B107

RAURIS

FUSCH

KESSELFALL

Stausee Wasserfallboden

Toll Booth

WORTH

● FERLEITEN

Stausee Mooserboden

Tauernmoossee

2571m Edelweisspitze

Hohe Tauern National Park

Mittertörl Tunnel

KOLM-SAIGURN

● FUSCHER TÖRL

FRANZ JOSEFS HÖHE

H O H E   T A U E R N

3798 Grossglockner

2504m Grossglockner Pass

● GUTTAL

Toll Booth

▭ Grossglockner

0 ——— 10 km
0 ——— 5 miles

HEILIGENBLUT

B107

southern end of the pass, but there's also fun to be had at the northern end, where the road tends to be steeper and tighter.

Located in the centre of the Hohe Tauern National Park, the Grossglockner is hemmed in by the skiing resorts of Kitzbühel and Schladming, with the nearest large cities, Innsbruck to the west and Salzburg to the north, a comfortable half-day's drive away. As you'd expect, so much snow falls on the High Alpine Road that it's impossible to keep it open all year round. In 1937 it took a team of 50 men 70 days to shovel the snow from just one lane of the pass in the spring. Now it takes modern snow-clearing machinery just 25 days to shift more than three times the volume of snow and clear the entire road. Barring freak weather the Grossglockner is closed from the beginning of November to the end of April. Once cleared in the spring, the road is open every day from 6am until 8.30pm, then 5am to 10pm in the height of the summer, with entry permitted up until 45 minutes before closing.

Unfortunately the cobbled corners that gave the mountainclimbers so much trouble have long gone.

In fact, many of the road's tighter turns have also been widened so that the numerous coaches that haul tourists up and down have more room to take a swing at the hairpins. The cobbles may have gone from the main Grossglockner route, but if you take the dead-end turn signed for Edelweisspitze, you're treated to a steep and bumpy cobbled spur road, which climbs through seven tight hairpins before depositing you at the 8,433ft (2,564m) viewpoint. If this is what the main road was like, Stuck and Lang really were heroes.

At the southern end of the pass there's another dead-end section, which leads to Franz-Josefs-Höhe, where the organizers of the 1938 Deutsche Bergmeisterschaft had hoped the second leg would reach its climax. It's not as high as the Edelweisspitze, but it does give you an amazing view across the vast battleship-grey expanse of the Pasterze glacier, Austria's largest.

The weather improved for the mountainclimb's second run and the three German aces really put on a show, with Stuck improving his first rain-affected run by 70sec, while von Brauchitsch pulled out all

the stops to complete the run more than a minute and a half faster than his tardy first run. Once the times were added together, Stuck retained his crown, with Lang heading the Mercedes pair to take second place. After a shaky start the Grossglockner had come good.

There would be one final Deutsche Bergmeisterschaft at the Grossglockner the following year, which Hermann Lang would take in contentious circumstances. When peace returned to Europe the grand old Grossglockner's surface had been ripped to shreds by the passage of tanks and heavy artillery, and by the time it had been repaired the mountains were seen as unsuitable places to unleash such extreme racing cars and the enthralling sport of mountainclimbing was lost to history. Thankfully a trip to Austria and the purchase of an £18 toll ticket buys you the chance to bring those distant memories back to life.

Below: The view over the Grossglockner Road from above the mountain pass through the Hohe Tauern National Park.

KLAUSEN PASS

DISTANCE: 13.4 MILES (21.6KM) **FIRST RACE:** 1922 **LOCATION:** SWITZERLAND

If you've ever driven through it, you'll know that Switzerland and speed don't mix. With a national motorsport ban still in force since the government imposed it in the immediate aftermath of the 1955 Le Mans disaster, the Swiss authorities' continued aversion to velocity most clearly manifests itself in the activities of the traffic police, who are among the most assiduous in the world.

It's an important point to bear in mind if you make the journey to this independent Alpine nation, for if you've travelled from Germany, where many stretches of autobahn are still derestricted, or Italy, where the *carabinieri*'s attitudes to making brisk progress are somewhat more relaxed, Switzerland will be something of a culture shock.

However, take a look back into motorsport's rich and varied history and you'll see that it wasn't always thus. In fact, for 13 glorious years Switzerland was the home of the Klausenrennen, a heroic competitive charge to the top of the 6,403ft (1,947m) Klausen Pass. At 13.4 miles (21.6km),

this tangled thread of mountain road was exactly equal in length to France's great mountain climbing venue, Mont Ventoux, and so shared the honour of being the longest climb in Europe. But with 136 corners – 35 of them severe switchbacks – a perilous tunnel and the 5,257ft (1,598m) Mont Clariden looming ever-present in the background, the Klausen Pass was arguably the greater driving challenge.

On a road map it appears as though the Klausen Pass is caught in a complex web of autoroutes, but in reality once you turn off the A3, which runs south from Switzerland's banking capital, Zurich, and head for the village of Linthal (where the Klausen Pass mountainclimb course starts), you're soon lost in this uplifting Alpine landscape. In fact, this entire region is a driver's paradise, with the highest concentration of mountain passes anywhere in the world. The St Gotthard, St Bernard, Susten, Splugen, Nufenen, Furka, Grimsel and Simplon passes are all within striking range. All are worth experiencing, but it's the Klausen that has the illustrious history.

Heading west through Linthal you'll have to be vigilant if you're to spot the start line, for despite an enthusiastic following among classic motorsport enthusiasts around the world, clues to the Klausenrennen are conspicuous by their absence in its place of origin. Eventually, perhaps more by luck than judgement, you'll see a hastily applied white line painted between the kerbs with 'Start' sprayed above it in scratchy freehand style. It's a less than fitting introduction to one of the world's great stretches of road, but then the pre-war European Mountainclimb Championship was never preoccupied with fancy buildings and sprawling facilities, preferring to focus on the purity of pitting man and machine against a monolithic mountain.

Although none of the competitors knew it at the time, August 1934 would be the final running of the Klausenrennen. It was a hotly contested event, thanks to the eagerly anticipated return of Rudi Caracciola after smashing his hip in a bad accident at the Monaco Grand Prix earlier in the year. It had been a severe injury, which left his right leg two inches (5cm) shorter than his left, yet despite being far from fully recovered he was keen to confound those who believed Monaco was his last truly competitive drive. His statement of intent was an all-out assault on the gruelling Klausenrennen: an event he had contested many time before, and one he felt would prove he was far from a spent force.

Three days of truly appalling weather almost thwarted the great man's mountain comeback. After 72 hours of virtually constant rain and snow the course was in a beleaguered state, with formerly babbling streams now raging torrents and the

Left: The Klausen Pass affords some stunning views of the Alpine landscape. **Opposite:** The snow capped mountain view of the Pass from Linthal to Altdorf.

remains of an avalanche partially blocking the only straight section of the climb at Urner Boden. Boulders loosened by the incessant rain began to tumble down the mountainside and the majority of the competitors were prevented from making any practice runs, which meant race day itself would be their first taste of the course.

By the time the weather improved and the course was returned to some semblance of order there was only time for one run for each competitor. While this instantly handed the advantage to those with prior experience of the Klausen Pass, everyone knew that the event was only ever really about the duel between Caracciola, driving for Mercedes, and Hans Stuck in his trusty Auto Union.

Having competed on the Klausen almost every year since 1924, Caracciola knew all 13.4 miles (21.6km) like the back of his string-gloved hand, but so too did Stuck, who was an equally formidable Grand Prix driver and a true mountainclimbing

specialist. Consequently the Klausenrennen was poised for one of the all-time great confrontations between the two finest and most exciting drivers of their day. Imagine Fernando Alonso and Kimi Raikkonen, each presented with their regular F1 mounts, a deserted mountain pass and their honour held in the ticking hands of a stopwatch, and you've got some idea of the event's significance.

With such drama on the cards it was no surprise that a sizeable throng of hardy spectators braved the elements to gain a panoramic vantage point from which to witness the action. As each car left the start in Linthal, no doubt in a flurry of wheelspin and tyre smoke, the noise must have echoed far and wide. Such an angry wall of sound would have heralded each car's arrival well before the gaggles of spectators caught a glimpse of the approaching projectile. None would have sounded, or looked, anything like Caracciola and Stuck's flying Silver Arrows.

The nickname for these superlative pieces of German engineering was never more appropriate than at the Klausen Pass, for the finish line was situated in Altdorf, the home of William Tell. Switzerland's answer to Robin Hood, Tell is said to have shot an apple from his son's head with a crossbow, having been forced to do so by a tyrannical ruler of the region in which Tell lived. Tell later shot said tyrant with another crossbow bolt after being imprisoned for his continued defiance.

Though successive historians have drawn the conclusion that the legend of Tell is nothing but a fable, Altdorf is clearly reluctant to give these heretical theories credence, and continues to celebrate the village's most famous son at every opportunity. While understandable, it seems a little

Below: One of the many mountainous switchbacks along the route which was built along the line of an old bridle path.

'The views – never less than bewitching – extend way down the valley, while the road, which is often little wider than two cars, uncoils invitingly through the windscreen'

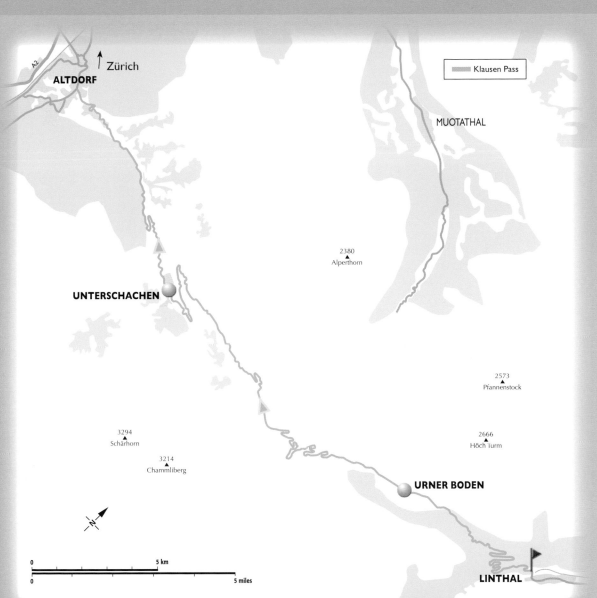

odd that a fictitious fruit-shooting folk hero should enjoy such a passionate following when the real heroes like Caracciola, Stuck and the other great drivers who took on the mighty Klausen Pass are all but forgotten by the general populace.

Forgotten by most, but remembered as though it was yesterday by those few spectators who survive, is the 1934 Klausenrennen. With huge reserves of power, both aces would have burst into view twitching and sliding their cars across the road's loose surface with furiously spinning rear wheels kicking clouds of shale and dust into the pristine mountain air. Stuck's car in particular took some hanging onto, its rear-mounted V16 engine and swing axle generating more traction than Caracciola's front-engined V12-powered Mercedes, but feeling much less stable when pushed to the limit. His exuberant driving style was a match for the Auto Union's malevolence, but a slight mistake led to a wayward moment, losing Stuck some time and, in all probability, his chance of victory.

Caracciola meanwhile was driving as never before, even by his exalted standards. Carving time out of his existing mountain record, he drifted through the Klausen's countless corners with total commitment. Blanking the pain from his still-healing hip and wringing every ounce of performance from his Grand Prix Mercedes, Rudi annihilated his previous best time of 15min 50sec set two years previously with an incredible run of 15min 22sec. Finishing just three seconds adrift, Stuck's climb was also an exceptional effort, but he surely headed back to Germany rueing the moment

the Auto Union's tail momentarily slipped his grasp.

Driving away from Linthal, you'll feel your chest swell with excitement as you cross the start and begin to drive the mountainclimb course itself. The views – never less than bewitching – extend way down the valley, while the road, which is often little wider than two cars, uncoils invitingly through the windscreen. It's awesome to think that apart from the new surface, which is now smooth tarmac, some road markings and a few token lengths of Armco barrier, Caracciola and Stuck would instantly recognize their old battle ground. So, little has changed on the Klausen since

those heady pre-war days, except for the tunnel, which must have been bypassed at some point. It's just a few miles from the start but hard to find as it lurks behind a wall and up a rocky path. There's a hole in the wall that's big enough to squeeze a car onto the path, at which point you can edge into the tunnel itself. Dank, dark and far from straight, the prospect of charging headlong into here in a car with no lights is enough to have you swallowing hard, and it's with increased respect for the courage of those pre-war racers that you gratefully make your escape and breath the clear air.

From the site of the disused tunnel the pass climbs steeply through hairpin after giddy hairpin. The temperature drops and the vegetation shrinks into the mountainside. Just as you think you must be coming to the summit, the road flattens, following a river as it runs straight through the centre of a meadow between two towering peaks. Though some of the flat section is gently meandering, this section – known as Urder Boden – features the Klausen Pass's only high-speed straight. It's a place where Caracciola and Stuck would have been doing 160mph (258kph) or more.

Such terrifying speeds are almost beyond comprehension, especially when wearing a leather helmet and flying goggles in a car with no seatbelts and a payload of fuel laced with highly volatile acetone for extra power. Yet compared to the endless stamina-sapping switchbacks that await you through the last 4 or 5 miles of the ascent, the relative freedom of this insanely fast stretch must have given Rudi and Hans enough respite to catch their breath and let the strength return to their stinging forearms before girding themselves for one last sustained attack.

After one last left-hand hairpin the road sweeps past some protective railings and across the finish line. Sprayed in yellow paint and subject to a similar level of indifference as the start in Linthal, it's worth pulling over and looking back down the valley's craggy cleft. Only then can you retrace the knotted bootlace of tarmac as it tumbles to infinity, savouring every twist and turn of a truly magnificent road.

Above: A Lotus 340R winds its way towards the summit.

175

MONT VENTOUX

DISTANCE: 13.4 MILES (21.6KM) **FIRST RACE:** 1902 **LOCATION:** FRANCE

They call it the 'Giant of Provence': an extinct volcano rising 6,263ft (1,903m) from the patchwork of vineyards and farmland that form the Rhône valley. Mont Ventoux's lazily sloping asymmetric outline presents a hulking presence on the Provençal skyline.

Perhaps it's because it looms so large over this beautiful region of southern France that people are constantly drawn to its precipitous flanks. Cyclists and drivers in particular have been seduced by Ventoux's siren call over the years, with the 13.42-mile (21.6km) road that clings to its slopes forging a fearsome reputation as one of the most gruelling ascents in the Tour de France cycle race, and one of Europe's most challenging competitive hillclimbs.

The first recorded ascent to Ventoux's summit is credited to the Italian scholar Francesco Petrarch on 26 April 1336. Whether he actually did clamber to the top remains open to conjecture, for his account was in a letter to a friend, which he's known to have composed many years after the supposed date of the climb as an autobiographical reflection on his own life. Whether it's a true account or scholarly yarn no one's quite sure, but the fact that Petrarch suggested he'd climbed Ventoux for no reason other than to enjoy the uplifting view from the summit is sufficient for him to be seen as the 'father of alpinism' by the climbing community.

One thing's for certain: if Petrarch did climb Mont Ventoux he must have picked his moment carefully, for although it isn't exceptionally high by alpine standards, it does experience true climatic extremes.

While the foothills enjoy wonderful Mediterranean weather, on the barren mountainsides temperatures can soar to more than 100°F (38°C) in the height of summer yet plunge to −27°F (−33°C) in the depths of winter. Winter also brings with it the vicious mistral, a wind that whips the southern side of the mountain. Squalls of up to 120mph (193kph) are not uncommon as you get close to the summit, while the highest recorded wind speed is closer to 200mph (322kph). No wonder the mountain's name is supposedly derived from the French word *venteux*, meaning windy.

Nearly six centuries after Petrarch's alleged climb, Mont Ventoux hosted its first motorsport event: a speed hillclimb open to cars and motorcycles. Like most mountain roads of the era, the surface was dressed with a loose layer of compacted rocks and gravel, and huge plumes of

dust rose into the late summer sunshine as a succession of cars and bikes scrabbled their way to the summit. The overall winner was a driver by the name of Chauchard, who manhandled his 13.7-litre Panhard to Ventoux's peak in a highly respectable 27min 17sec, averaging 29.5mph (47.5kph). By contrast the quickest motorcycle took a little under 42mins.

To appreciate the significance of such hillclimbing you first have to understand motoring itself. At the turn of the 20th century the automobile was a new and largely unreliable contraption, its frail mechanical health meaning long or steep gradients were often regarded as insurmountable obstacles. With minimal power and feeble brakes (often only fitted to the rear wheels) ascents usually ended in a cloud of steam, while descents were a pastime for the brave, foolhardy or desperate.

Left: A winter view of Mont Ventoux from one of the many Provençal vineyards. **Right:** The gradient is gentle near the foot of the mountain, but gets gradually steeper as you climb.

The early motorist had to plan his or her journey with military precision to avoid any potentially tricky topography, so competitive hillclimbing was by far the most meaningful real-world measure of a car's performance, both for the manufacturers and the wealthy car-buying public. As a result the sport rapidly grew in both significance and popularity, with Mont Ventoux standing proudly among the earliest, toughest and most prestigious venues.

By the 1930s hillclimbing was taken just as seriously as Grand Prix racing, although this meant the sport had long since left the practical needs and interests of the motorist behind in favour of high-octane drama. With the arrival of factory teams and professional drivers the supremacy of the German Mercedes and Auto Unions was inescapable. Not content with dominating their home hills and mountains, both German teams also made Ventoux their own.

Mercedes were first to do so, in 1931, thanks to the genius of Rudolph Caracciola's driving skills and the formidable pace of his wailing, supercharged SSK sports car. He won again the following year – this time driving his own Alfa Romeo – but it was Auto Union that left the most lasting impression in 1934, when the acknowledged mountain master Hans Stuck took his rear-engined supercharged V16 Grand Prix car to an awe-inspiring victory. In a bravura performance, Stuck literally tore his way up the mountain, power sliding the 550bhp projectile out of every corner, oblivious to the precipice to his left and the solid rock face to his right. It remains one of the most spectacular hillclimb efforts in history.

After World War II the cars and bikes returned to Ventoux in 1949, and the event remained keenly contested right up until 1976, by which time it was being tackled in Formula Two single-seaters complete with slick tyres and large wings. By this time the two modern enemies of such a classic old-school venue – money and safety – had begun to threaten the event. It took many hundreds of police, fire and rescue personnel to ensure the safety of competitors and spectators, and the hillclimb course was shortened to 9.57 miles (15.4km) in an effort to ease the burden on resources. Sadly this stopgap measure couldn't save the event, and 1976 was the last time Ventoux hosted a dedicated hillclimb event.

As you turn off the A7 autoroute at Avignon and head towards Carpentras on the D492 you're less than an hour from Mont Ventoux's hallowed tarmac. With Châteauneuf-du-Pape and other prime wine-growing areas within striking distance it's no surprise to find yourself winding through endless vineyards, the neatly clipped branches groaning under the weight of ripening bunches of sun-purpled grapes.

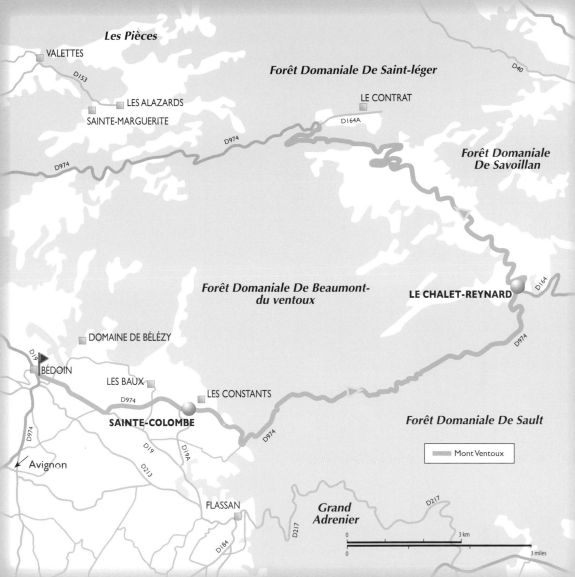

Top: The old green and white kerbstones are still visible as the climb enters the beech wood. **Above:** The famous Chalet Reynard – a popular stop-off point for cyclists.

Once in Carpentras you quickly pick up the D974, which you then follow all the way up Mont Ventoux and back down the northern face to Malaucène. With anticipation building fast, you begin to climb Ventoux's most distant southern foothills long before you're anywhere near the official start of the hillclimb course in Bédoin. Gently at first, then steadily gaining in gradient, the D974 begins to square up to the spent volcano's slopes, lifting you from the hot, bright vineyards and into the leafy cool and dappled shade of a sizeable beech wood.

The road here is smooth and fast, punctuated with snappy combinations of barrier-lined hairpin bends to keep you amused on the way to the hamlets of Sainte-Colombe and Les Bruns. Look at a detailed map and you'll see how the D974 coils around Ventoux like a belt, the hillclimb route starting on the south side and working

anticlockwise to the summit, its tortured twists and turns promising great things.

After the fertile plains and serenely sheltered woodland, signs of life begin to dwindle as you approach Chalet Reynard, one of Ventoux's two modest ski resorts sitting some 10 miles (16km) into the ascent. The road looks odd here: a large and extremely wide hairpin, with another road (the D164 to Sault) merging from the right. Old photos show this corner to have resembled a larger, less severe version of the Nürburgring Nordshleife's Karussel, with a dished concrete section to aid cornering. It's long been filled in, but with the Chalet Reynard's restaurant terrace overlooking the curve you get a real sense that this must have been one of Ventoux's most popular spectating zones.

There are just 3.5 miles (5.6km) of the hillclimb remaining, but the D974 has saved the best until last, for as you watch Chalet Reynard fade in your

'as you watch Chalet Reynard fade in your rear-view mirror, all signs of vegetation also begin to peter out, leaving nothing but bare slopes of bleached limestone'

rear-view mirror, all signs of vegetation also begin to peter out, leaving nothing but bare slopes of bleached limestone. Up until the 12th century much of the mountain was forested, but it was ruthlessly stripped of trees to feed the burgeoning shipbuilding trade in the port of Toulon. Reforestation began in the late 1800s, when many of the beech trees were planted on the lower reaches of the mountain, but the top remains breathtakingly bald.

The starkness of Ventoux's upper slopes is mesmerizing and also faintly unsettling. There's something alien about a view that comprises just azure sky and bone-white rocks, and as you snatch glimpses of the frankly bizarre-looking weather station and gargantuan barber's pole of a television mast the illusion of a lunar settlement is complete.

Exposed to the elements all year round the road surface is coarse and abrasive. Giant 10ft-high (3m) snow poles line the edges of the road to guide the snowplough drivers who clear the road each spring, while sporadic strips of barrier do little to appease your sense of vertigo as you skirt the abyss.

Impressively you'll still be encountering cyclists, their engorged calf and thigh muscles pumping the pedals as they strain their way up the mountain like proto-Lance Armstrongs. The great American may

be a giant of Le Tour but he wasn't a match for the Giant of Provence, never winning the stage. If our Lycra-clad friends knew what he had to say about Mont Ventoux they might not have felt up to its challenge: 'Nineteen hundred meters [6,232ft] up there is completely different from 1,900 metres any place else. There's no air, there's no oxygen. There's no vegetation, there's no life. Just rocks. Any other climb there's vegetation, grass and trees. Not there on the Ventoux. It's more like the moon than a mountain.'

As you get within reach of the summit you'll doubtless find a gaggle of riders gathered around a large marble memorial to the great British cyclist

Top left: The road through the wooded section is smooth and fast, but eventually opens out into a much more barren landscape **(above)**.
Above left: A plaque commemorates the climb record set in 1936.

Tommy Simpson, who literally rode himself to death here in the 1967 Tour. Riding in fierce heat and less than a mile from the peak, Simpson began to weave to and fro across the road before taking a tumble. Delirious but still utterly focused on completing the climb he was heard asking spectators to 'put me back on my bike' and even managed to resume his ascent, but almost immediately collapsed once more and

died, still clipped to his pedals. A post mortem revealed traces of amphetamines and alcohol in his blood stream, and controversy has stalked the sport ever since.

In addition to the cyclists, you may, if you're lucky, also spot a pre-production prototype car being subjected to Mont Ventoux's extremes by teams of test and development engineers. The combination of gradient, altitude, heat and possibility of a fast brake-testing descent makes Ventoux a prime natural proving ground for many of the world's biggest car manufacturers. Hmm, that sounds like a familiar tale...

While the thought of grabbing a lucrative scoop shot is a nice idea, the real reason to come to Mont Ventoux – aside from the road, of course – is the extraordinary view from the summit. There's a large south-facing parking area just below the surreal antenna, and if conditions are right you'll find yourself peering down on the clouds, like skydiving with your feet firmly on the ground. On a crystal clear day you'll see France rolling out before you until it meets the Mediterranean. Sunsets here are among the most spectacular you'll ever see, while sunrise is as inspirational as the road itself. Perhaps Petrarch did make it here after all.

PIKES PEAK

DISTANCE: 12.4 MILES (19.9KM) FIRST RACE: 1916 LOCATION: COLORADO, USA

Describing the annual dash to the 14,110ft (4,289m) summit of Pikes Peak simply as a hillclimb is a masterpiece of understatement. Perhaps that's why competitors and fans of the Pikes Peak International Hill Climb refer to it by an altogether more evocative and appropriate name: The Race to the Clouds.

Held every year, on or as close as possible to American Independence Day (4 July), the PPIHC is a unique and spectacular event, attracting fearless racers and hardy spectators from around the world. Most incredible of all is the fact that for the rest of the year (weather permitting) the Pikes Peak Highway is a toll road open to the general public.

Though Native Americans have been familiar with its brooding silhouette for millennia, Pikes Peak takes its name from Zebulon Pike, the leader of an expedition that trekked through the area in 1806. Terrible weather prevented him and his men from making the summit, but his discovery was enough to win him immortality. Another explorer, a botanist by the name of Edwin James, successfully climbed the mountain in the summer of 1820. There was some dispute over the mountain's name, some calling for 'Pike's Peak', others for 'James' Peak'. In the end Pike's supporters won the argument. The final twist in the tortured naming process happened in 1871, when the newly formed US Board on Geographic Names recommended against the use of apostrophes in names, at which point Pike's Peak became officially known as Pikes Peak.

Rising from the Great Plains of Colorado and defining the eastern edge of the Rocky Mountains, Pikes Peak is a colossal and inspiring landmark. At sunrise it casts a shadow some 50 miles (80km) long, and when driving south towards the city of Colorado Springs on Interstate 25, it is visible from a distance of more than 130 miles (209km). After a carriage ride to the summit in 1893, Katherine Lee Bates was stirred to write the words to the song 'America the Beautiful', while today the vast granite monolith is a National Historic Landmark and proudly known as 'America's Mountain'. With an apostrophe.

In 1916, Spencer Penrose, a shrewd beneficiary of Colorado's gold rush years, rebuilt the carriage road travelled by Bates, and inaugurated the new Pikes Peak Highway with an automobile hillclimb. The Race to the Clouds was born. Its first winner, Rea Lentz, completed the gruelling course in a time of 20min 55.40sec. Today, some 91 years later, Pikes Peak is the second-oldest surviving motorsport event after the Indianapolis 500, with the quickest competitors now taking less than half Lentz's winning time to reach the summit.

Located 10 miles (16km) west of Colorado Springs in El Paso County, the Pikes Peak Highway is a 19 mile (31km) road that starts a few miles up the Ute Pass in Cascade. It's easy to find, and initially easy to negotiate, for the first half of the highway is surfaced with tarmac. You need to drive around 7 miles (11km) before you reach the start line for the PPIHC course. It's not obvious, for there are no grandstands or other permanent structures, but if you keep your eyes peeled it's possible to spot a white line painted across the road.

Opposite: The tortuous switchbacks of Pikes Peak are a unique challenge; few roads in the world take you past scenery as stunning.
Below: Louis Unser tackles Pikes Peak in his Federal Automotive Special in 1952.

'defining the eastern edge of the
Rocky Mountains, Pikes Peak is a colossal and inspiring
landmark'

If you visit in the months immediately following the race, snaking trails of burned rubber provide a more graphic clue!

Once past the start line, not only are you continuing along a road travelled by more than 300,000 visitors every year, you're also following in the wheeltracks of some legendary race and rally drivers. Homeland heroes Al and Bobby Unser, and Mario Andretti are all past winners of the oldest competitive class – the Open Wheel division – manhandling fearsome single-seater racing cars along every one of the 12.42 miles (19.99km) to the summit. Europe's finest rally drivers have also been drawn to the challenge of Pikes Peak, including the German former World Rally Champion, Walter Röhrl, and the Flying Finn, Ari Vatanen, whose death-defying efforts were captured in the 1989 award-winning film *Climb Dance*.

Even at a more sedate pace, you don't need to stretch your imagination too far to appreciate the skill and courage each PPIHC competitor summons when pitting their wits against the mountain. The tarmac curves are smooth and inviting, but the transition to unmetalled gravel is sudden, the surface stark and alien. When driven at normal speeds in a comfortable family car, the change of surface isn't a problem, but attempting to drive flat out on old man Penrose's dusty trail road in a tremendously powerful, twitchy racing car is an epic challenge.

In almost every respect bar the machinery that takes to the mountain every year, the PPIHC is a throwback to an era of motorsport long since left behind. It's rare enough to find a competitive event still taking place on closed sections of public road. To find one that is still running on the same course – a course that's essentially devoid of modern safety measures – after almost a century of competition is unique.

That's not to say the event is impervious to the advances of the Fun Police, but the changes being forced upon the Pikes Peak Highway are more to do with politics than public safety. Like the thousands of miles of trail road that criss-cross Colorado's portion

of the Rocky Mountains, Pikes Peak has a loose surface. However, unlike the rest of the trail roads, Pikes Peak's 12.42 miles (19.99km) are among the most famous and emotive in all America.

As a consequence, it has been singled out by the Sierra Club – a powerful body similar to the UK's National Trust – as a major cause of pollution of the surrounding reservoirs, thanks to soil erosion from the unmetalled surface. This places the Peak, and therefore the city of Colorado Springs, in breach of the Clean Water Act, which, in the finest American tradition, means one thing: litigation.

A court settlement was reached in 1999, in which the city rubber-stamped a 10-year plan to stabilize the road's surface. That doesn't sound too catastrophic, but in practice means the entire road will eventually be surfaced with tarmac. So far a number of key sections have been surfaced, including the 'The Ws', and Armco barrier have also been installed in certain supposed danger spots. Work is scheduled for completion by 2012.

Right: Rod Millen at the Glen Cove section of the Pikes Peak Hillclimb in 2000. **Far right:** Larry Ragland in his GMC Envoy on his way to victory the same year.

ROD MILLEN – PEAK PERFORMER

There have been countless legendary drivers at Pikes Peak, but no one has completed the 12.42-mile (19.99km) ascent of the Pikes Peak International Hill Climb course faster than New Zealander Rod Millen.

Driving his self-built Toyota Celica Turbo (seen on the right at the 2002 Goodwood Festival of Speed in England) – a crazy 850bhp, all-wheel drive monster capable of hitting 100mph (160kph) in around 5 seconds – Millen completed the run in 10:04.06min to take overall victory in the 1994 event and setting an the all-time mountain record that stands to this day.

Despite returning with a new machine – the even fiercer and faster Pikes Peak Toyota Tacoma – adverse weather conditions thwarted his repeated attempts to duck under the magic 10min mark. Now aged 55, Millen has called time on his Pikes Peak efforts, deciding there's little to be gained from effectively racing against an eight-year-younger and sharper version of himself. Having already held three hill records and won the event outright six times, Millen has nothing left to prove, while with the course now changing out of all recognition, any time comparisons have been rendered irrelevant.

Millen moved from New Zealand to the west coast of the United States in 1978 to pursue his motorsport career. It was a wise move, for, in addition to his dominant presence at Pikes Peak, Millen has also won numerous titles in a multitude of categories, from rallying and circuit racing to off-road truck racing. He also won the annual Race of Champions in 1997, beating the best drivers from the World Rally Championship.

Still an enthusiastic competitor and a firm favourite at the Goodwood Festival of Speed after beating all comers – including current F1 cars and drivers – in his record-holding Pikes Peak Celica, Millen remains a popular and intensely competitive figure in world motorsport.

Together with his son, Rhys, who is one of the leading competitors in the US Formula D drift series, they are some of the most sought-after precision stunt drivers in the world. Constantly in demand for specialist driving roles in big-budget TV commercials and Hollywood blockbusters Rhys and Rod are affectionately known by the nicknames 'Mad Skillz' and 'Mad Skillz Jnr' by US drift fans.

Millen Snr's vast experience in designing and engineering his successful purpose-built Pikes Peak machines has led to the foundation of Millen Works, a company specializing in the creation of anything from one-off operational concept cars and entertainment rides for theme parks to the altogether more serious business of designing and fabricating highly advanced manned and unmanned military vehicles for specialized combat and reconnaissance missions.

Left: A timely reminder for drivers at the unprotected roadside.

For now, though, much of the road is still unpaved, just as it always has been. The distinctive reddish pink gravel is hard-packed and regularly graded to form a surface halfway between a forest track and a Speedway oval. It's free from ruts and surprisingly stable, so even the lowest sports cars should be able to make the ascent without difficulty.

Although it's operated as a toll road, you actually get to drive roughly half-way up what constitutes the PPIHC course before you reach the toll booth itself, at a place called Glen Cove. There's plenty of fun (and frights) to be had before you hand over your ten bucks, with a few longish straights and a whole bunch of tight and twisty hairpins, including Engineers Corner and Brown Bush Corner, before you enter the mouth-parching Blue Sky. A perfectly named multi-apex left-hand bend with nothing but the tips of a few pine trees and a whole lot of fresh air between you and a bumpy ride down to

Colorado Springs, it's one of the most famous parts of the PPIHC course.

To get a sense of the kind of altitude you're dealing with at Pikes Peak it pays to appreciate that the PPIHC startline is just over twice as high as Britain's highest mountain, Ben Nevis. By the time you reach Glen Cove you've climbed another 2,000ft (608m) or so, but from here on in the climb gets more serious, and much steeper. Not long after this halfway point the trees wither, then disappear altogether, leaving you with a stark view and nothing to distract you from the edge of the road, which looks more like the edge of the world.

As you've gathered by now, many of Pikes Peak's 156 corners have been given some pretty lurid names over the last 90-odd years. Ragged Edge is a long, gently curving straight along which the quickest PPIHC racers will be topping 110mph (177kph). Such is the graphic nature of the drop to your right your heart will be pounding at 150bpm at a fraction of that velocity.

It's not just the stomach-churning drops that leave you breathless. At some 2.5 miles (4km) above sea level, the air is thin and vapid, containing just 60 per cent of the oxygen found at more habitable heights. On race days this manifests itself most clearly to the racers in the distinct deterioration in their cars' engine performance as they get closer to the summit. For spectators and, on non-race days, visitors to the summit's souvenir shop, simply walking or climbing requires real effort. Splitting headaches are common, with more severe cases of altitude sickness not unheard of. To avoid feeling unwell make sure you drink plenty of water, and take care not to overexert yourself, but if you do start to feel unwell, it's best to head back down.

With Ragged Edge a distant sweaty-palmed memory your focus shifts to 'The Ws', which are like a super-sized set of alpine switchbacks. On any other road they would be the highlight, but here they're just welcome for the familiarity of some low-speed zigzags and a windscreen filled with terra firma instead of wide blue yonder.

If the Ws calm your nerves, the prospect of what The Devil's Playground has in store will get them jangling once more. According to Pikes Peak legend, the name springs from the region's spectacular and violent electrical storms when lightning can be seen leaping from rock to rock. If you get to Bottomless Pit and wonder how it got its name, pull into the side of the road and have a peep over the low wall on your left. The 2,000ft (608m) plunge to oblivion should provide you with a clear answer.

As you approach the summit, the scenery is so divorced from anything you're likely to have seen before you could almost be driving through a Martian mountain range. Meanwhile, Boulder Park could well be where the gods go to play marbles; such is the gargantuan size of the countless smooth, rounded rocks that lie scattered across the mountainside.

By now the altitude will be playing tricks with your car, with inclines it would race up at sea level now requiring a lower gear and plenty of throttle

thanks to a 40 per cent drop in power. Olympic is the last corner of the course, and it's a real tight one, with a frankly gobsmacking drop to its outside, but as you have to take it slowly, its knee-knocking effects are largely psychological. Besides, any collywobbles you might be feeling are soon washed away with the wave of euphoria you get on reaching the 14,100ft (4,286m) summit.

Short of climbing Everest, it's hard to imagine a greater sense of elevation. Of course, being in America, you can still buy a celebratory coffee and

donuts together with a T-shirt emblazoned with the legend 'Real Men Don't Need Guardrails.'

That may well be the case, but thanks to the Sierra Club the Pikes Peak Highway is getting them anyway. If you want to experience one of the all-time great and largely original mountain roads before the do-gooders desecrate it, get yourself to Colorado.

Above: The Race to the Clouds really is just that – the summit of Pikes Peak is a truly unique place.

REST AND BE THANKFUL

DISTANCE: 1 MILE (1.6KM) **FIRST RACE:** 1949 **LOCATION:** SCOTLAND

Two of the greatest champions in the history of Formula One have driven here. Okay, so Jim Clark and Jackie Stewart weren't Grand Prix gods when they each travelled across Scotland's Western Highlands to compete on the historic Rest and Be Thankful hillclimb course, but it was on this solitary mile of scabby tarmac that they began to refine their skills.

It's been the best part of four decades since any competitive hillclimb event took place here. Looking at the decaying surface – a lumpen patchwork of potholes and moss – you could be forgiven for thinking it's been at least twice that, yet thanks to the scenery, ever-changing weather and the road's intriguing history, this curious place still has soul and atmosphere in abundance.

Dwarfed by the finest mountainclimbs of mainland Europe, Rest and Be Thankful was comfortably the longest and most demanding course in Britain. With its mountainous surroundings, it could also lay legitimate claim to sharing something of the French, Swiss and Austrian giants' spirit, if not their colossal scale.

The road was completed in 1753, but can trace its roots right back to the Scottish rebellion of 1745 and the major road-building initiative that the government instigated in the wake of the rebels' defeat. With the rapid transit of troops and supplies a top priority in the isolated Highlands, Major William Caulfield was given the responsibility of directing the completion of the road network that had been started by his comrade General Wade when sent to Scotland in 1724 by King George I to investigate reports of political unrest. Of the 1,100 miles (1,771km) of road they constructed between

Left: The Rest and be Thankful Mile Hill Climb in 1949.
Right: General Wade's military road marker.

them – including the spectacular Great Glen Road from Fort William to Inverness – Rest and Be Thankful is the best known.

Caulfield had a paltry budget but access to a literal army of men, yet he still preferred to follow the path of least resistance, hugging the valley floor to the last possible moment before hauling the road up the 850ft (258m) elevation to the summit. When completed, a stone inscribed with the words 'Rest and Be Thankful' was placed at the top, dispensing sage advice to those who had just completed the breathless slog. One such hiker was a certain William Wordsworth, who walked the road to the summit of Glen Croe in the autumn of 1831 and was sufficiently inspired to write the poem '"Rest and be Thankful!" At The Head of Glencroe'.

The full extent of this particular military road runs from Dumbarton along the shores of Loch Lomond to Inveraray on the western shores of Loch Fyne (now the A82 and A83), and as such formed a vital link between Glasgow and the Western Highlands. The tiny piece we're interested in is a gated portion, which spurs off the modern A83, nestled into the valley floor of Glen Croe, midway between the heads of Loch Fyne and Loch Long.

Up until World War II, Caulfield's 'old' road was the only road, and his penny-pinching hairpin crescendo was the cause of many an early motorist's nightmares. Indeed, such was its notoriety, that the Royal Scottish Automobile Club (RSAC) used the spot for reliability trials. By the end of the war a new piece of road was built to ease the climb out of Glen Croe, and it's this route that today's A83 takes, cut into the flank of Ben Arthur – also called 'The Cobbler' – running higher but parallel with the original Rest and Be Thankful route.

The new road might have made the great original instantly redundant, but it provided the RSAC with

a golden opportunity to create a new hillclimb venue. No time was wasted and the first event was held in 1949. Despite the less than convenient location for many of the competitors, and its lack of RAC Championship status, the inaugural meeting was well supported, with many of British motorsport's leading lights in attendance.

With the intervention of World War II, racing car development had ceased, which explains why the quickest drivers were still pedalling pre-war Grand Prix machinery. Not that it mattered, for the sight of a bellowing Alfa Romeo 8C and wailing ERA, complete with twin rear wheels for added traction, hammering through a Highland glen was a soul-stirring spectacle so soon after the privations of the war.

The RSAC had spent £2,000 on improving the already crumbling road surface but Rest and Be Thankful was never less than bumpy. In the end it was Raymond Mays – the elder statesman of British motorsport – who posted the fastest time, completing the mile-long (1.6km) sprint in 68sec to set the first hill record.

You'd need nerves of steel and the mechanical sympathy of a joyrider to get close to that time today. To be completely truthful, you'd also require

'You'd need nerves of steel and the mechanical sympathy of a joyrider to get close to that time today'

Above: A 1992 Sylva Phoenix making its way up the climb.
Right: The Rest and Be Thankful hillclimb passing through hilly heathland in Argyll Forest Park.

the permission of Andrew Davidson, who owns the land through which the Rest and Be Thankful runs. Fortunately Davidson is a car nut, and regularly allows car clubs, rallies and historic events to use the road, so it's quite possible you can arrange access so long as you're prepared to pay the toll: a bottle of decent malt whisky.

The decrepit state of the surface and the relentless march of weeds and slippery moss may not be the most inviting combination for spirited driving, but if you look at old images taken at some of the RSAC events you'll see that it's always been pretty flaky. Despite repeated efforts to improve the surface dressing during the Rest's active years, the surface was only ever consistent in its inconsistency, which makes the gradual reduction in the hill record both impressive and genuinely comparable.

It's possible to see the whole of the Rest from the new A83, which provides a fascinating if somewhat deceptive perspective on the course. From up here it looks a cinch, with a modest left-hander and the climbing hairpin at the finish seemingly all there is to it. Once at ground level you'd best check that your bottle is still in your possession, for it looks a whole lot more challenging from behind the wheel of your car.

The start line rises gently but runs reasonably true for a few hundred yards before the ducking and weaving begins. There are series of dips: two modest followed by one sufficiently abrupt dip and crest for the quicker cars' wheels to leave the ground. You would have had to be sure of your line over the yump for the road is never more than a car-and-a-half wide. Dropping a wheel off the crumbling edge at racing speeds really wasn't

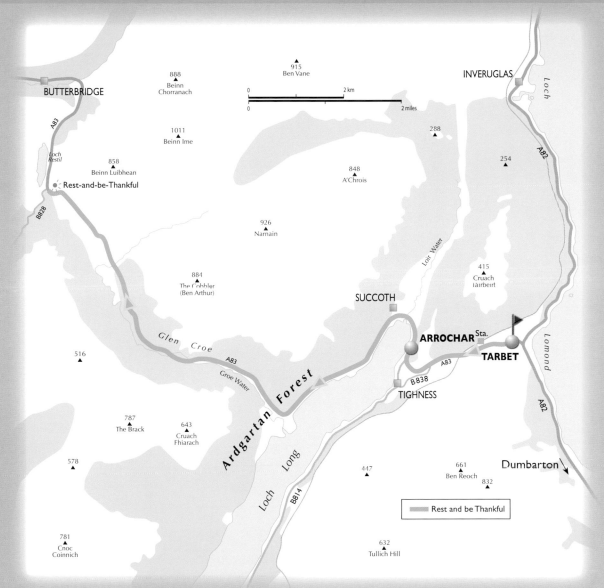

an option, for if the grassy banks didn't trip your car into a roll the hidden rocks would doubtless amputate a wheel or two. That is, of course, if you didn't tumble down the glen towards the white farmhouse…

One of the most exciting sections is the snaking dip across Stone Bridge, which as its name suggests is where the Rest crosses a craggy drop. The angle of your approach means you don't enter the bridge square. Your line is unsighted too, so all you have to aim at is the heft stone parapet. Pictures show cars driting through this daunting left-hander, carried by sheer momentum and a pinch of blind faith, before tweaking right into the next unsighted corner, between a sturdy metal fence on the left and a rocky bank on the right.

This was a crucial section on a timed run, but so too was the tighter left that followed it, complete with a worrisome unfenced drop to the inside. A final straight blast was your reward for clearing the left-hander, allowing you time to decide just how much speed you were going to carry through the left-right-left before you coming steaming into Cobbler, a tighter left-hand turn with the inspiring arc of road rising ahead of you towards the long and awkwardly cambered hairpin and the run to the finish.

Being a hillclimb, the fun didn't stop with the completion of your first run, and with the A83 lay-by forming the top paddock for those with a road-legal car it was but a short blast back down to rejoin the competitors waiting to make their ascent. As veterans of the Rest mischievously testify, that return drive among dawdling holidaymakers could be just as much fun as the hillclimb itself…

By the late 1950s and early 60s the Rest was being tackled by all sorts of wild and wonderful machines. A young Jim Clark was proud to take a class victory in a Porsche 356 supplied by his mentor Archie Scot Moncrieff and his racing team the Border Reivers, while a few years later Jackie Stewart served his apprenticeship in a Marcos sports car.

Left: A 1936 Austin Grasshopper and a 1935 Aston Martin Ulster negotiate their way through the rain across the twisting, crumbling tarmac.

The very quickest cars were the kind of strange hybrids born from the unique demands of hillclimbing. The pre-war Grand Prix cars had long given way to the lighter, smaller and more disposable rear-engined racers, but some still preferred the challenge of big-banger machinery, including a courageous chap called Martin Brain, who thought it quite reasonable to fire himself up the Rest strapped into a 7.2-litre V8 Cooper-Chrysler. Two four-wheel-drive single-seaters were also campaigned, yet both crashed: one after a mechanical failure after the yump, the other skittering through the railings and down the bank at Cobbler. Despite the Rest's unforgiving terrain and frequent spills, no one was killed in more than two decades of competition.

By now the fastest drivers had torn almost 20sec out of Raymond Mays' original hill record in the space of a mile, with the absolute hill record of 50.09sec set by Peter Boshier-Jones in 1964 driving his agile and powerful supercharged Lotus 22.

Despite the growing enthusiasm for the Rest all was not well. The organizers were fighting a constant and expensive battle with the mouldering road surface, and while there were masses of spectators in attendance they were all parked along the A83 for a free and panoramic view of the proceedings. In the end the numbers simply didn't add up and so, reluctantly, the action ceased in 1970.

After all this time there's much fondness for Rest and Be Thankful. The years haven't been kind to it, but this grand old road's unique setting and simple charm made it a firm favourite with the drivers. Their affection is also tinged with a deep respect, for the Rest was undoubtedly the toughest challenge in British hillclimbing. Though it'll cost you a bottle of Scotch to experience it firsthand, the exchange rate is more than fair for you'll get priceless memories in return.

Record
Breaking

The 'Turbinator', driven by Don Vesco, established a new World Land Speed Record for wheel-driven vehicles of 458mph (737kph) on 18 October, 2001. Photo by Ron Christensen.

BONNEVILLE SALT FLATS

DISTANCE: 10 MILES (16KM) **FIRST RACE:** 1912 **LOCATION:** UTAH, USA

It's called 'salt fever': an indiscriminate, highly contagious illness that preys on vulnerable car enthusiasts visiting the Bonneville region of Utah. Speed, and lots of it, is the only known cure.

People have been drawn to the salt for centuries, the earliest recorded journey being those made by the early American settlers, who completed the arduous and potentially life-threatening trek on foot during the 19th century. By 1912 people had ventured out onto the salt in their cars. As it's often said, motor racing was almost certainly born when two cars pulled alongside each other for the very first time, and it's safe to assume that those pioneering drivers hadn't made the trek out to the flats just to admire the view. However, it was the construction of a highway crossing the barren, salt-crusted lakebed in 1925 that cemented Bonneville's connection with the car.

As part of the highway's opening ceremony a young Utahan motorcycle racer by the name of David Abbott Jenkins, or 'Ab' as he was known, was enlisted to drive an automobile along the new road in a race against a train running along the adjacent railway. He rose to the challenge and beat the locomotive by a handful of minutes. No stranger to speed, Ab was seduced by what he saw out on the flats, believing that if properly utilized and promoted, their endless space and hard, level

surface was perfectly suited to setting land speed records. Salt fever had found its first victim.

Seven years later he was back on the salt with a 12-cylinder-engined Pierce-Arrow – an American car company he had become involved with through his racing activities – in which he intended to drive 2,400 miles (3,864km) in 24 hours as a means of demonstrating the car's performance and Bonneville's suitability for speed attempts. Having marked a 10-mile (16km) circular course out on the salt he pulled the wheelarches and windscreen off the Pierce-Arrow, primed his friends with stopwatches, slapped some grease on his face as a primitive form of sunblock, donned his goggles and drove. And drove. And drove.

Stopping every two hours to refuel, Jenkins never stepped out of the car. When he finally did emerge, 24 hours after setting off, he had been rendered temporarily stone deaf by the bellowing engine, but had covered an extraordinary 2,710 miles (4,363km) at an average speed of 112.916mph (181.794kph), and his impromptu effort had almost bagged him a world record.

He returned the following year, this time to set an official endurance speed record in the same car. Shortly after beginning his run, the flats were swept by a violent storm, but as his support crew began to pack anything away that wasn't securely tied down, Ab ploughed on, cutting lap after lap at 125mph

(201kph) or more, eventually setting a new world 24-hour distance record of 127.229mph (204.838kph).

By now his efforts had been noticed by the great British speed merchants John Cobb, Malcolm Campbell and Sir George Eyston, who all came to Bonneville with the express intention of taking records back to Blighty. A consummate sportsman, Jenkins vacated the salt for Cobb's attempt and even played a vital role in Cobb taking a new endurance record when he loaned the Englishman his tools and equipment. It was a pivotal moment in the early history of Bonneville, for Jenkins' selfless actions and magnanimous conduct set the tone for future generations of salt flats drivers, who would go on to take the land speed record to more than 600mph (966kph), before the limitations of Bonneville's salt prevented higher speeds from being attained and the LSR attempts moved to the Black Rock desert in neighbouring Nevada.

Assisting Cobb in his record-breaking efforts was by no means Ab's last moment of Bonneville glory. In fact he'd be back countless times in a succession of incredible cars which he called the Mormon Meteor. His finest hour, or rather 24 hours, came in

Below: The salt flats can be a lonely place. **Right:** The JCB Dieselmax land speed record attempt in 2006. The car set a new record for a diesel-powered vehicle of 350.092mph (563.648kph)

'the distance somehow makes the scene all the more spectacular as the very fastest cars skim through your field of view like a slapped ice hockey puck'

1940, when, together with his relief driver, Cliff Bergere, he set an astonishing new record of 161.180mph (259.499kph), in the mammoth aero-engined Mormon Meteor III. It was just one of 21 records Jenkins and the car broke that year. More incredible still is that it would take half a century of car development and a team of no less than eight drivers before Ab's 24-hour record would fall.

By the late 1930s the movement had become big enough to need some serious organization, and in 1938 the South California Timing Association was founded as a means of unifying the many clubs that gathered on the flats, and also to give the speed-chasing sport a much-needed sanctioning body. Seventy years later the SCTA remains in control, managing events at both Bonneville and El Mirage dry lake, just 100 miles (160km) to the east of Los Angeles (see page 212), with the same authoritative but welcoming manner it always has.

The salt flats themselves are one of the natural wonders of the world, covering 159sq miles (412sq km) of northwestern Utah, close to the casino town of Wendover, which lies just across the state line in Nevada. It's the largest of the numerous salt flats to be found west of the Great Salt Lake, which gives its name to the capital of Utah (Salt Lake City) and currently covers around 1,700sq miles (4,403sq km). In turn, the Great Salt Lake is the largest remnant of the prehistoric Lake Bonneville, which was formed 32,000 years ago and covered more than 19,691sq miles (51,000sq km), which in European terms is an area approximately the size of Belgium.

Apologies for the condensed geology lesson, but until you know how the salt flats were formed, and the huge areas they cover, you simply can't hope to appreciate the vastness of this dazzling sodium desert.

Now classified as public land, the flats are overseen by the Bureau of Land Management. Every summer, once the salt has dried, the Utah State Highway Department mark out the courses that comprise the

Left: The Honda F1 Team sets a new land speed record for a Formula 1 car by narrowly beating the 400kph mark (248.6mph) in July 2006.

so-called Bonneville Speedway: a 10-mile (16km) straight for the very fastest vehicle classes, a shorter 5-mile straight (8km) for the cars capable of around 200mph (322kph) or less and an oval or circular track that can be anything between 10 and 12 miles (16–19km) in circumference (depending on the condition of the salt) for any budding 'Sons of the Salt' to follow in Ab Jenkins' wheeltracks.

Just 88 miles (142km) west of Salt Lake City on the Interstate 80, the salt flats are easy to find, as you'd expect of a vast, level expanse of pure white. The nearest town to the flats is Wendover, which started life as an isolated petrol station in the 1920s when that first road was constructed. Aside from its proximity to Bonneville, Wendover's other claim to fame is that the Boeing B-29 bomber *Enola Gay* took off from here to drop an atom bomb on Hiroshima. Now its main role in life is to provide travellers with an oasis of moral turpitude on the Nevada side of the state border with the God-fearing Mormon state of Utah.

If you're not there for the girls and the gambling then you can only be there for the salt, in which case you're more than likely to bump into a recovering victim of salt fever to show you the way to the Speedway. If you don't, there's no need to worry: just drive through back through town in the direction of Utah, where you'll soon spot signs for the Bonneville Speedway. After a few miles you'll see the entrance to the self proclaimed 'Fastest Place on Earth'.

If your trip coincides with the main Speed Week meeting in August or the World of Speed meeting in September you'll be met either by someone from the SCTA or the Utah Salt Flats Racing Association, who will relieve you of some dollars and direct you along a graded 'road' in the salt to the parking and spectating areas.

Driving on these salt approach roads is a peculiar sensation for the blinding whiteness and lack of landmarks make it almost impossible to get any perception of distance or motion. It can also be more of a challenge than you might expect, for although the surface is normally firm and crusty, when there's been rain it can become soft and

gloopy. Either way it makes a mess of your car, which explains why most if not all car rental companies for miles around specifically forbid driving on the salt flats. It also explains why there's such a long queue for the carwash in Wendover at the end of the day.

If the flats aren't being used for speed runs then you've pretty much got them to yourself. Be careful, for such is the salt's popularity with film crews shooting car adverts and Hollywood blockbusters you're unlikely to be the only one out there, but you just might not see them until it's too late. The surface is also surprisingly slippery, proffering

Above: The sign welcoming you to the Bonneville Salt Flats International Speedway. **Right:** The stark expanse of the salt flats at dawn.

around half the grip and traction of tarmac, but the sense of space and silence remains almost incomprehensible. An immense pan of pure white, surrounded by ragged mountain ranges silhouetted against a cobalt sky, the view is so pristine and uninterrupted you can actually see the curvature of the Earth. The curve and the shimmering heat create the illusion that the surrounding mountains are floating above the surface of the salt. To feel so small and isolated is a humbling and inspirational experience.

But then so too is seeing some of the quickest vehicles in the world come streaking across the salt. The SCTA is an organization run by volunteers from the numerous racing and hot rod clubs who come to Bonneville and El Mirage. It's an approach that helps ensure Bonneville isn't like other forms of motorsport, where big budgets and rampant commercialism rule. Dedication and innovation are what counts out on the salt, and whether you're a sun-baked veteran or sunblocked newbie, you'll be just as welcome and equally enthralled.

With myriad classes that encompass everything from the more conventional looking road cars and bikes through classic hot rods, streamliners and lakesters (dragsters built to run on the dry lakes), to awe-inspiring jet, turbine and rocket-powered cars and motorbikes, Bonneville is one of the last bastions of the intrepid weekend warrior breed.

ART ARFONS – JUNKYARD GOD

Bonneville's vibrant history is peppered with colourful characters, but none are more memorable than Art Arfons.

Born in 1926 in Akron, Ohio, Art Arfons was a man with a genius for turning what other people would regard as scrap into blindingly fast machines. He was once described as the 'junkyard genius of the jet set', thanks to his remarkable series of 'Green Monster' dragster and land speed record cars, which he built around ex-military jet engines. The unusual name for these invariably ugly cars

came from the fact that he and his brother, Walt, painted their first creation with some green paint left over from painting a tractor. The hue became something of a trademark and the name stuck.

The holder of three world land speed records, Arfons also held the record for the world's fastest car crash, when his Green Monster lost a wheel at 600mph (965kph) and flipped, rolled and tumbled down the salt for more than a mile before finally coming to rest. The car was a tangled mess of metal, but Arfons emerged unscathed.

In 1967 Arfons decided he would attempt the world water speed record, but rather than build a bespoke craft, he decided to adapt one of his earlier Green Monsters, the so-called 'Cyclops', by attaching a pair of sponsons. As if this wasn't hair-brained enough, Arfons also fitted a pair of wheels, which protruded a few inches from the bottom of each sponson, the theory being that he would be able to 'drive' along the surface of the water once he had exceeded 150mph (240kph). His continued survival is testament to his decision not to go for the record.

One of the best places to view the action is at the 5-mile (8km) stage on the long course, for it's here you'll see each car as it passes through the all-important measured mile, filling the white and blue void with its straining, almost mournful engine note and a tight comet-tail of salt. You're a quarter of a mile away from the action, yet the distance somehow makes the scene all the more spectacular as the very fastest cars skim through your field of view like a slapped ice hockey puck, devouring the salt at 400mph (644kph) or more.

In fact, the only place better than watching from the 5-mile marker is from the driving seat of a purpose-built Bonneville racer. It's a rare and privileged position, but there's many a spectator who came thinking they'd never drive the salt for real, only to return years later with a car they've spent all their spare time and cash building. Beware: salt fever is bad for your wealth.

And when you do get out there on the long course, what will you see? Salt, obviously: scuffed and rutted in the push-start area where the quickest cars and bikes are shoved up to speed by their support crews' pickup truck. Then you'll pick up a thick black line, which marks the centre of the long course lane. Short swirls of polished

Above: Sunrise on the salt flats.

salt glint in the sunshine, highlighting the point where impatient drivers applied a fraction too much power a fraction too soon and spun-up their car's rear wheels. As your speed builds the surface begins to feel smoother, then, as the orange marker cones flash past with increasing pace the run takes on an edge of urgency. Huge forces start to pummel the car; the bumps feel more severe, pulverized salt hammers into the wheelarches and your heart pounds as the white surface speeds beneath you. And all the while those distant mountains remain nailed to the horizon, the seemingly infinite space sucking away the impression of speed.

As your run reaches its crescendo and you reach the end of the measured mile, you immediately begin the process of steadily slowing down. Ease off the power, let the car settle, dip the clutch then throw your parachute and feel your harness straps squeeze into your shoulders as the slipstream grabs the billowing canopy. As the speed bleeds away, you can kill the engine and gently turn off the marked lane, exhaling as you finally come to a halt. Deafened by the silence and tingling with adrenaline you wait for your crew to tow you back to the pits and prepare the car for another run. Faster than the last, of course.

Left: Spectator vehicles as they would have appeared in 1962. This was re-created for a scene in the 2005 film *The World's Fastest Indian*.

FRANKFURT–DARMSTADT AUTOBAHN

DISTANCE: 9.7 MILES (15.6KM) **FIRST RACE:** 1937 **LOCATION:** GERMANY

Thanks to the autobahn, Germany is one of the world's last strongholds of speed. Every day these derestricted stretches of motorway enable ordinary Germans to drive as fast as they feel appropriate for the car they're driving and the prevailing weather conditions. After enjoying this unique personal freedom for more than 70 years, such rapid progress isn't just a German driver's privilege, it's a birthright.

As a result, though they are coming under increasing environmental and political pressure, the limit-free autobahn remains an integral part of German life. For many it's a highly emotive issue, as revealed by German Transport Minister, Wolfgang Tiefensee, when speaking to the *Financial Times Deutschland*: 'Derestricted driving on the autobahn is to the Germans what pesto is to the Italians and the baguette is to the French. No one in Italy or France would dare to try and ban the cultural characteristics of their country.'

But then the autobahns have never been strangers to politics. The brainchild of Adolf Hitler's Nazi government, when they were constructed they made a dual statement of intent: in the corridors of power they were regarded as the conduits to mobilize an army, while in public they were a network of roads to be used by German citizens in their Volkswagens, or people's cars. Either way, they were pivotal in the plan to demonstrate Germany's increasing industrial, financial and engineering power.

As, of course, were the Silver Arrows: a succession of ever-faster and more spectacular racing cars built by Mercedes-Benz and Auto Union. As you've no doubt read in many of the other classic motorsport routes contained within this book, the impact these fabulous silver cars had on pre-war motorsport is something that will never be repeated. Utterly dominant from 1934 until the outbreak of World War II in 1939, the Silver Arrows were seemingly able to crush the opposition in whichever discipline they chose, be it Grand Prix racing, mountainclimbing or, as we're about to discover, land speed record breaking.

One of the first autobahn stretches to be completed ran between Frankfurt and Darmstadt. Given the somewhat sinister name Reichsautobahn (imperial motorway), it was a pair of two-lane concrete carriageways that cut a stark swathe through the surrounding pine forests. As the battle between Mercedes and Auto Union (fuelled by Hitler's government subsidy of 250,000 Reichmarks for each team) intensified, this section of autobahn would witness scenes of unparalleled triumph and, ultimately, bitter tragedy.

Not content with the two German teams essentially fighting among themselves for Grand Prix wins, the governing body of German motorsport, the Oberste Nationale Sportbehörde für die Deutsche Kraftfahrt (mercifully abbreviated to the ONS), actively encouraged the two teams' rivalry to extend to the autobahnen, where they could break speed records for the glory of the Reich.

To this end the head of the ONS, Korpsführer Adolf Hühnlein, initiated Rekordwoche (Record Week) on the Reichsautobahn in the autumn of 1937. Just a few weeks before the Berlin Motor Show, the purpose of Record Week was clearly for one of the teams to generate a headline-grabbing achievement that could be announced to the world at the show.

In many ways Rekordwoche was the zenith of the German teams' obsession with setting extraordinary speeds on public roads. Both Mercedes and Auto Union had been setting world records for various time and distance classes since 1934, from the shorter Standing Mile to sustained One Hour and 100 Miles average speed disciplines. As each team pushed its engineers to create increasingly specialized machines, and the drivers – the same crack wheelmen who drove for the teams in Grand Prix racing – dug deeper and took greater and more frequent risks, the speeds increased dramatically. Hühnlein was happy, but, in private at least, the drivers were becoming concerned.

By 1937 both teams had streamlined cars that were exceeding 240mph (386kph) in race trim, and with Auto Union's new star – Bernd Rosemeyer – pestering the team to be given the chance to go for some records, the Reichsautobahn was pressed into use in June, a full four months before the proposed Rekordwoche. Rosemeyer made the most of the opportunity, setting one world record and six class records in one morning. In the process of setting them – the fastest being his Flying Mile record of 242.09mph (389.76kph), the most incredible his 10 Mile world record of 223.89mph (360.46kph) – he had cheated death several times, when gusts of wind blew his Auto Union onto the grass dividing strip between the north- and southbound carriageways.

As an 'official' event, both Mercedes and Auto Union were required to participate in Rekordwoche. In truth neither would have dreamed of missing it, as both were desperate to be the first to reach the magic 400kph/250mph mark. To do so, both came equipped with astonishing machines: Mercedes with an all-enclosed 5.6-litre V12-engined car, Auto Union with an equally slippery-bodied 6.3-litre V16-engined brute.

Rosemeyer and Auto Union took first blood with a 252mph (406kph) run, then proceeded to take a fistful of records throughout the week. By contrast

Right: The Frankfurt–Darmstadt autobahn in 1935.

'The pressure was on Auto Union, and in the team's haste to reclaim their record, fatal errors of judgement were made'

Mercedes had a dismal time; their number one driver, Caracciola, refused to continue driving the streamlined Benz after it almost took off at close to 250mph (403kph). His colleague, Herman Lang, was pressed to drive the car and experienced the same hair-raising trait. Mercedes cut their losses and went back to Stuttgart.

Had there been less pride at stake, it's conceivable that Rekordwoche would have been the end of it, but Mercedes weren't done with the autobahn. Using a contact that was in Hitler's inner circle, Mercedes asked for the chance to make another attempt on the records. Permission was granted and the Reichsautobahn was once again closed to public traffic.

This time it was Mercedes that got off to the better start. Having worked tirelessly over the winter, the team had built a vastly improved car and Caracciola was clearly revelling it its new-found stability. His first run yielded a speed of 268mph (431kph) and with subsequent runs he quickly exceeded Rosemeyer's record, reaching a peak speed of 271mph (436kph). The pressure was on Auto Union, and in the team's haste to reclaim their record, fatal errors of judgement were made.

The speeds were so high that weather and, more specifically, wind conditions, were critical factors. Mercedes had made their attempts early, in the relative calm of early morning, but even so

Caracciola had encountered some destabilizing crosswinds at the fastest section of the autobahn. By the time Auto Union were ready, the conditions had deteriorated, but although the team advised Rosemeyer to wait until the following day, he insisted on commencing his runs. The first passed without incident, apart from Rosemeyer complaining that the engine had struggled to reach its optimum temperature in the chill January air. Alterations were made to the radiator intake before he set off once more. He was never to return.

Many theories have been voiced as to why Rosemeyer crashed, but the most plausible is that he was caught by a freak gust of wind while travelling at 270mph (435kph). Blown onto the grass in the centre of the autobahn he used his exceptional reactions to correct the slide, but in rejoining the carriageway he somehow over-corrected, which destabilized the car once more and sent it hurtling up the wooded embankment close to the Langen-Morfelden bridge.

In the resulting crash the car was almost completely destroyed, while the hapless Rosemeyer was thrown clear, eventually being found slumped among some trees, unmarked and looking for all the world as though he was sleeping. Those first on the scene detected a faint heartbeat, but he died a few hours later. The ONS immediately declared the Reichsautobahn unsafe for record attempts, and while the national obsession with speed would continue until the war, Rosemeyer's death had deprived Germany of a much-loved hero.

Evidence of the enduring affection for Rosemeyer can be found in a lay-by alongside the southbound carriageway of the A5 autobahn, heading towards Darmstadt. Sheltered amongst the trees it marks the spot where poor Bernd was found, barely alive after his terrible crash. Fresh flowers are still placed at the site by those unwilling to forget his sacrifice.

It's a moving and inspiring place, for just a few yards to the left is the autobahn itself. Still resolutely without a speed limit, the spirit of this road remains unchanged, even if its size and appearance would be almost unrecognizable to Rosemeyer and Caracciola. Now divided by Armco

Right: A Porsche Carrera GT enters the derestricted zone on the autobahn

Left: Looking back over the rear of the Porsche Carrera GT as it powers down the autobahn.

and spreading across four lanes in each direction instead of two, the A5 is one of Germany's busiest roads, with a constant stream of lumbering trucks. Consequently congestion applies its own speed limit along here for most of the day.

That's not to say it isn't possible to enjoy big speeds, you just have to bide your time, as Rudi and Bernd did during Rekordwoche. Dawn is the best chance of finding a clear run between junctions 23 and 25, which is the stretch where records were chased seven decades ago. Handily there's a service area positioned roughly halfway between them, which provides a scruffy but reliable source of high-octane petrol and caffeine-based fluids.

As you edge out onto the autobahn it feels strangely intimidating knowing that you can drive as fast as your car, or nerve, will allow. It's not that you feel pressure exactly, but being let off the leash on a public road brings a unique tingle in the pit of your stomach.

How much fun you have depends largely on how fast a car you have, but it pays to make a few dry runs if you can, just to see what lies in store. What does is pretty sobering, for instead of being the arrow-straight road of your imagination, the A5 actually kinks just enough to obscure your view through the whole corner before opening out onto a reasonable but far from endless straight. With converging junctions and that service station feeding yet more variables into what might pull onto the road, you'll be glad you set your alarm so early, for once the morning rush hour begins you've got no chance of paying your respects to Rosemeyer in the most appropriate manner.

However, if the gods are smiling it's still possible to feel something of what those intrepid Silver Arrow pilots felt as you attempt to wring every last mile-per-hour from your car, just as they did. Don't get too carried away, though, for even if you get yourself a 252mph (406kph) Bugatti Veyron and pin its throttle to the stop you'll still have to keep your eyes on your mirrors, scanning the road behind you for the fast-approaching ghosts of this haunting and historic road.

EL MIRAGE
MOJAVE DESERT

DISTANCE: 6 MILES (9.7KM) **FIRST RACE:** 1946 **LOCATION:** CALIFORNIA, USA

Are you a 'Gear Grinder' or a 'Sidewinder', a 'Rod Rider' or a 'Road Runner'? It's something you need to give serious consideration to if you're going to visit El Mirage, for this parched dry lakebed in the middle of the Mojave Desert is where rival groups of speed junkies have been coming to get their fix – and settle a few friendly scores – for more than half a century.

Back in the 1920s and 30s the mildly anarchic youth of the day discovered that they could modify their cars to extract more speed. To test their work and to blow off some steam, they would race each other on the streets. It was a dangerous and antisocial pastime, and the authorities soon began to clamp down. The hot-rodders needed to find a better venue if they were to stay out of trouble.

Thanks to its proliferation of large, flat and isolated dry lakebeds and its convenient location just 100 miles (160km) from the sprawling city of Los Angeles, the high desert of the Mojave came to their rescue. At first the rival groups' rodders took their 'hopped-up' racers to the Muroc Dry Lake to hold their fledgling speed trials. However, when America's war effort increased they were displaced once more, as Muroc became part of the rapidly expanding Edwards Air Force Base, where an altogether greater quest for speed had begun.

Designated as the Air Force Flight Test Centre, Edwards became home to both the United States Air Force Test Pilot School and NASA's Dryden Flight Research Centre. It was at Edwards that the race to develop world-leading aerospace technology began in 1946 with the legendary X-plane programme. The following year, Chuck Yeager flew the bright orange Bell X-1 through the sound barrier, and by 1967 the X-15 had set an all-time manned flight record of mach 6.7. Indeed, 'The Right Stuff' can still be found at Edwards to this day.

With Muroc out of bounds, hot-rodders looked for another alternative and found one, in the shape of the 6-mile long (9.7km) El Mirage Dry Lake. It was less suited to high-speed driving than Muroc, being smaller, more dusty and peppered with hillocks, but the rodders were used to improvising – it was how they built their cars after all – and so they adopted a slightly curving course to avoid the natural hazards.

Before the unifying influence of the South California Timing Association, safety and organization weren't high on the list of the essentially underground hot-rodding community's priorities. Avoidable accidents happened. Under the SCTA's steadying influence, safety was improved, a structure evolved, classes were established and records were set. With officially verified benchmarks to aim at, the racing scene at El Mirage flourished, and people have been breaking records there – both official and personal – ever since.

Like Bonneville, El Mirage is controlled by the Bureau of Land Management, which does an excellent job in providing and maintaining the Off-Highway Vehicle Recreation Area. Well signed and with good access from main roads, the El Mirage OHV Area lies west of Adelanto between US Highway 395 and the Los Angeles County line. The most common entry route is via Highway 395, from which you need to follow signs for the town of El Mirage. The perimeter of the lake is fenced to control the points of access, so you'll need to follow Mountain View Road, which will take you to the official OHV Area.

The lakebed itself is a flat playa formed by silt and clay deposited in the undrained basin during periods of heavy rainfall. With nowhere to flow, the water is evaporated by the searing desert sun, gradually exposing the mud and baking it into a

hard, flat, bone-dry pan. Though extremely dusty, the surface is smooth and durable. Being desert, the temperature is subject to massive fluctuations: in summer daytime highs can reach 120°F (49°C), while the nights can be chilly. In winter temperatures can fall to just 5°F (–15°C), although during the day temperatures can still be as warm as a good English summer!

Most of the region's rainfall occurs during the winter, but you should always be watchful of summer thunderstorms, which strike rapidly and with spectacular force. If there's been recent rainfall, the Bureau of Land Management is likely to close the OHV Area to prevent the lakebed from becoming rutted, but notices will be posted at the Mountain View entrance. If you're planning a trip, it's always worth calling the dedicated phone line (760/388-4411) beforehand for a recorded announcement on weather conditions and other information that may affect the OHV Area.

Once you get to El Mirage you have 24,000 acres (9,700ha) to explore. There's no speed limit out on the open lakebed, but you are responsible for your own safety and culpable for your actions. It's bizarre and sobering to think that whatever you arrive in, be it a Hertz-hired Mustang or a Bugatti Veyron, you could point it at the horizon and drive it as fast as it's ever going to go. While the atmosphere remains resolutely relaxed, the California Highway Patrol, San Bernadino County Sheriff and BLM Rangers regularly patrol the OHV Area. Don't worry: they're not there to stop you having fun, simply to ensure everyone is respecting each other's safety and the desolate beauty of El Mirage.

Part of El Mirage's charm as a speed trials venue is that it has remained low-key and true to it roots, although this is largely due to its restricted size

Below left: A Ford Mustang Cobra crosses the Mojave desert.
Above left and right: El Mirage remains a mecca for hot rodders.

relative to the vast expanse of Bonneville rather than any conscious decision on the part of the SCTA. In its heyday Bonneville could accommodate a strip of 10 miles (16km) or more, whereas El Mirage musters less than half that. Consequently, while speeds continued to rise on the salt flats – reaching a peak of 617.602mph (994.339kph), when Gary Gabelich broke the LSR at Bonneville in his rocket-powered car, The Blue Flame – El Mirage has remained a club venue, where ordinary people can chase their extraordinary dreams.

The most successful of these is a man by the name of Alex Xydias. After being discharged from the United States Army Air Corps (where he served as an engineer on B-17 bombers during World War II) Los Angelino Xydias (a 'Wheeler', in case you're wondering) founded the SO-CAL Speed Shop in 1946. One of the first hot rod shops in Southern California, and therefore the world, his Burbank premises soon became a place where like-minded hot-rodders would meet.

The cars built by SO-CAL were formidable machines, setting records almost immediately, and eventually becoming the first hot rods to breach 160, 170, 180 and 190mph (258, 274, 290 and 306kph). The first car Xydias built was designed around a teardrop-shaped 315-gallon (1,432-litre) drop tank from a World War II P-38 Lightning fighter plane. Powered by a 1939 Ford V8 engine and using an adapted Model T Ford chassis, as was typical of 1940s hot rods, the SO-CAL Lakester made an immediate impression at El Mirage, scoring a class record speed of 130.155mph (209.549kph) in the summer of 1948.

It was a tight fit in there for Xydias. Crammed into the nose section of the drop tank, the bellowing V8 engine was mounted amidships, just behind his shoulders. The fuel tank and rear axle were located behind that, in the tank's tail. With an adapted Perspex aircraft canopy in place above his head, the noise, heat and fumes must have been

'With an adapted Perspex aircraft canopy in place above his head, the noise, heat and fumes must have been almost unbearable'

almost unbearable, but by all accounts Xydias thought driving the Lakester was a blast: a human pea in a very fast aluminium pod.

Over the winter of that same year, Xydias removed the belly tank bodywork and commissioned Dean Batchelor to redesign the chassis, which was then clothed in a larger streamlined body built by a local metal shop. Using the same engine as the Lakester, the new Streamliner set a two-way average speed of 156.39mph (251.79kph) at Bonneville, which increased to almost 190mph (306kph) when they decided to fit a bigger and more powerful V8. The following year, still swapping between engines, they set new class records yet again, this time exceeding 200mph (322kph) for the first time.

In 1951 the Streamliner crashed at Daytona Beach. The car was a wreck: those components that survived were sold to other hot-rodders, what was left went to the scrap dealer for $4. While the experience was enough for Batchelor to quit racing, Xydias wanted to continue and teamed up with Dave DeLangton, who had just built more advanced Belly Tank racer...

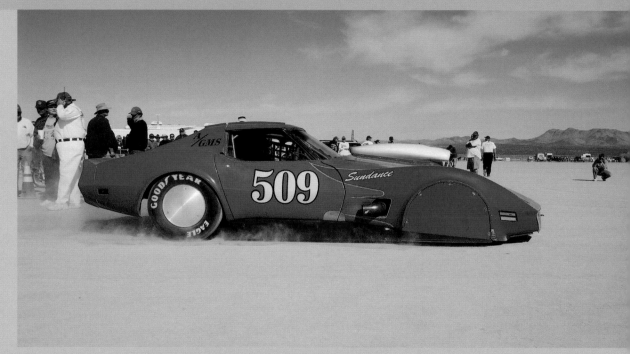

The SO-CAL legend continued, both at El Mirage and Bonneville until 1961, when Xydias closed the shop to take up a role within the Petersen Publishing group, working on a succession of hot rod magazines before founding the forerunner of the world-leading SEMA auto show for specialist tuners. In 1997 the SO-CAL name was revived by another hot rod legend, Pete Chapouris, who had won international plaudits for completing a sensational restoration of... Xydias' old SO-CAL Belly Tank Lakester.

So-Cal are just one of many hot-rod shops who continue to race at El Mirage. The SCTA hold five one-day races per year, in May, June, July, September and October, with a longer two-day meeting in November. Each race day starts early with a drivers' briefing, which is held out on the open lake in the bright morning sun. Then the marshals and start area officials discuss the day's plan before the assembled drivers, crews and officials gather to sing the national anthem. Then the racing starts, and continues for as long as the lake surface, weather and, ultimately, daylight allows.

Above and right: El Mirage still has the feel of a club venue for the amateur – the variety of customized hotrods that turn up to compete is huge.

Out on the lakebed the action's just the same as it's always been. In fact many of the cars and even some of the drivers are the same, too. Hot rods handed down from father to son to grandson aren't uncommon. Those not lucky enough to inherit a rod, lakester or streamliner simply do what their dads did and build a rod of their own, with a little help from their genetic inheritance.

Either way, as you pass through the gates off Mountain View Drive you're entering a world almost untouched by time: a place where life gets no better than squinting against the dazzling glare, straining to be the first to make out the brightly coloured speck that's hustling over the horizon and being chased by the intensifying holler of a race-tuned V8. If you love hot rods, El Mirage isn't just a dry lake in the middle of the Mojave Desert, it's the cradle of civilization.

SILVER STATE CLASSIC

DISTANCE: 90 MILES (145KM) FIRST RACE: 1988 LOCATION: NEVADA, USA

It sounds like something from one of those 'When Drivers Go Bad!' television shows: two middle-aged guys in an ex-NASCAR racer go screaming through the high desert of Nevada. Running flat out at speeds well in excess of 200mph (322kph) they drive for 90 miles (145km) towards Las Vegas, eventually stopping when they reach the town of Hiko, where the road is blocked.

When they eventually emerge – sweaty but laughing – from their car, what do you think they face? The barrel of a police-issue Colt 45? Death row? Life imprisonment? Actually no, none of the above. In a country with some of the most vigilant highway patrols in the world, far from losing their driving licences and liberty, these two desperados get a trophy, a slap on the back and a place in the *Guinness Book of World Records* as the new holders of the Public Highway Land Speed Record. No, this isn't a joke: it's the Silver State Classic Open Road Challenge Series.

Despite all the evidence shouting to the contrary, the Silver State Classic is a legal and officially sanctioned open road time trial. Run since 1988, it now attracts more than 200 competitors from all over the world, and boasts a diverse field of cars spanning everything from factory standard family saloons to retired NASCARs and other equally fearsome racetrack refugees.

If you've ever driven through Nevada you'll be intimately familiar with what it means to be frustrated. The main highways are incredible, rolling endlessly ahead of you like a tarmac treadmill. Driving at legal speeds, even a little above, you feel like you've been nailed to the spot, the widescreen scenery resolutely refusing to move as you crawl along seemingly at walking pace, but what is in reality 70mph (113kph). With such enormous distances to cover and little in the way of natural obstacles, the straights extend into the shimmering horizon, while most of the corners are really just the gentlest of curves and require minimal steering input to negotiate. Ten minutes of this torment and you're grinding your teeth in desperation, while the voice in your head begs for suspension of the speed limit.

Thanks to Silver State Classic Challenge Inc. that's exactly what's on offer, twice a year in May and September. With the full support and co-operation of the State of Nevada and the Nevada Highway Patrol, some 90 miles (145km) of Route 318 is closed to the public. Passing through White Pine, Nye and Lincoln Counties on its way south, the Silver State Classic route starts in the town of Lund, near Ely in northern Nevada, before heading almost directly south to Hiko.

While nothing but a miserable exercise in self-control when driven at the prescribed speed limits, for two days a year Route 318 is transformed into the fastest competitive closed road stage in the world. Picture yourself driving in the Unlimited class and just reading through the course notes is enough to send a shiver down your spine. From the start line you accelerate for half a mile before encountering a gentle left-hand bend. Unless you're in a really quick car you're unlikely to need to brake, and as the bend opens out a 3-mile (5km) straight lies before you. Four miles (6.5km) in and you encounter an uphill right-handed sweeper, which carries you onto a massive 7-mile (11km) straight.

The 7-miler is just a warm-up. Before reaching the more technical section of the course, which begins 58 miles (93km) in and peaks with a treacherous 3-mile (5km) canyon stretch called 'The

Left: A competitor in the Silver State Classic flashes past the timer.
Right: The interior of the Nissan 350Z driven by the owner of *Option*, a Japanese car magazine.

216

'Blow-outs are quite common, and almost always result in crashes of aircraft proportions'

Narrows', there are 14-mile, 5-mile and 11-mile (23, 8 and 18km) straights to dispatch. After The Narrows there are just a few more gradual bends and a couple of 4-mile (6.5km) straights to the finish. The quickest cars in the Unlimited Class will complete the 90 mile (145km) course in a little over 25 minutes. Our friends – Chuck Shafer and Gary Bockman – in the NASCAR are the current record holders, having averaged 207.78mph (334.32kph) for the duration of the course. But even they couldn't eclipse Silver States' instantaneous-trap-speed record of 227mph (365kph), set by pizzeria owner Rick Doria in an ex-IMSA racing Corvette. Wonder if he delivers…?

Despite cars being released singly at 2-minute intervals, running at these sorts of speeds for sustained periods of time makes the Silver State is a high-risk sport. Tyres are the major weakness and the biggest source of potential disaster. Blow-outs are quite common, and almost always result in crashes of aircraft proportions. Rick Doria built his record-setting Corvette around the 630bhp Chevy V8 he salvaged from the pulverized remains of his last Silver State car, which was destroyed during the 1999 event when it blew a tyre at 190mph (306kph). When you consider that at that speed, each of his Corvette's tyres would have been

completing a mind-blowing 45 rotations per second it's no wonder they let go from time to time.

Of course not everyone drives such ballistic beasts. In fact, of the 230 or so cars that take part in each event, the awesome Unlimiteds make up less than 5 per cent of the entry. The rest are divided into classes according the speed you decide you or your car is capable of averaging. Starting at 95mph (153kph), these classes go up in 5mph (8kph) increments all the way to 180mph (290kph). Any faster and you're in with the NASCARS guys and Doria's Pizza Express.

Most crews compete in the classes between 95mph (153kph) and 150mph (241kph) in standard or near-standard cars. Completely standard cars with no additional safety equipment can run in anything up to the 110mph (177kph) Touring class, which makes the Silver State Classic one of the most accessible forms of motorsport you can do. If you want to go faster the general rule of thumb is that as speeds increase the more safety equipment your car will need to be fitted with.

Unlike the Unlimited cars, which simply attack the course with the intention of completing it as quickly as possible, to win a prize in the lower classes you need to cross the finish line at the precise second dictated by the target time for your class. This is calculated by dividing the 90 mile (145km) course distance by the class speed. For example, if you're competing in the 100mph (160kph) class then your target time is 54min dead, while the 110mph (177kph) class should take 49.0909min. It may not sound as gung-ho as the Unlimited category, but it's a far from simple challenge. For starters, you'll need a diligent co-driver with nerves of steel and a keen eye for landmarks, for most crews chart their progress using a 'Flight Plan', checking their time through the course against as many as 40 pre-determined waypoints. These are most often roadside mile markers, but can be anything really, so long as you're sure you'll be able to pick it out at high speed!

Right: The American-built SSC Aero: 1183 bhp, and designed to be capable of over 270mph (435kph)

Map

Silver State Classic

- 50
- McGILL
- ELY
- Schnell Creek Range
- 6
- 50
- 3503 Duckwater Pt.
- LUND
- Great Basin N.P.
- CURRANT
- Railroad Valley
- 318
- 3434 Troy Peak
- 93
- 2982 Indian Pt.
- WARM SPRINGS
- PIOCHE
- 2864 Highland Pk
- MODENA
- HIKO
- 56
- RACHEL
- CALIENTE
- 2048 Panaca Summit
- BERYL JCT.
- 1704 Hancock Summit
- Las Vegas
- 2859 Bald Mtn.
- ALAMO
- ELGIN

Left: A Japanese-tuned Nissan 350Z waits its turn. **Above left:** En route in a Dodge Magnum. **Above right:** A Ford Mustang prepares to take the start.

It's a proven method, but one that requires a pre-Silver State recce, as you need to be precise with your trip readings. The exercise is made doubly tricky because even if you're in the slowest class you won't be able to complete a practice run at representative speeds. Anyone who tries, and is caught doing so within a month of the Silver State Classic itself, is automatically banned from the event.

Since the first event in 1988, the Silver State organizers have initiated a number of measures to increase safety and ensure that the drivers are as well prepared as they can be for the unique demands of the event. If you're a Silver State rookie, you first select the speed at which you want to run and then you are required to attend a driver-training session at the Las Vegas Motor Speedway. Held on the Thursday before the event itself, you drive on the Speedway's infield course while being assessed by a professional race instructor to ensure you are capable of driving at the speed you've entered. Your car will also be subjected to a technical inspection to make sure it's safe for the Silver State.

While the build-up is a serious business, there's also plenty of time for fun and relaxation. Once each driver has registered the entire field embarks on a 240-mile (386km) drive from Las Vegas to Ely – the official home of the event – where everyone attends a cocktail party held in their honour. The excitement and adrenaline starts to ramp up on Friday with the opportunity to take part in the Silver State Speed-Stop Challenge, which is a kind of 0–100–0 competition to test the acceleration and braking capabilities of your car. In the evening all the cars drive through Ely in a Silver State Parade. The partying continues on Saturday with a car show and BBQ before Silver State competitors have the option of taking part in the High Noon Shootout, which is held on closed half-mile and mile sections of Highway 490. Then you're left with a sleepless night before an early start on Sunday morning to take full advantage of the cool desert air.

At 8am sharp the first of 230 competitors is flagged away from the start line in what has to rank as the greatest single example of organized anarchy in America. It's also completely egalitarian. Wherever you come from, whatever you do, when you arrive in Ely you leave your normal life behind. Wander around the assembled competitors and you'll see accountants rubbing shoulders with actors, IT experts with office workers, all united by their love of fast driving.

Unsurprisingly the Silver State has a few celebrities who enter, and a few more eccentric characters, who bring an added dimension to this already extraordinary event. One recognizable face in the crowd is John Schneider, the car-loving actor who played good ol' boy Bo Duke in *The Dukes of Hazzard*. Partnered by his father, John Snr, he has been a regular Silver Stater for years. And his chosen mode of transport? What else but an orange 1969 Dodge Charger, which he had built specially at a cost of some $125,000.

Another notable Silver State competitor is the Japanese publishing magnate Daijiro Inada. Normally found at the wheel of a sensationally modified Japanese car – most recently a Nissan 350Z complete with carbonfibre body and turbocharged 700bhp engine – Inada is frighteningly committed, and has cornered the market in hair-raising crashes, which include completely destroying said Nissan only 7 miles (11km) into the course after a tyre blow-out, then crashing the rebuilt Nissan the following year before the Silver State Classic had even begun, when he out-braked himself while competing in the High Noon Shootout.

Like the other 229 drivers, Inada is hooked by the Silver State's compelling combination of pure speed and the nefarious thrills to be gained from experiencing it on the public road. The real magic of the Silver State it that so long as you're over 18 years old and hold a driving licence, it's a thrill that you can feel for yourself.

Index

Acknowledgements

The Automobile Association would like to thank the following photographers, companies and picture libraries for their assistance in the preparation of this book

Abbreviations for the picture credits are as follows – (**t**) top; (**b**) bottom; (**c**) centre; (**l**) left; (**r**) right; (**AA**) AA World Travel Library.

1 Artemis Images/Pikes Peak International Hill Climb; **2/3** The Klemantaski Collection; **5** LAT; **8** evo Magazine/Malcolm Griffiths; **12/13** Antony Fraser; **14** Johnny Tipler; **15** Antony Fraser; **16tl** The Klemantaski Collection; **16tr** AA/R Strange; **17** Antony Fraser; **18/19** Johnny Tipler; **19t** The Klemantaski Collection; **20tl** Antony Fraser; **20/21** Johnny Tipler; **22** AA/A Mockford & N Bonetti; **23** Antony Fraser; **24** Mark Bramley; **25tl** Antony Fraser; **25tr** Mark Bramley; **26cl** Antony Fraser; **26bl** Antony Fraser; **27** Mark Bramley; **28tl** Antony Fraser; **28/29** Antony Fraser; **30/31** The Klemantaski Collection; **31t** The Klemantaski Collection; **32** LAT; **33** Antony Fraser; **34/35** Antony Fraser; **35tr** Antony Fraser; **36** Antony Fraser; **37tc** AA/C Sawyer; **37tr** Antony Fraser; **38c** McKlein; **38/39** Antony Fraser; **40** Perfect Prints Tasmania; **41** Perfect Prints Tasmania; **42/43** Perfect Prints Tasmania; **44bl** Perfect Prints Tasmania; **44bc** Perfect Prints Tasmania; **44tr** Perfect Prints Tasmania; **45** Perfect Prints Tasmania; **46** LAT; **47** Antony Fraser; **48bl** Antony Fraser; **48tr** LAT; **48br** Antony Fraser; **49b** Antony Fraser; **49tr** LAT; **50/51** LAT; **52** Stephen Davison/Pacemaker Press International; **53** Stephen Davison/Pacemaker Press International; **54/55** Stephen Davison/Pacemaker Press International; **55b** Stephen Davison/Pacemaker Press International; **56/57** Stephen Davison/Pacemaker Press International; **58** LAT; **59** LAT; **60** LAT; **61** LAT; **62/63** Antony Fraser; **63br** JDHT; **64tl** LAT; **64/65** Antony Fraser; **66** evo Magazine/Andy Morgan; **67** sutton-images.com; **68/69** sutton-images.com; **69br** LAT; **70/71** LAT; **72/73** sutton-images.com; **72tr** LAT; **73br** sutton-images.com; **74** LAT; **75** LAT; **76/77** LAT; **77b** LAT; **78tr** LAT; **79l** LAT; **79tr** LAT; **80** LAT; **81** JDHT; **82/83** Antony Fraser; **83tr** LAT; **83cr** Antony Fraser; **85** LAT; **86/87** McKlein/LAT; **88** McKlein; **89** LAT; **90/91** AA/J Blandford; **91tr** LAT; **92** AA/J Blandford; **93tl** LAT; **93tc** LAT; **94** Ebrey/LAT; **96/97** Ebrey/LAT; **97r** Ebrey/LAT; **98/99** Ebrey/LAT; **100** LAT; **101** Ebrey/LAT; **102l** Ebrey/LAT; **102/103** Ebrey/LAT; **104/105** Ebrey/LAT; **106** LAT; **107** AA/B Smith; **108/109** McKlein/LAT; **110/111** McKlein/LAT; **112tl** McKlein; **112/113** McKlein/LAT; **113br** LAT; **114** McKlein/LAT; **115** McKlein/LAT; **116l** McKlein/LAT; **116/117** McKlein/LAT; **118** McKlein/LAT; **119** McKlein/LAT; **120tc** Ilkka Rytkönen; **120/121** LAT; **122** McKlein; **123** AA/B Tomms; **124** sutton-images.com; **124/125** sutton-images.com; **126** sutton-images.com; **127** McKlein; **128/129** LAT; **130** LAT; **131** LAT; **132b** LAT; **132/133** LAT; **134tr** Photo4/LAT; **135l** LAT; **135tr** LAT; **136** LAT; **137** LAT; **138** Joe Windsor-Williams; **139t** Antony Fraser; **139cl** LAT; **140/141** LAT; **141tr** Antony Fraser; **143** LAT; **144l** LAT; **144/145** evo Magazine/Kenny P; **146** LAT; **147tl** Antony Fraser; **148/149** evo Magazine/Mark Bramley; **150** LAT; **151** LAT; **152/153** LAT; **154** LAT; **155** LAT; **156** LAT; **157** The Klemantaski Collection; **158/159** LAT; **159t** LAT; **160/161** LAT; **162/163** LAT; **164/165** LAT; **166** Klaus Rauth; **167** Klaus Rauth; **168/169** AA/A Baker; **170** evo Magazine/Gus Gregory; **171** AA/S Day; **172/173** AA/S Day; **174/175** evo Magazine/Gus Gregory; **176** David Shepherd; **177** David Shepherd; **178/179** David Shepherd; **179bl** David Shepherd; **180tl** David Shepherd; **180c** David Shepherd; **180/181** David Shepherd; **182** Porsche AG; **183** Artemis Images/Pikes Peak International Hill Climb; **184c** LAT; **184/185** LAT; **186/187** Porsche AG; **187bl** LAT; **188/189** evo Magazine/Gus Gregory; **190** LAT; **191** AA/J Carnie; **192l** Lochside Photography; **192/193** AA/K Paterson; **194** Lochside Photography; **196/197** Ron Christensen; **198** Martyn Goddard; **199** LAT; **200/201** LAT; **202tl** LAT; **202/203** LAT; **204/205** Ron Christensen; **205tl** LandSpeed Productions/George Callaway; **205tr** Ron Christensen; **207** AKG-Images/Ullstein Bild; **208/209** evo Magazine/Kenny P; **210/211** evo Magazine/Kenny P; **213tl** SCTA-BNI; **213tr** SCTA-BNI; **213** evo Magazine/Andrew Yeadon; **214** SCTA-BNI; **215** SCTA-BNI; **216** Joe Windsor-Williams; **217** Joe Windsor-Williams; **218/219** Joe Windsor-Williams; **220/221** Joe Windsor-Williams; **221tc** Joe Windsor-Williams; **221tr** Joe Windsor-Williams

Every effort has been made to trace the copyright holders, and we apologise in advance for any accidental errors. We would be happy to apply the corrections in the following edition of this publication.

Classic MOTORSPORT *Routes*

Written by **Richard Meaden**

Original concept **Nick Otway**
(with thanks to Tim Hughes)

Design concept **Damian Smith**

All design work **Nick Otway**

Picture research **Lesley Grayson**

Image retouching **Michael Moody**

Production **Rachel Davis**

Copy editor **Stephanie Smith**

Indexer **Marie Lorimer**

Managing Editor **Paul Mitchell**

Produced by AA Publishing
© Automobile Association Developments Limited 2007

This edition published in 2008 by Motorbooks, an imprint of MBI Publishing Company, Galtier Plaza, Suite 200, 380 Jackson Street, St. Paul, MN 55101 USA

All Cartography produced by the Mapping Services Department of AA Publishing with additional information supplied by the FIA and Bobby Willis of RallyMaps.

The information in this book is true and complete to the best of our knowledge. All recommendations are made without any guarantee on the part of the author or Publisher, who also disclaim any liability incurred in connection with the use of this data or specific details.

A03642

MBI Publishing Company titles are also available at discounts in bulk quantity for industrial or sales-promotional use. For details write to Special Sales Manager at MBI Publishing Company, Galtier Plaza, Suite 200, 380 Jackson Street, St. Paul, MN 55101 USA.

The views expressed in this book are those of the author, and are in no way representative of the policies of Automobile Association Developments Limited.

Colour separation by Imaging.MM, London
Printed in Dubai by Oriental Press

Library of Congress Cataloging-in-Publication Data

Meaden, Richard.
  Classic motorsport routes : 30 legendary routes you can drive today / by Richard Meaden.
    p. cm.
  ISBN-13: 978-0-7603-3431-7 (hardbound w/ jacket)
  ISBN-10: 0-7603-3431-5 (hardbound w/ jacket)
  1. Automobile travel. 2. Automobile racing. I. Title.
GV1021.M43 2008
796.7206'8--dc22

                                    2007046687

Mapping in this title produced from:

 This product contains mapping data licensed from Ordnance Survey® with the permission of the Controller of Her Majesty's Stationery Office. © Crown copyright 2007. All rights reserved. Licence number 100021153

ORDNANCE SURVEY®
OF NORTHERN IRELAND This product includes mapping based upon data licensed from the Ordnance Survey of Northern Ireland® by permission of the Chief Executive, acting on behalf of the Controller of Her Majesty's Stationary Office. © Crown Copyright 2007. Permit No. 8316.

Republic of Ireland mapping based on Ordnance Survey Ireland. Permit No. 70037. © Ordnance Survey Ireland and Government of Ireland.

© MAIRDUMONT/Falk Verlag 2007.

Map Data © New Holland Publishing (South Africa) (Pty) Ltd. 2007.

© Hema Maps Pty Ltd. 2007.

© Tele Atlas N.V. 2007

© 2007 Navigation Technologies B.V. All rights reserved.

Mountain High Maps ® copyright © 1993 Digital Wisdom, Inc.